# The Profits of Distrust

The burgeoning bottled water industry presents a paradox: Why do people choose expensive, environmentally destructive bottled water, rather than cheaper, sustainable, and more rigorously regulated tap water? *The Profits of Distrust* links citizens' choices about the water they drink to civic life more broadly, marshalling a rich variety of data on public opinion, consumer behavior, political participation, geography, and water quality. Basic services are the bedrock of democratic legitimacy. Failing, inequitable basic services cause citizen-consumers to abandon government in favor of commercial competitors. A vicious cycle of distrust undermines democracy while commercial firms reap the profits of distrust – disproportionately so from the poor and racial/ethnic minority communities. But the vicious cycle can also be virtuous: excellent basic services build trust in government and foster greater engagement between citizens and the state. Rebuilding confidence in American democracy starts with literally rebuilding the basic infrastructure that sustains life.

MANNY P. TEODORO is Associate Professor at the Robert M. La Follette School of Public Affairs, University of Wisconsin-Madison. He works at the intersection of politics, policy, and management, with a focus on water in the United States. His research involves utility governance, regulation, and environmental justice. A prolific speaker, blogger, and author of *Bureaucratic Ambition* (2011), Teodoro has advised water sector leaders for more than 25 years.

SAMANTHA ZUHLKE is Assistant Professor at the School of Planning and Public Affairs, University of Iowa. She applies novel methods of spatial analysis to investigate important problems in public policy, public administration, and environmental politics. Her current research examines how partisan politics shape the U.S. nonprofit sector.

DAVID SWITZER is Assistant Professor at the Harry S Truman School of Public Affairs, University of Missouri. He researches environmental policy, politics, and administration. His work focuses on local government water policy in the United States, examining the how the interactions between institutions, citizens, and the environment inform the implementation and development of public policy at the local level.

Business and Public Policy

*Series Editor:*

ASEEM PRAKASH, University of Washington

*Series Board:*

Sarah Brooks, Ohio State University
David Coen, University College London
Nathan Jensen, University of Texas, Austin
Christophe Knill, Ludwig-Maximilians-University, Munich
David Konisky, Indiana University
David Levi Faur, Hebrew University, Jerusalem
Layna Mosley, University of North Carolina, Chapel Hill
Abraham Newman, Georgetown University
Leonard Seabrooke, Copenhagen Business School
Mike Vandenberg, Vanderbilt University
Edward Walker, University of California, Los Angeles
Henry Yeung, Singapore National University

This series aims to play a pioneering role in shaping the emerging field of business and public policy. *Business and Public Policy* focuses on two central questions. First, how does public policy influence business strategy, operations, organization, and governance, and with what consequences for both business and society? Second, how do businesses themselves influence policy institutions, policy processes, and other policy actors, and with what outcomes?

*Other books in the series:*

JANE L. SUMNER *The Cost of Doing Politics: How Partisanship and Public Opinion Shape Corporate Influence*

KATHRYN HOCHSTETLER *Political Economies of Energy Transition: Wind and Solar Power in Brazil and South Africa*

PAASHA MAHDAVI *Power Grab: Political Survival through Extractive Resource Nationalization*

STEFAN RENCKENS *Private Governance and Public Authority: Regulating Sustainability in a Global Economy*

SARAH BAUERLE DANZMAN *Merging Interests: When Domestic Firms Shape FDI Policy*

LILIANA B. ANDONOVA *Governance Entrepreneurs: International Organizations and the Rise of Global Public-Private Partnerships*

NATHAN M. JENSEN AND EDMUND J. MALESKY *Incentives to Pander: How Politicians Use Corporate Welfare for Political Gain*

*(continued after the index)*

# The Profits of Distrust

## Citizen-Consumers, Drinking Water, and the Crisis of Confidence in American Government

MANUEL P. TEODORO
*University of Wisconsin–Madison*

SAMANTHA ZUHLKE
*University of Iowa*

DAVID SWITZER
*University of Missouri–Columbia*

CAMBRIDGE
UNIVERSITY PRESS

# CAMBRIDGE
## UNIVERSITY PRESS

Shaftesbury Road, Cambridge CB2 8BS, United Kingdom

One Liberty Plaza, 20th Floor, New York, NY 10006, USA

477 Williamstown Road, Port Melbourne, VIC 3207, Australia

314–321, 3rd Floor, Plot 3, Splendor Forum, Jasola District Centre, New Delhi – 110025, India

103 Penang Road, #05–06/07, Visioncrest Commercial, Singapore 238467

Cambridge University Press is part of Cambridge University Press & Assessment, a department of the University of Cambridge.

It furthers the University's mission by disseminating knowledge in the pursuit of education, learning, and research at the highest international levels of excellence.

www.cambridge.org
Information on this title: www.cambridge.org/9781009244862

DOI: 10.1017/9781009244893

First published 2022

A catalogue record for this publication is available from the British Library.

ISBN 978-1-009-24486-2 Hardback
ISBN 978-1-009-24485-5 Paperback

*For our parents:*
*Dee and Reynaldo*
*Susan and Dwayne*
*Victoria and Sheldon*

Whoever can be trusted in small matters can also be trusted in great ones, but whoever is dishonest in small matters will also be dishonest in great ones.

Luke 16:10

# Contents

# Figures

# Tables

# *Preface*

Fittingly, this book was written in the midst of a pandemic.

As we were crafting a theory about basic service failures, trust in government, citizen-consumer behavior, and democratic legitimacy, a worldwide coronavirus outbreak put governments at every level under stress. Failures in public health, education, transportation, energy, and other areas of public management ensued as the virus rampaged from 2019–2022. Much of the public distrusted advice from public health officials, disregarding pleas to wear masks in public and refusing vaccination. At the same time, racial tensions over law enforcement sparked protest and violent outbursts in cities across the country. Joe Biden prevailed in a particularly acrimonious presidential election against Donald Trump. Angry at the outcome and questioning the election's legitimacy, thousands of President Trump's supporters assaulted the US Capitol on January 6, 2021, disrupting the electoral vote count. These events cast in stark terms the crisis of legitimacy that American government now faces and how they link to basic services.

One event in early 2021 resonated with us especially strongly. A week after we submitted the initial draft of this book's manuscript to our publisher, Texas experienced a once-in-a-century winter storm. For the first time ever, every county in the Lone Star State was under a winter storm warning. This book was born from relationships forged at Texas A&M University, and one of its authors still lived in Texas during the catastrophe. It is one thing to theorize about the consequences of basic service failure; it is quite another to experience service collapse firsthand and to witness declining trust in government in real time.

Extreme cold from the February 2021 winter storm in Texas knocked gas-, wind-, and coal-sourced power offline. The Electric Reliability Council of Texas (ERCOT), the entity that oversees Texas's power grid, instituted rolling blackouts in order to protect

Texas from monthslong, uncontrollable power blackouts. Utility workers toiled heroically to provide power and water during the emergency, but failures were built into the systems that they operated. On February 16, at least 4.5 million Texans were without power; by February 21, more than 10 million people had no access to safe drinking water. According to official records, the storm and its aftermath were responsible for 151 deaths statewide – including that of an 11-year-old boy in Conroe.

As with so many other disasters, scholars, politicians, and practitioners will likely dissect the causes of the Texas energy disaster in terms of its human, political, and social failings. For us, some of the consequences of this event are already clear. The Texas winter storm underlines that basic services are critical components of a functioning society and the linchpins of government legitimacy. People suffer terribly when such basic services fail. But beyond physical damage, people's trust in government also suffers following the failure of basic services.

In this book, we argue that people who experience or observe basic service failure learn to distrust the government and then seek solutions to their service problems from private, commercial firms. The relationship between government distrust and consumerism was evident during the 2021 Texas winter storm. H-E-B, a popular Texas grocery chain, is well known for providing emergency services following disaster events. One Texan described H-E-B as the "moral center of Texas" (Montgomery, Rojas, & McDonnell Nieto del Rio 2021). In a *San Antonio Express-News* column entitled "Opinion: Why H-E-B Comes through in a Crisis When Texas Government Doesn't," Greg Jefferson (2021) described why Texans substitute H-E-B for government: "H-E-B keeps its customers fed, if not comfortable, when a crisis hits. And they remember – which is one reason . . . so many Texans look to H-E-B almost as a de facto arm of government." Jefferson continued,

One of the barbs tossed around frequently on Twitter last week – more wistful than angry – was that we'd all be better off if H-E-B took over the Texas power grid.

It would have been hard to argue the point, especially while sitting in a cold, dark house or apartment. . . . It's a shame [Texas politicians] refuse to do the hard work of governing to earn the same kind of respect.

As ERCOT failed to provide power during Winter Storm Uri, Texans turned to H-E-B for food – provided free of charge to customers when H-E-B's electricity failed (Gonzalez 2021) – and fuel (Redman 2021). As water utilities failed, commercial companies like Zen Water, Publix Super Markets, and Proud Source Water donated enough bottled water to fill twenty-one trailer loads – more than 725,000 bottles – to food banks across the state (Redman 2021).

H-E-B's assistance to struggling Texans stood in contrast to political leaders' responses. Governor Greg Abbott (falsely) blamed power grid problems on renewable energy (Jefferson 2021). Senator Ted Cruz fled for warmer weather in Cancún, only to return later with excuses and apologies. Meanwhile, Winell Herron, a vice president at H-E-B, expressed the grocery chain's solidarity with Texans: "H-E-B is here for Texas, and we will do everything we can to support those in need across our great state" (Redman 2021). This contrast did not go unnoticed by the public; many Twitter users called for H-E-B to run for governor or president, or made other observations comparing the actions of H-E-B and the government (Velasco 2021):

> "In Texas, we can only trust HEB [sic] to take care of Texans"
> – @yoomsters
> "Our institutions are failing, but we aren't" – @jhenderson010
> "HEB is doing more for texas [sic] than its own senator"
> – @Moniccaa1013

Our book echoes these themes: basic service problems damage trust in government and drive people toward commercial alternatives. But commercial firms, however well intentioned, are not accountable to the public. As former Texas residents, we are all H-E-B devotees, but H-E-B is not the government. H-E-B is "a company that knows its customers and their needs intimately," as Jefferson's column observed. "It's a master at selling groceries and pharmaceuticals, not at governing." Ultimately, H-E-B's responsibility is to its bottom line, and disaster relief is a profitable strategy that builds brand loyalty and a consumer base. On the other hand, liberal democracies like the United States derive their power from the consent of the governed; citizens collectively decide what is important, and government manifests those values into services. When governments fail to provide basic services, crises of legitimacy ensue. Exit to commercial firms drains political support and resources from government, further increasing the chance of basic service failure and increasing government distrust.

We believe this cycle can be reversed. Our book ends with insights into how to reset the relationship between government and citizen-consumers. We call for government to rebuild trust with citizen-consumers by providing for excellent, open, and equitable basic services. In 2011, Texas experienced a less severe deep freeze that revealed the power grid's vulnerability, but ERCOT and elected officials failed to address the grid's shortcomings in the decade before Winter Storm Uri. Imagine if they had – an alternative reality where all Texans had reliable electricity, heat, and drinking water during the February 2021 winter storm. The stories we would tell would center on government as a legitimate provider of people's basic needs. When basic services work, they instill faith and trust in American government. Instead, we tell stories of how a private grocery chain stepped up in the wake of government failure; citizen investment in government is replaced by loyalty to private, commercial firms.

Our arguments about basic services, trust, and government legitimacy transcend time, but they are more salient than ever in light of the disasters and political strife of 2020–2021. The lives lost in the disasters of these years are irreplaceable. It will take time to upgrade Texas's public infrastructure, repair damage from 2020 police protests, recoup economic losses from the COVID-19 pandemic, and recover from other regional disasters. Trust in government will be much harder to rebuild, but we believe excellent, open, and equitable basic services are the building blocks to reconstructing state legitimacy. We hope this book can be part of that reconstruction.

Drinking water is a great place to start.

# Acknowledgments

We were fortunate to be supported by several organizations, colleagues, and research assistants in the development of this book.

A strength of this book is its use of data from a wide variety of sources. We thank the Institute for Science, Technology, and Public Policy at the Bush School of Government & Public Service for sharing NEXUS survey data; the US Water Alliance for sharing their Value of Water survey data; and Providence Water for sharing their lead-testing data. The Truman School of Government and Public Affairs and the Kinder Institute on Constitutional Democracy at the University of Missouri provided funding for a Cooperative Congressional Election Study module that allowed for our questions to be included. Texas A&M University provided financial support for this work in the form of a faculty development leave (for Teodoro) and graduate fellowships from the Texas A&M Office of Graduate and Professional Studies and the College of Liberal Arts (for Zuhlke).

We are grateful to seminar participants at Texas A&M University, the American Political Science Association, Visions in Methodology, the American Water Works Association (AWWA) Annual Conference and Exposition, and the Water Environment Federation's/AWWA Utility Management Conference. Colleagues at those events who witnessed early versions of this work asked difficult questions and provided insightful feedback. In particular, we thank Scott Cook (Texas A&M), Robert Maranto (University of Arkansas), and Casey Petroff (Harvard University) for suggestions that improved our thinking and the final manuscript.

We thank our research assistants – Jun Deng, Devika Marwaha, McKenzie Speich, and Dana Villalobos – who provided invaluable perspective, time, and help at various stages of the project. We also thank the Texas A&M Aggie Research Scholars Program, a unique program that pairs undergraduate students seeking research experience with graduate students seeking research assistance. The spring

2017 program made the collection of our kiosk data possible, and we were fortunate to work with six bright, dedicated, and talented Aggies: Crystal Arteaga, Kara Cassano, Teodora Gutierrez, Michael Miguad, Frazer Mulugeta, and Aaron Mathew Vasquez.

Finally, we thank our partners and families, whose patience during the pandemic made the writing of this book possible. Life proceeds alongside research, and over the course of this project's development one of its authors got engaged (Zuhlke), one got married (Switzer), and one saw his children graduate from high school and college (Teodoro). As we passed these milestones, our families were sounding boards for our ideas and enthusiastic supporters of our work, lifting our spirits when they flagged.

Our deepest gratitude is to our parents, who instilled in each of us an abiding curiosity about the world and passion for making it better.

# 1 | Basic Services and Trust in Government

## The Glorious, Tragic Legacy of America's Water Systems

Political power is that power . . . given up into the hands of the society, and therein to the governors, whom the society hath set over itself, with this express or tacit trust, that it shall be employed for their good.

John Locke,[1] *Second Treatise of Government*

The use of drinking water is the only interaction that every American is guaranteed to have with their government every day.

Seth M. Siegel,[2] *Troubled Water*

This book is about basic services and trust in American government. Basic services – the services that are required to maintain a safe, healthy, and productive life – are the bedrock of government legitimacy. The core of liberal political theory is the idea that the authority of any government rests on its ability to provide for its people's basic needs. How do people respond when government fails to provide for those needs? What choices do people make about the basic services they receive, and what are the cumulative consequences of those decisions?

In democracies with market economies such as the United States, people may choose to receive basic services collectively through government or from private commercial firms. A government's people – its citizens – are also consumers; in the United States, most consumers are also citizens. When experiencing problems with basic services, these "citizen-consumers" may demand improvements from government and continue to rely on collectively provided basic service, or they may abandon public services in favor of private, commercial alternatives. In the pages that follow, we argue that individuals' decisions as citizens are bound up in their decisions as consumers. Consumers' spending choices reflect, in part, their identities as citizens, and citizens'

---

[1] Locke ([1690] 1980, chapter XV, section 171).    [2] Siegel (2019, 255).

political decisions reflect their assessments of value as consumers. When government produces and/or regulates a basic service, the citizen-consumer's choice between the public provider and a private, commercial firm reflects, in part, her trust in the institutions of government. This book explores the ways that basic service quality relates to trust in government, the ways that commercial firms exploit basic distrust, the ways that citizen-consumers react to basic service failures, and how government responds (or does not respond) to citizen demands for improvements.

Building on insights from political science, economics, and psychology, we advance a theory of the citizen-consumer that connects the quality of basic services to trust in government, trust in government to consumer behavior, consumer behavior to citizen political participation, and citizen political participation back to the quality of basic services. Distilled to its essence, our argument is that when basic services are sound, citizens trust the institutions of government; when basic services fail, citizens distrust those same institutions. Trust in government then manifests itself in consumer behavior: People who trust government rely on public services, whereas those who distrust government opt instead for (usually more expensive) commercial alternatives. Consumers who use public services have a strong interest in safeguarding quality, so they are politically active as citizens. On the other hand, consumers who abandon public services in favor of commercial providers have less incentive to engage with government, so they tend to withdraw from political life. These patterns of political participation feed back into the quality of services. More trusting, active citizen-consumers demand high-quality public services and support investments in those services; their governments respond with strong service quality. Distrustful, disengaged citizen-consumers demand little from government and oppose public investments as wasteful; starved of both resources and attention, governments' service quality will decline. The relationship between government and citizen-consumer is thus reciprocal.

In this opening chapter, we argue that the choices Americans make about the most basic of basic services they receive – the water they drink – reveal deeper lessons about civic life. Our subject is drinking water in the United States, but the ideas that we develop in this book could easily apply to health care, law enforcement, firefighting, housing, postal service, food, transportation, or any other basic service. The chapters that follow trace the cyclical logic that connects basic service quality, trust in government, consumer choices, and political participation. Although the picture that emerges is often dismal, it also shows that basic services can (re)build trust in the institutions of government in a skeptical and politically polarized age.

## Water and Trust

Water is literally essential to human life. All polities, from the smallest, most primitive societies to the most advanced industrial state, must secure and maintain water supplies. Unlike much of what government does, providing drinking water is universally important and immediately relevant every day: In virtually every corner of the country, people brush their teeth with, flush their toilets with, bathe with, cook with, clean with, and drink water every day.

Drinking water is at once a political phenomenon and a consumer product. In the United States, federal and state governments are jointly responsible for regulating drinking water health for all drinking water systems in the country. American local governments are the main owners and operators of community drinking water systems. Even where community water systems are owned and operated by investor-owned firms, state agencies regulate their quality and pricing. As such, government is responsible for the *provision* of tap water, even when tap water service is *produced* by privately owned utilities. With water systems so heavily regulated and largely owned by local governments, water policy and management are intensely and inherently political in ways that most other goods and services are not. If basic services are the bedrock of government legitimacy, then water is the foundation of the edifice of the state.

The rise of the bottled water industry in the United States is an alarming indication of cracks in that foundation. An increasing share of Americans report that they do not drink the water that flows from their taps. Consumption of bottled and other commercial drinking water in the United States has skyrocketed over the past two decades, as the dashed line in Figure 1.1 shows. According to the International Bottled Water Association (IBWA), Americans purchased 5.1 billion gallons of unflavored, noncarbonated bottled drinking water in 2001, generating $6.9 billion in wholesale revenue. Over the next twenty years, the bottled water industry in the United States nearly tripled to

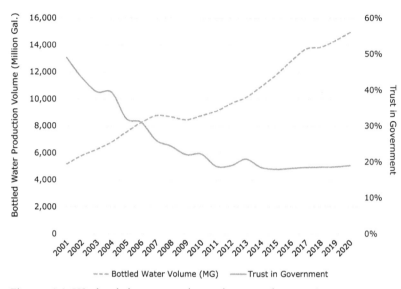

**Figure 1.1** US bottled water sales volume and trust in government, 2001–2020.

*Sources:* International Bottled Water Association; Pew Research Center. Trust in Government is percentage of survey respondents who trust the government in Washington to do what is right always or most of the time.

15.0 billion gallons of annual volume and $20.1 billion in wholesale revenue (Rodwan 2020). In 2016, the bottled water industry passed a major milestone when bottled water surpassed carbonated soft drinks as America's most popular bottled beverage, accounting for nearly a quarter of all bottles sold. In 2020, Americans spent more than $36.2 billion retail on bottled water. The robust and rapidly expanding commercial water industry in the United States presents a puzzle: *Why do Americans opt for more expensive commercial drinking water when high-quality tap water is widely available?*

The commercial water industry's remarkable rise has come at a time of declining trust in American institutions generally, and declining trust in government specifically (Gramlich 2019). According to the Pew Research Center, the share of Americans who "trust the government in Washington to do what is right always or most of the time" fell from 49 percent in 2001 to 17 percent in 2019 – an astonishing 32-point drop over eighteen years. The solid line in Figure 1.1 shows the concomitant fall of trust in government from 2001 to 2020. The two lines – the rise of bottled water sales and the decline of trust in government – run in opposite directions, with eerily similar, though divergent, long-term trends: Over the period shown in Figure 1.1, bottled water volume grew by an average of 5.9 percent annually and trust in government fell by 4.6 percent annually.

This book aims to demonstrate that the two trends in Figure 1.1 are neither coincidental nor inevitable. The steady, alarming decline in Americans' trust of government has emerged as a major focus of political anxiety and social research in recent years. The chapters that follow articulate the logic that connects basic service quality (in our case, tap water) to trust in government, trust in government to consumer behavior, consumer behavior to citizen political behavior, and citizen political behavior back to government performance. This opening chapter examines the significance of water systems in American political development, the rise of commercial water, and the role of local, state, and federal governments in drinking water provision. As we will see, the evolution of drinking water in America raises fundamental questions about the reciprocal relationship between citizens and the state.

## A Legacy of Infrastructure

Government legitimacy and drinking water provision are intimately tied. American political development is in many ways a story of water infrastructure development. In the late nineteenth century and for much of the twentieth century, water utilities in the United States earned well-deserved reputations for delivering reliable, high-quality, potable drinking water. The rise of drinking water systems and sanitary sewers in the United States eliminated waterborne diseases such as cholera and typhoid that had ravaged cities for centuries. With improved water systems came improved public health and economic performance. Along with urban sewer and sanitation systems, America's drinking water utilities were a collective triumph in urban infrastructure.

That triumph is a mark of government success. Historian Jon Teaford (1984) observed that, in late nineteenth-century America,

Municipal officials were employing the latest engineering technology to create systems of water supply and drainage of unrivaled size. American municipalities administered a larger network of mains than any other governing body in the world; they provided a greater supply of water than any other city worldwide; and they sponsored unmatched schemes of engineering. *The waterworks and sewer systems of America were objects worthy of pride.* (225, italics added)

For example, in 1908, Jersey City, New Jersey, became the first city in the United States to disinfect its water through continuous chlorination – a move that dramatically reduced typhoid fever and several other waterborne diseases (McGuire 2013). Within a decade, half of the nation's water utilities had followed suit. By the 1930s, American governments' water supply systems were almost entirely chlorinated, and the nation had largely conquered "the waterborne diseases which ravaged America during the late nineteenth and early twentieth century" (Douglas 1976, 502). These miracles of urban infrastructure were credit-claiming opportunities for public officials, as American cities leapt ahead of their European counterparts in the scope and quality of their water infrastructure. With iron and concrete, water and sewer systems helped transform American cities from squalor to prosperity.

Politicians built the modern American party system as they built these water systems, with the credibility of the former resting in part on the integrity of the latter (Teaford 1984). Far more than utilitarian, water supply facilities were testaments to civic achievement and the burgeoning nation's political leadership. When the City of Saginaw, Michigan, completed its water treatment plant in 1929, top-hatted politicians made speeches and held citywide celebrations (Reinsch 2016). A parade through Saginaw ended at the city's new treatment plant and featured the ceremonial burial of a hand pump to symbolize the dawn of modern in-home water service. Beautifully designed, the plant featured state-of-the-art treatment technology and the works of local artists. Over the front door of the new Saginaw plant, a sign declared, "The World's Best Water." This scene repeated itself across the country as new plants opened in the late nineteenth-century and early twentieth-century heyday of American drinking water system construction. From New York to Cincinnati to Seattle to Miami, reservoirs, water towers, and treatment plants were both functional and beautiful. The monumental architecture that accompanied these facilities stood as testimonies to their social and political value. Drinking water and sewer systems improved life in American communities, immediately and tangibly, inspiring confidence in the governments that created them. Just as in the ancient Roman Empire, aqueducts and sewers brought health and prosperity to flourishing American cities, simultaneously serving as powerful reminders of the state's political genius and might.

New contaminants began to threaten drinking water supplies in the mid-twentieth century as American industry grew and matured, and federal regulatory reforms in the 1970s made important strides in controlling water pollution and bolstering drinking water quality in the United States. Congress passed the 1972 Clean Water Act and 1974 Safe Drinking Water Act (SDWA), along with other landmark federal environmental laws. These laws sparked important advancements in water treatment technology and produced a generation of environmental and water quality engineers through investments in research and education. In 1996, major amendments expanded the SDWA to enhance risk assessment and, especially, to increase transparency and public confidence in water supplies.

This legacy of government water provision and regulation means that Americans' relationships with their water shape and reflect their relationships with the institutions of American government at every level: local, state, and federal. In the United States, electricity, gas, and telecommunications utilities are overwhelmingly owned and operated by private, investor-owned firms. But about 85 percent of Americans receive their drinking water from a water utility operated by a local government. Where local governments provide water service, citizens own the infrastructure that serves them. Most of these systems are parts of municipalities, counties, special districts, tribal agencies, or other authorities managed by elected officials and public administrators. Where investor-owned utilities operate drinking water and sewer service, these water systems are heavily regulated and governed by state agencies under a host of environmental, health, safety, and financial laws. Overseeing these hundreds of state agencies and thousands of water utilities are federal regulatory agencies. Put simply, American government is responsible for the provision of drinking water, and the legitimacy of American governance institutions was built in no small part on public confidence in public water systems.

## The Rise of Commercial Drinking Water

Despite America's legacy of inexpensive, widely available, highly reliable, high-quality tap water, the commercial drinking water industry –

that is, bottled and kiosk water – in the United States has exploded over the past two decades, as Figure 1.1 indicates. Once rare, bottled water is now commonplace. Luxury brands such as VOSS and FIJI Water sell for up to $15 per bottle, with a handful of elite brands absurdly selling for thousands of dollars. But far more prevalent are half-liter plastic bottles sold in ubiquitous cases at grocery and discount stores under brands such as Aquafina, Arrowhead, Ozarka, and Crystal Geyser. Wheeled out of big-box stores and into catered lunches and home refrigerators, these bottles have become part of everyday American life. Such growth would be remarkable for any industry, but the rise of bottled water in the United States is particularly striking because most Americans have easy access to a more carefully regulated, often qualitatively superior, and always far less expensive alternative: tap water.

State and federal agencies regulate tap water quality in the United States under the SDWA, which requires regular testing, imposes specific limits on contaminants known to endanger human health, and obliges water utilities to report drinking water quality and other issues to the public.[3] Unlike tap water, bottled water quality is largely unregulated at the state level. With bottled water classified as "packaged food," production facilities are subject to inspection by the US Food and Drug Administration (FDA) at the federal level, and formally bottled water is supposed to meet the same contaminant limits that the SDWA requires for tap water. However, bottled water often fails to meet SDWA-level quality standards when subject to rigorous testing (Ikem et al. 2002; Pip 2000; Sharp & Walker 2002), and it can expose consumers to leachate from plastic containers (Mason, Welch, & Neratko 2018; Wagner & Oehlmann 2009; Westerhoff et al. 2008). Moreover, bottled water manufacturers are not subject to the SDWA's public reporting requirements.

Beyond water quality concerns, bottled water carries significant environmental impacts. The production of plastic water bottles requires energy and petrochemicals. Gleick and Cooley (2009) estimated that in 2007 the production and distribution of bottled water required between 32 and 54 billion barrels of oil. Water is also quite heavy, so distributing bottled water from factory to consumer requires

---

[3] One American tribal government, the Navajo Nation, also regulates drinking water quality within its jurisdiction.

significant surface transportation costs, sometimes across great distances. Perhaps the most famous – or notorious – example is FIJI Water. Extracted from an artesian aquifer on the remote South Pacific island, FIJI Water is transported more than 10,000 kilometers to consumers in the United States. Bottled water also generates significant waste, as less than a quarter of bottles are recycled (Gitlitz & Franklin 2007). Instead, used bottles become litter or are diverted to landfills, where they degrade very slowly (Gironi & Piemonte 2011). Jungbluth (2005) estimates that the environmental impact of one liter of bottled water is more than 100 times the impact of a liter of tap water. Taken together, these externalities take a heavy toll on the environment. Despite these concerns, a growing number of Americans apparently are willing to *pay far more* for *a more lightly regulated* product that harms the environment.

## Urban Water Kiosks in the United States

Similarly puzzling is the recent proliferation of commercial drinking water kiosks in American cities. Water kiosks are privately owned, automated vending machines that dispense drinking water in exchange for payment. Journalists and academic researchers have spilled plenty of ink on the growth and pathologies of bottled water, but relatively little is known about water kiosks in the United States.[4] Kiosks can be located within businesses or freestanding. These automated vending machines are frequently located in parking lots in front of dollar stores and provide "purified" drinking water to customers. Individuals travel to kiosks, bring their own containers, insert cash or pay with a credit card, fill their containers with the purchased water, and then leave. Typically priced at 25–35 cents per gallon, kiosk water is cheaper than bottled water, but still far more expensive than tap water on a volumetric basis. For instance, basic residential water and sewer prices in Houston averaged 1.5 cents per gallon in 2019. In Cleveland it was 1.9 cents per gallon; in Boston and Detroit it was 1.3 cents; in Memphis, Phoenix, Pasadena, and Salt Lake City, a gallon of residential water service cost less than a penny.

---

[4] The few studies that exist focus on the relationship between water quality, demographics, and kiosk location in rural, southern Texas *colonias* (Jepson 2012; Jepson & Brown 2014; Jepson & Vandewalle 2016).

Kiosks draw their water supply from the municipal drinking water utilities where they are located, and their operators claim to apply additional filtration within the kiosk prior to dispensing. But in the United States, water kiosks operate mostly in a regulatory lacuna. Kiosks are not subject to state or federal SDWA rules (except insofar as their tap water sources must comply with the SDWA). Some jurisdictions regulate kiosks under local building codes for also structural safety or as vending machines for fraud prevention. But extensive review found no state or federal guidelines that regulate the quality of water from kiosks, the maintenance of kiosks, or public reporting about kiosks. A 2002 Environmental Law Foundation study tested water quality samples from California water kiosks, finding that more than a third dispensed water that violated state water quality standards and roughly two-thirds of the tested units failed to attain their claimed water purity (Sharp & Walker 2002). Furthermore, the reverse osmosis treatment processes that kiosk companies claim to apply generate by-products that flush into urban sewer systems without measurement or monitoring. Water kiosks are effectively unregulated in the United States, and their claim of dispensing water superior to what flows from the tap is almost entirely untested.

Drinking water kiosks are common in the developing world, where access to potable water is scarce, public water is unreliable, and commercial water is often clearly preferable despite its high price. And predictably, water kiosks established some of their first footholds in the United States in regions with very poor tap water quality, with unreliable potable water utility service, or where tap water is entirely unavailable, such as the Rio Grande Valley of South Texas (Garcia & Hernandez 2011; Jepson 2012) and parts of rural Appalachia (Appalachian Regional Commission 2015; Arcipowski et al. 2017). But commercial water flourishes not only in poor, isolated communities with histories of water quality problems. Kiosks are also common in communities that boast strong tap water utilities – they abound in Houston, Phoenix, and other major cities with professionally managed utilities and excellent SDWA compliance records, as Figure 1.2 shows.

To summarize, drinking water utilities provide water at a much lower unit cost than bottled water and water kiosks, are far less environmentally destructive, and are subject to quality and public reporting requirements that commercial drinking water sellers are not. Millions of Americans are nonetheless willing to buy loosely regulated commercial drinking water at vastly more expensive prices than the highly regulated water that flows from their taps. Although water utility rates have risen sharply in recent years and affordability has emerged as an urgent political issue in the United States (Bartlett et al. 2017; Kane 2018; Teodoro 2018, 2019; Teodoro & Saywitz 2020), tap water prices remain very low compared with most other essential household expenses (e.g., housing, health care, food, taxes, or home energy). More importantly for present purposes, tap water is *far* less expensive than its commercial alternatives, with prices much cheaper than bottled or kiosk water on a volumetric basis (Hu, Morton, & Mahler 2011).

(a)

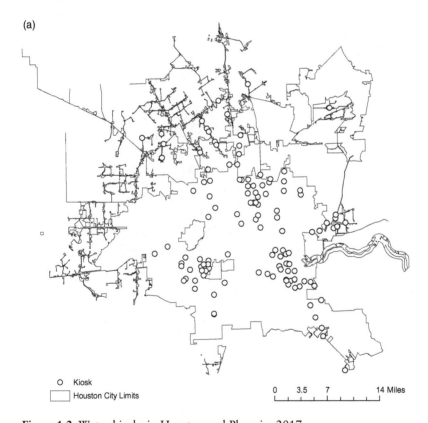

○ Kiosk

☐ Houston City Limits

0     3.5     7          14 Miles

**Figure 1.2** Water kiosks in Houston and Phoenix, 2017.

(a) Watermill Express and Ice House America Kiosks in Houston, TX | *Source*: Original data.

(b)

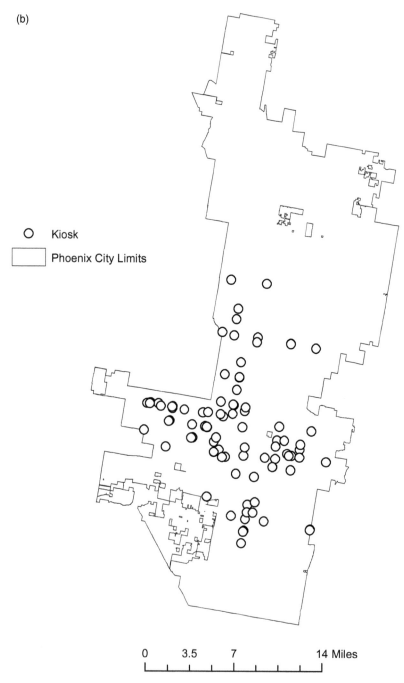

○  Kiosk

☐  Phoenix City Limits

0        3.5        7                    14 Miles

**Figure 1.2** (*cont.*) (b) Watermill Express and Ice House America Kiosks in Phoenix, AZ | *Source*: Original data.

## Puzzling Perceptions

The burgeoning bottled water business and the emergence of water kiosks in major US cities thus present a paradox. What causes consumers to opt for far more expensive and environmentally destructive commercial water of dubious quality, rather than cheaper, environmentally sustainable, and more rigorously regulated tap water? *What explains the decline in tap water consumption and the concomitant growth of bottled water and drinking water kiosks in America?*

If consumers are rational, then people who choose to drink commercial water must *believe* that its quality is different from and superior to tap water quality in some important way. Empirical investigation affirms this expectation: Several recent studies link bottled water consumption to a perception that bottled water is safer than tap water (Doria, Pidgeon, & Hunter 2009; Levêque & Burns 2017, 2018). Of course, in some situations tap water quality really *is* questionable or outright dangerous (Siegel 2019). American tap water is safe, by and large; however, some utilities are poorly managed, and regulatory regimes are often slow to address new contaminants. Drinking water contamination events sometimes occur, and natural or manmade disasters can objectively harm public drinking water supplies. As we will see in the chapters ahead, such disasters can shake confidence in tap water long after and far away from any actual danger.

Beyond safety, drinking water appearance, taste, and odor might cause consumers to buy more expensive bottled or kiosk water instead of tap water; such aesthetic considerations certainly drive consumer behavior in other retail markets. Recent studies affirm that perceptions of aesthetics are associated with bottled water consumption (Graydon et al. 2019). But blind taste testing yields no consistent evidence of differences in taste between bottled and tap water (Debbler et al. 2018), which suggests that perceptions that commercial water tastes better than tap water are mostly illusory.

It might be tempting to dismiss this curious and growing perception of commercial water's superior quality as an economic oddity. Consumers buy many luxury goods that confer social status or other psychological benefits that justify their higher prices relative to qualitatively similar substitutes. In the case of drinking water, consumer preference for expensive commercial water from supermarket shelves or drive-up kiosks is not necessarily a public policy problem. If bottled water carries negative environmental externalities, then the appropriate policy response is to manage or reduce those externalities through taxation or regulation (Switzer 2019b). Costly alternatives to tap water do not in themselves threaten public welfare, much less the legitimacy of democratic institutions.

But a peculiar pattern in this consumer behavior indicates that purchasing bottled or kiosk water is not a simple story of a self-indulgent luxury good. Something more than affluence and evolving tastes is driving the spectacular rise of commercial water in the United States.

## The Curious Demographics of Commercial Drinking Water

Commercial drinking water consumption in the United States is neither random nor even across the country. Plotted geographically, the distribution of 2017 average per household bottled water sales in Figure 1.3 hints at how drinking water purchasing varies across US counties. Kiosks also hint at visual patterns when mapped across the United

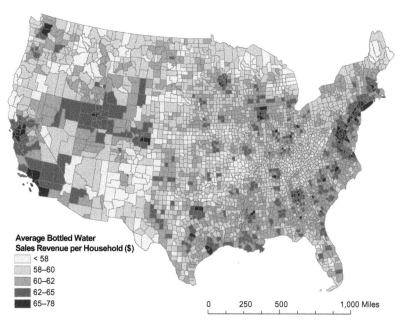

**Figure 1.3** Average bottled water sales per household by county, 2017.
*Source*: Household average bottled water sales (2017) from SimmonsLocal.

States. Unlike bottled water, water kiosks are fixed in geographic space, so they provide an extraordinary opportunity to analyze the spatial distribution of commercial water consumption. Figure 1.2 showed the distribution of kiosks operated by Watermill Express and Ice House America in Houston and Phoenix; Figure 1.4 shows 2017 kiosk locations across the United States.

A cursory look at these maps suggests nonrandom spatial patterns in commercial water consumption. If consumer preference for commercial water is driven mainly by aesthetics, then perhaps differences in source water quality across the country lead to more or less commercial water demand in different regions. It is harder to explain why people prefer commercial water to tap water in different neighborhoods within a single city (as the maps of Houston and Phoenix in Figure 1.2 suggest) when a single utility provides tap water to all.

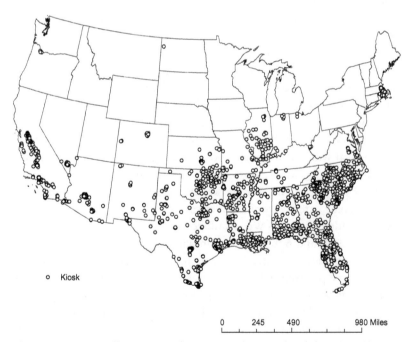

**Figure 1.4** Watermill Express and Ice House America kiosk locations, 2017.
*Source*: Original data set; see Appendix B for information on data collection.

## Bottles and Jugs for the Poor

In spite of its reputation and pricing as a luxury product, commercial drinking water spending in the United States is inversely related to income. A raft of research over the past decade has found that bottled water is most popular among low-income households in the United States and that more affluent American households are likely to drink tap water. In separate studies of National Health and Nutrition Examination Survey data, teams led by researchers at the University of Washington (Drewnowski, Rehm, & Constant 2013) and Penn State University (Rosinger et al. 2018) found that bottled water consumption was greatest among lower-income respondents, whereas higher-income individuals were much more likely to opt for tap water. College-educated people were more than twice as likely to drink tap water and significantly less likely to drink bottled water, compared to individuals without a college education. A 2019 survey of roughly 1,200 Los Angeles County residents found the same pattern, with well-educated and higher-income households more likely to drink tap water and less-educated, lower-income households more likely to drink bottled water (Family et al. 2019). A survey of Phoenix residents led by an Arizona State University team found that bottled water consumption was inversely related to income: As household incomes increased, tap water consumption increased and bottled water consumption decreased (York et al. 2011). The findings in Phoenix are especially notable because a single water system serves the desert city's entire population of 1.7 million.

Kiosk locations within cities also fit awkwardly with a depiction of commercial water as a luxury good. Although their product is cheaper than most bottled water, kiosk water is still far more expensive than tap water. Even so, Figure 1.5 shows that kiosks seem to be located in lower-income areas within American cities (i.e., kiosks locate in lighter-shaded areas). We examine kiosk locations in detail in Chapters 3, 4, and 6, but even an initial look at Figure 1.5 casts doubt on any depiction of water kiosks as luxury retailers. The upper- and middle-class preference for tap water and popularity of commercial drinking water among the poor suggest that the perception of commercial water as a luxury good is an illusion. The negative correlation of income and commercial water consumption is also difficult to square with the argument that taste preference drives the growth in bottled and kiosk water. Why would lower-income people prefer the taste of bottled water and middle- or upper-income people prefer the taste of tap water?

## Race, Ethnicity, and Drinking Water

Equally striking are the ethnic and racial patterns of commercial water consumption in the United States. The line of research that revealed the surprising socioeconomics of bottled water demand found similarly stark racial and ethnic patterns in drinking water behavior. Perhaps most notable is the difference in drinking water behavior among Hispanic consumers in the United States. Bottled water consumption is markedly higher among Hispanics in recent National Health and Nutrition Examination Survey

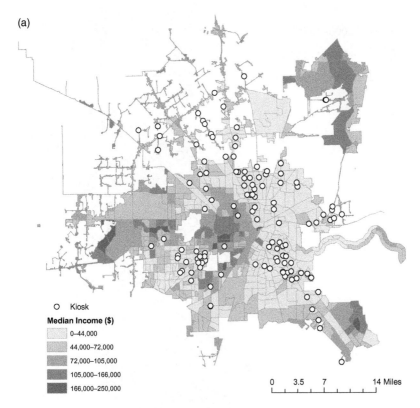

**Figure 1.5** Kiosk locations and median household income by census tract, 2017.

(a) Kiosk location by 2016 census tract median income in Houston, TX. Labels rounded to the nearest $1,000. Categories set with Jenk's Natural Breaks. | *Source*: Kiosk data original, 2016 Median Income from U.S. Census Bureau.

(b)

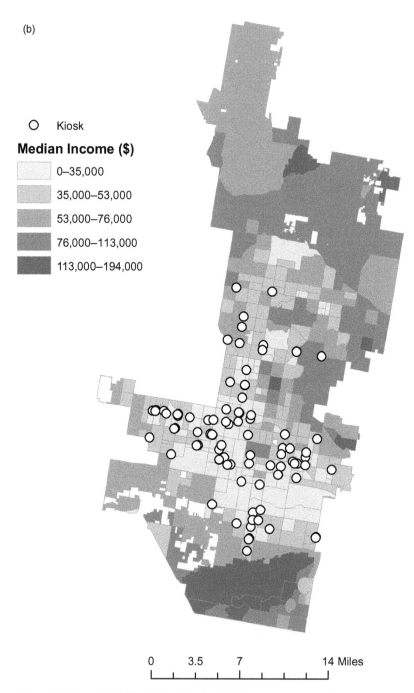

Figure 1.5 (*cont.*) (b) Kiosk location by 2016 census tract median income in Phoenix, AZ. Labels rounded to the nearest $1,000. Categories set with Jenk's Natural Breaks. | *Source*: Kiosk data original, 2016 Median Income from U.S. Census Bureau.

analyses (Drewnowski et al. 2013; Rosinger et al. 2018). After adjusting for age, education, and income, Rosinger et al. (2018) find that, compared with non-Hispanic whites, Hispanics were half as likely to drink tap water and more than twice as likely to drink bottled water. The geographic distribution of 2017 kiosk locations in Figure 1.6 is consistent with those studies (i.e., kiosks are located in areas shaded darker).

The prevalence of bottled water consumption among Hispanic Americans is sometimes attributed to "culture" or water habits that recent immigrants developed in home countries before arriving in the United States (Scherzer et al. 2010). However, the disparity in bottled

(a)

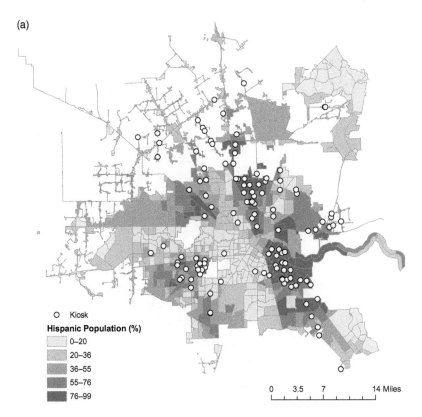

**Figure 1.6** Kiosk locations and percent Hispanic population by census tract, 2017.
(a) Kiosk location by percent Hispanic population (2016) in Houston, TX. Categories set with Jenk's Natural Breaks. | *Source*: Kiosk data original, 2016 Hispanic population from U.S. Census Bureau.

(b)

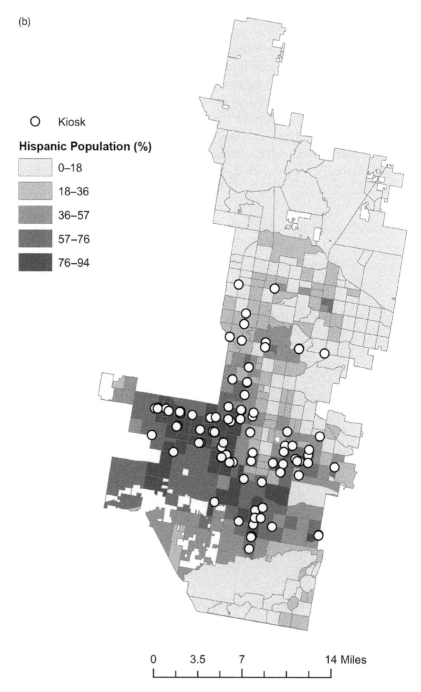

Figure 1.6 (*cont.*) (b) Kiosk location by percent Hispanic population (2016) in Phoenix, AZ. Categories set with Jenk's Natural Breaks. | *Source*: Kiosk data original, 2016 Hispanic population from U.S. Census Bureau.

water consumption between Hispanic and non-Hispanic whites remains large, even after accounting for immigration status or time since immigrating (Hobson et al. 2007; Rosinger et al. 2018). Also countering the idea that Hispanic bottled water consumption is an imported cultural behavior is the similar prevalence of bottled water consumption among Black people who were born and raised in the United States. National Health and Nutrition Examination Survey data show that overall bottled and tap water consumption among Blacks and Hispanics are similar (Drewnowski et al. 2013; Rosinger et al. 2018). Figure 1.7 hints that kiosk locations in Houston and Phoenix might correlate with neighborhoods' racial composition.

(a)

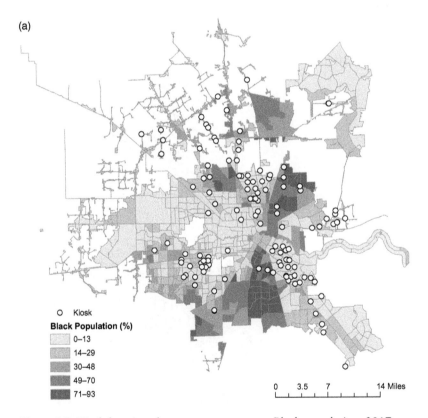

**Figure 1.7** Kiosk locations by census tract percent Black population, 2017. (a) Kiosk location by percent Black population (2016) in Houston, TX. Categories set with Jenk's Natural Breaks. | *Source*: Kiosk data original, 2016 Black Population from U.S. Census Bureau.

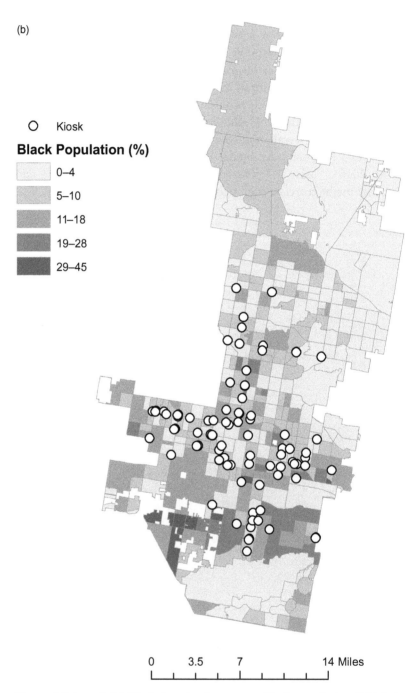

**Figure 1.7** (*cont.*) (b) Kiosk location by percent Black population (2016) in Phoenix, AZ. Categories set with Jenk's Natural Breaks. | *Source*: Kiosk data original, 2016 Black Population from U.S. Census Bureau.

## Patterns of Perception

The large and rapidly growing commercial water industry implies that a significant share of consumers believes that water from bottles and/or kiosks is qualitatively superior to tap water. A 2011 survey of more than 3,200 Americans by researchers at Iowa State University and the University of Idaho found that perceived tap water quality was the single strongest predictor of bottled water consumption: Compared with people who trust their home tap water, respondents who did not believe that their tap water was safe were nearly five times as likely to use bottled water as their primary drinking water source (Hu et al. 2011; see also Abrahams, Hubbell, & Jordan 2000; Saylor, Prokopy, & Amberg 2011).[5] Growing evidence indicates that perceptions of tap water quality vary markedly by income and across racial and ethnic groups. Analysis of American Housing Survey data by UCLA researchers found a strong, positive correlation between household income and perceived tap water quality (Pierce & Gonzalez 2017). The same studies found lower trust in tap water among Blacks and Hispanics, compared with non-Hispanic whites (see also Javidi & Pierce 2018). Similar racial and ethnic patterns of distrust in tap water emerge in studies of African Americans in urban settings (Huerta-Saenz et al. 2012) and rural Hispanic communities (Scherzer et al. 2010).

These racial and ethnic disparities in tap water versus commercial water perception and consumption defy easy explanation. Is trust or distrust of tap water rooted in fact and reason? Are perceptions of water quality reflexive responses to sensational media? Is widespread distrust of tap water little more than superstition?

Leaving aside whether consumers can really perceive differences in taste between tap water and commercial water, it is difficult to imagine why taste in drinking water would vary systematically across racial or ethnic groups. An argument that Hispanics eschew tap water because they are socialized with cultural norms that value commercial water over tap water effectively begs the question. Simple cultural explanations cannot account for mistrust of tap water among native-born Black Americans or differences in perceptions about tap water quality among rich and poor and among high school educated and college

---

[5] Hu et al. (2011) also found that people who relied on private wells – which are effectively unregulated and of uneven quality – were *less* likely to use bottled water than customers of municipal utilities.

educated – especially when people receive tap water from the same system. Immigrants' experiences with and expectations about tap water from their countries of origin may explain some of the disparity in distrust (Pierce & Gonzalez 2017), but an explanation of distrust in tap water rooted in past ethnic experience is more rational than cultural. That is, if Hispanic mistrust of tap water originates with failing water systems in other countries, then Hispanic immigrants' preference for commercial water is a rational response to expectations about the institutions that provide drinking water.

## Institutional Trust at the Tap

Whether problems with tap water are real or merely perceived, the proliferation of bottled water and kiosks suggests that people choose these more expensive products because they perceive tap water quality as inferior to commercial water quality. Crucially, perceptions of tap water vary in part *because tap water comes from government.* Perceptions of tap water quality, therefore, are a function of people's trust in government: To trust tap water is to trust the government.

### *Distrust and Defensive Spending*

It could be that Hispanic and Black populations are disproportionately burdened by poor-quality tap water in ways that sow broader distrust of water utilities. The 2015 water crisis in Flint, Michigan, captured national headlines not only for the city's contaminated water, but also because Flint's plight framed drinking water in terms of race, socioeconomic class, and democracy (Pauli 2019). A majority of Flint's population is Black, and at the time of the crisis more than 40 percent of its households had incomes below federal poverty levels. Victims of Flint's drinking water contamination crisis were thus disproportionately poor and Black, whereas the state politicians and regulatory officials whose actions precipitated the crisis were mostly white and middle class. Popular accounts and official investigations of what came to be known as the "Flint water crisis" cast the event as a case of environmental injustice rooted in failures of governance (Davis et al. 2016). More than a public health disaster, the Flint water crisis's environmental justice frame evoked political identity for Blacks specifically and poor people generally (Čapek 1993). For many, the message of the Flint water crisis to the people of the United States was this: *Your tap water may be contaminated because the government does not care about you – especially if you are poor and Black.*

Flint is not alone, unfortunately. Analysis of US Environmental Protection Agency (EPA) data on community drinking water systems across the country reveals serious and significant racial, ethnic, and socioeconomic disparities in SDWA compliance. SDWA water quality violations are more common in communities with higher Black and especially Hispanic populations; moreover, these racial and ethnic disparities are greatest in poorer communities (Switzer & Teodoro 2017, 2018). That is, drinking water contamination is most common where people are both poor and nonwhite. Distrust of tap water among low-income and/or racial and ethnic minority populations seems more reasonable in light of these findings: For people who have experienced tap water that endangers human health, a preference for expensive alternatives is entirely rational. However, for people who have not experienced tap water that endangers human health, the preference for expensive alternatives is puzzling. Socioeconomic, racial, and ethnic differences in water consumption persist even within communities served by water utilities with sound records of drinking water quality (Javidi & Pierce 2018; Patel 2019). Distrust of tap water among poor and minority populations seems to grow not only from direct lived experience, but also from a shared identity with those who have experienced drinking water problems.

Black and Hispanic preference for bottled water follows in part from these systematic disparities in SDWA compliance, argue economists Kip Viscusi, Joel Huber, and Jason Bell (2015). High-profile contamination events lead consumers to "defensive spending" on commercial water in response to perceived health risks from far less expensive tap water (Dupont & Jahan 2012). This defensive spending is rooted in a deep distrust of tap water, even where there are no apparent health problems with tap water or health benefits to commercial drinking water.

## *Merchants of Thirst*[6]

Commercial water firms' marketing tactics and growth strategies align eerily with defensive spending as a source of profit. Consider the Primo

---

[6] The phrase "merchants of thirst" was the headline of a *New York Times* story about commercial water providers in the developing world (Schwartzenstein 2020).

company, for example. Primo is a commercial drinking water firm that provides direct delivery to home and business dispensers, operating self-service kiosks across North America and Europe. Consumer distrust of tap water is central to Primo's appeal to consumers.

Primo's advertising explicitly appeals to health concerns and stokes consumer fears about the quality of tap water. The company's slogan is "Drink Big. Drink Healthy," and in 2021 visitors to Primo's website were greeted with the words "HEALTHIER LIVES THROUGH HEALTHIER WATER" and "Drinking safer water should be a no-brainer." The advertisements that adorned water kiosks operated by the Primo company in Houston raised the specter of tap water contamination with the image of a rusty pipe. "Your tap water can hang out in some pretty seedy joints," the Primo sign warned consumers. "It's time to rethink your water." The advertisement's appeal to consumer fear was notably larger than its claims about the Primo kiosk's "9-step purification process." Commenting on the design of a commercial water kiosk, columnist Thomas Hine (1995) observed, "In a subtle way, this machine tells people that safe water is something that has to cost extra. Rather than spur improvement in public water, which might result in higher water rates, consumers prefer to make sure their own water is pure."

More than mere marketing, distrust of tap water born of failing infrastructure is key to Primo's corporate growth strategy. In 2019, Primo's filings with the Securities and Exchange Commission (SEC) told its investors,

*The water and wastewater infrastructure in the United States and Canada was given a D- grade by the American Society of Civil Engineers* in 2017. Trillions of dollars will be required to bring water treatment and drinking water distribution into compliance with applicable laws and standards over the next twenty years. In addition, many sources of drinking water are now contaminated with known and emerging contaminants which will likely require sophisticated water treatment technologies to render tap water safe. *Providing safe drinking water now will fall to forward thinking companies such as Primo who not only provide water that consumers trust* but also provide products that align with a sustainable, environmentally friendly business model.[7]

---

[7] Primo Water Corporation, 2019 Proxy Statement, Securities and Exchange Commission Schedule 14A (italics added).

In identifying the company's competitive strengths, Primo's 2021 SEC filing declared that consumer "concerns about deteriorating municipal water quality" represented the company's principal "new growth opportunity."[8] In discussing Primo's competition and threats to its market share, the same filing noted that "consumers may choose to drink from municipal water sources instead of purchasing bottled water." Ironically, the filing noted that Primo relies on municipal water for its supply.[9]

In 1984, a group of commercial water industry leaders established the Drinking Water Research Foundation (DWRF).[10] The innocuously named foundation's stated mission is to "conduct research and disseminate information regarding the sources, evaluation and production of safe and affordable drinking water, including bottled water, tap water and filtered water." With less than $300,000 in assets and annual revenue of less than $120,000, the DWRF apparently conducts little or no scientific research.[11] Rather, the DWRF issues press releases defending the commercial water industry and tracks news on legislative and regulatory developments related to commercial water. The foundation's website, thefactsaboutwater.org, publishes press releases, provides "expert views" on bottled versus tap water, and offers links to a carefully curated set of published scientific studies on the health benefits of hydration and health risks associated with tap water.[12]

---

[8] Primo Water Corporation, 2021 Proxy Statement, Securities and Exchange Commission Schedule 14A, p. 5.

[9] Primo Water Corporation, 2021 Proxy Statement, Securities and Exchange Commission Schedule 14A, p. 8. The same filing identified threats to municipal water sources as a risk factor that could hurt the company's financial performance: "[I]f any of our municipal water sources were curtailed or eliminated as a result of, for example, a natural disaster, work stoppage, or other significant event that disrupted water flow from such municipal source, we may have to purchase water from other sources, which could increase water and transportation costs" (p. 14).

[10] The Drinking Water Research Foundation of Alexandria, Virginia, is unrelated to the similarly named Water Research Foundation of Denver, Colorado.

[11] Google Scholar searches conducted at the time of writing yielded just one published study linked to the Drinking Water Research Foundation: a nonrefereed edited volume entitled *Safe Drinking Water: The Impact of Chemicals on a Limited Resource* (Rice 1985). The volume includes a chapter entitled "Bottled Water: An Alternative Source of Safe Drinking Water" by Jerry T. Hutton, vice president of food and drugs company Foremost-McKesson.

[12] The most-cited expert on thefactsaboutwater.org is Jack West, a bottled water industry consultant and chairman of DWRF's board of trustees.

On one hand, the DWRF declares bottled water to be "a safe and healthful alternative to other beverages," with a seal to ensure that "the safety of the water is uncompromised." On the other hand, "the quality of tap water depends mainly on factors outside the consumer's control." The DWRF is not so much a research enterprise as it is an advertisement for commercial water and an investment in doubt about tap water quality – all with a scientific veneer.

Just as the builders of the American state made their political fortunes on trust in tap water, much of the commercial water industry's profit springs from distrust in tap water. Some commercial water companies specifically target racial and ethnic groups in their marketing, capitalizing on distrust in government institutions – a practice that we examine further in Chapter 6. In the United States, commercial water success depends on encouraging and capitalizing on distrust in tap water – a collective service regulated by and mainly provided by government. Sowing distrust in tap water means growing distrust in government.

## The Argument in Brief

Trust or distrust at the tap has far-reaching consequences for governance writ large. Chapter 2 elaborates the logic that connects basic services to government trust and legitimacy, grounding each step in existing research; here, we briefly summarize the core argument as applied to drinking water.

Trust has two main dimensions: *competence* and *morality*. People trust government's competence when they believe that government leaders and employees are capable of carrying out public policy effectively; we call this *performative trust*. People trust government's morality when they believe in the basic benevolence of government leaders and employees; we call this *moral trust*. Belief in government's competence and morality contributes to trust in government, whereas perceived government ineptitude or malevolence drives distrust. To be trustworthy, it is not enough for governments to produce qualitatively good outcomes (e.g., my tap water is good and affordable); government administration also must be procedurally fair, respectful, and honest (e.g., my utility communicates clearly and respects me).

### Wellsprings of (Dis)trust

Three main factors account for a citizen-consumer's trust or distrust of government. First, *lived experiences* with and observations of government affect trust. People who enjoy benefits from government programs and services tend to trust government insofar as they recognize that government provides these benefits. Trust operates both directly (e.g., I trust my tap water because it is safe, reliable, and tastes good) and indirectly (e.g., I trust my tap water because my city's libraries, police, and fire departments are good). Second, public *agency reputations* contribute to trust in government. Reputations are widespread beliefs about government agencies' technical acumen, past performance, ethics, and fairness. Reputations emerge from politicians' and mass media depictions of government agencies and their work. Third, a person's trust in government is partly a function of his own *identity*. Members of social groups that enjoy privileged status or sizable political influence are inclined to view government institutions as benevolent and competent. Individuals from politically marginalized groups are likely to be more skeptical about government's intentions. Objective conditions are thus evaluated through a lens of identity. People who share racial, ethnic, socioeconomic, or other elements of social identity with victims of government failure will perceive government failure elsewhere as confirmatory evidence that government itself is untrustworthy.

Citizen-consumers who are dissatisfied with the quality of government service provision may either *voice* their concerns to officials in hopes that governments will improve conditions or *exit* by purchasing goods or services from commercial firms. The choice between voice and exit turns on the citizen-consumer's expectations about the effectiveness of her voice and the cost of commercial alternatives. If distrust arises from government incompetence, then the citizen-consumer may rationally respond with voice. Citizens may be dissatisfied with outcomes but nonetheless maintain faith in the moral decency of government as an institution. In such cases, citizens may voice concerns through the political process in hopes of improving conditions. However, if the citizen-consumer distrusts government's basic morality, then she distrusts government as a political institution and will always exit for available commercial alternatives. Indeed, distrustful citizen-consumers who exit for commercial providers may oppose efforts to improve government services because such efforts are seen as costly and futile. The citizen-consumers most distrustful of government will abandon government providers for commercial providers rather than demanding improved service or regulatory enforcement from government.

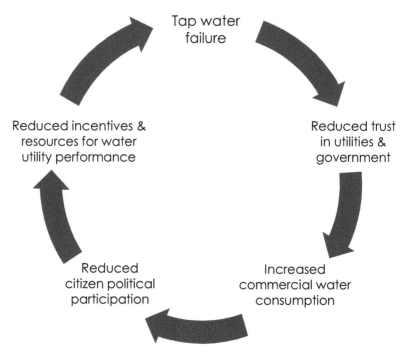

**Figure 1.8** The vicious cycle of distrust in tap water.

*Note*: This water-specific model depicts the vicious cycle of distrust, and recurs throughout the book as a conceptual model. In Chapter 2 we introduce a version of this model that applies to all basic services.

### A Vicious Cycle

When tap water failures occur – locally, regionally, or nationally – citizen-consumers abandon utilities in favor of commercial water, with the most distrustful and politically marginalized people most likely to opt for bottled water. Already politically weak, marginalized citizen-consumers have less to gain from engagement with the state and thus withdraw from political participation and civic life more generally as they exit to private alternatives. Politicians have little reason to respond to the demands of populations who do not participate in politics. As citizen-consumers withdraw from civic life, the government agencies that produce and/or regulate water have weaker incentives and fewer resources to provide excellent water utility service. With less oversight, a less active citizenry, and fewer resources, water utility service quality continues to erode: Tap water failures become more common, trust declines further, and a feedback sets in. Distrust becomes alienation, and the perception of government failure becomes self-fulfilling. Figure 1.8 depicts this vicious cycle of distrust and serves as a conceptual model that recurs throughout the book.

## The Profits of Distrust

As this vicious cycle proceeds, private firms capture profits in the form of a *distrust premium*, paid by citizen-consumers who believe that governments provide inferior service. In the case of drinking water, the distrust premium is readily observable in the vast volumetric price differences between tap water and its commercial alternatives. Commercial growth and profit depend in large part on the size and scope of that perceived gap in quality. Charges of poor or inequitable government service, valid or not, will find their most receptive audience among the politically marginalized, so citizen-consumers who distrust government readily pay the distrust premium. In the case of water, commercial water companies stoke fears about tap water quality and assert the superior quality of bottled and kiosk water to attract consumers – especially among the poor and members of racial and ethnic minority groups. The private firms that provide alternatives to government goods and services have strong incentives to rub raw the sores of distrust.[13]

## A Virtuous Cycle?

Fortunately, this vicious cycle can also be virtuous. Just as failure and distrust lead to exit and cynicism about government, trust can lead to engagement with and support for better government. In the tradition of Putnam's (1993) classic work on the political effects of social capital, we argue that the quality of basic services drives trust in the institutions of government, which leads to greater public engagement, which in turn leads to better government performance. Drinking tap water is a sign of trust in government: The citizen who drinks from the tap implicitly entrusts her health to the agencies that provide and/or regulate her water. Reliant on tap water and trusting in the institutions of government, she will support investments in public water utilities and demand quality from politicians and managers. Buoyed by or at least mindful of those demands, regulatory officials and utility operators will fulfill that trust with the high-quality water and sewer services that helped establish the legitimacy of the state more than a century ago.

Basic services are the foundation of state legitimacy. In the book's last two chapters, we show that the vicious cycle in Figure 1.8 can turn

---

[13] With apologies to Saul Alinsky.

virtuous, with excellent basic services building trust in the institutions of government and fueling greater citizen engagement. For visionary political leaders, then, rebuilding American civic life starts with literally rebuilding the infrastructure that sustains life.

## Plan of the Book

This has been a brief introduction to the argument that we develop and support in the chapters ahead. Chapter 2, "The Profits of Distrust," presents our argument in detail, tracing the logics of consumer behavior, public administration, psychology, and politics that drive the profits of distrust. Chapter 2 is concerned mainly with theory, generalizing the conceptual model in Figure 1.8 beyond drinking water to all basic services. Rooted in scholarship across multiple disciplines, Chapter 2 is aimed mainly at scholars; the chapter culminates in a series of hypotheses linking basic service problems to trust in government, citizen-consumer behavior, and citizen political participation. Readers who are chiefly interested in drinking water and less interested in social scientific theory may safely skim Chapter 2 or proceed directly to the empirical chapters that follow.

Chapters 3–7 lay out the empirical evidence for our claims about the relationships between service quality, trust in government, commercial markets for government alternatives, and politics. Each of these chapters opens with an anecdote that illustrates our argument and connects the chapter's substance to the broader conceptual map in Figure 1.8. Analysis of data on drinking water, consumer behavior, public opinion, and political participation in the United States follows in each of these chapters. The empirical investigation starts in Chapter 3, "(Dis)trust at the Tap," which explores the relationship between tap water quality and performative trust. We show that people who experience problems with their drinking water trust government less, and that failures in tap water provision predict local commercial water demand.

Chapter 4, "Hyperopia and Performative Trust," continues the exploration of performative trust with an analysis of the relationship between water quality compliance and the prevalence of commercial drinking water kiosks. Spatial analysis shows that the effects of tap water failure on public trust transcend political and service area boundaries. In other words, tap water problems in one place affect citizen-consumer perceptions of tap water in other places. Distrust at the tap is contagious, particularly among low-income populations and members of racial and ethnic minority communities. For the politically marginalized, tap water failure anywhere undermines trust everywhere.

In Chapter 5, "Speaking Up or Opting Out," we demonstrate the individual citizen-consumer logic at the heart of our argument. Citizen-consumers who are dissatisfied with their tap water may complain to their utilities in an effort to improve service (i.e., voice) or buy commercial drinking water instead (i.e., exit). We show that low-income Black and Hispanic individuals are less likely than higher-income white and non-Hispanic people to voice their discontent with tap water to governments. Drawing on data from multiple public opinion surveys and nationwide bottled water sales data, we show that distrust in government predicts "exit" from tap water to the commercial drinking water market. Crucially, we also find a marked demographic and socioeconomic skew to these patterns of distrust and exit: Low-income and nonwhite people are most likely to opt for commercial drinking water. We then show that this choice of "exit" over "voice" extends to broader political participation – as bottled water sales rise, voter turnout declines.

Chapter 6, "Geographies of Alienation," focuses on patterns of political marginalization and drinking water behavior that emerge in three parts of the United States. Analysis of water kiosk locations and bottled water sales shows that kiosks are disproportionately located in areas where significant portions of the population have been politically marginalized through decades – or even centuries – of institutional bias or neglect. Exactly which populations are politically alienated varies across this diverse country; this chapter explores three of them: Blacks in the American South, rural populations in Appalachia, and Hispanics in the Southwest.

The analysis comes full circle in Chapter 7, "When Trust Pays." We show that political support for public investment in water infrastructure is greater among people who drink tap water and lower among commercial water drinkers. Utilities thus benefit from greater public support when citizen-consumers trust government enough to drink deeply from their taps. The payoff to citizen-consumers comes in the form of better performance: Utilities comply with tap water quality rules where voter turnout is higher.

The book concludes by linking basic services – in our case, the humble, ubiquitous pipes that lie beneath our city streets – to foundational principles of government. The rise of commercial water and concomitant decline of trust in government reveal something essential about the relationship between citizen and state. If governments establish their legitimacy by ensuring the basic security, health, and welfare of their people, then maintenance of these basic services is a key to maintaining state legitimacy. The rise of commercial water in America is a subtle but persistent sign that Americans do not trust their governments. Breaking the cycle of distrust and restoring institutional legitimacy require restoring public confidence in government's ability to provide for basic services. Chapter 8, "Basic Services and Rebuilding Legitimacy," offers a series of guidelines for restoring faith in the promise of democracy through excellence, openness, and equity in basic services. To that end, we close the book with "The Plan," a set of practical reforms to improve water service in America, and so to restore faith in the promise of democracy.

# 2 | *The Profits of Distrust*
## A Political Theory of the Citizen-Consumer

Instead of stimulating improved or top performance, the presence of a ready and satisfactory substitute for the services [a] public enterprise offers merely deprives it of a precious feedback mechanism.

Albert Hirschman,[1] *Exit, Voice, and Loyalty*

What Fiji and other bottlers understand is that people can be made to fear the quality of water that comes out of their taps. We don't know where it comes from. We don't know what's done to purify it. And we're distrustful of the governments or corporations that have the responsibility to clean, protect, and deliver it.

Peter Gleick,[2] *Bottled and Sold*

Presented with a choice between commercial and government suppliers, why do people opt for loosely regulated, socially or environmentally destructive commercial products that are qualitatively indistinguishable from and vastly more expensive than their public alternatives? Why do people with the fewest resources choose the more expensive commercial products? Why do democratically elected governments fail to provide high-quality basic services, even though citizens value those products and services and are evidently willing to pay a premium for them? The paradoxes of drinking water in the United States outlined in Chapter 1 lead to more fundamental questions about basic services and democratic governance.

This chapter widens the scope of inquiry beyond drinking water to take up these fundamental questions. We advance a political theory of citizen-consumer behavior that links the quality of basic services to trust in governance institutions, consumer choices, and political participation. In focusing our model on the "citizen-consumer," we begin from the premise that citizens are also consumers. Consumer choice

---

[1] Hirschman (1970, 44).    [2] Gleick (2010, 17).

can be a form of political behavior, and political factors can shape consumer choice. At the same time, consumer behavior and commercial factors can shape political decisions. We argue that citizen-consumers' choices of products reflect their trust in government, and so the firms that compete with government have an incentive to stoke distrust in government. As citizen-consumers opt out of government services in favor of services from private providers, their incentives for engagement with government decline. Distrust and the choices that follow are most pronounced among people who are most politically alienated. In turn, rational government officials have less incentive to satisfy the needs of citizen-consumers who abandon the public forum in favor of the private market. The government failures that follow further erode trust in government, reinforcing a cycle that alienates citizens and boosts the bottom lines of the commercial firms that compete with government.

## Basic Service Provision

Although our empirical subject is drinking water, our theory is general insofar as it applies to any context where government agencies and commercial firms provide similar or identical products and services *in direct competition with one another*. Familiar examples in the twenty-first-century United States include public versus private schools, public versus private hospitals, libraries versus bookstores, the US Postal Service versus private delivery companies such as FedEx and UPS, and, of course, commercial versus tap water. We are especially concerned with *basic* services: the services that are required to maintain a safe, healthy, and productive life. Examples include law enforcement, firefighting, medicine, housing, food, sanitation, energy, and drinking water.

Importantly, we argue that governments must *provide* for basic goods and services, not necessarily that governments must *produce* those goods and services. That is, the government must sustain conditions in which all citizens receive what they need to be safe, healthy, and productive, but the government itself need not produce services to meet all of its citizens' basic needs. Most Americans receive their basic services from a mix of government and private entities. For example, with few exceptions, law enforcement, firefighting, and flood protection in the United States are provided and produced by governments.

Meanwhile, food and housing in the United States are overwhelmingly produced by private firms, but regulated and/or subsidized to various degrees by government. Sanitation, solid waste disposal, energy, and water services in the United States are all government regulated, but produced by a mix of public, private, and nonprofit entities. Government is responsible for ensuring basic services, but those goods and services may be produced directly by government agencies or by private-sector entities under government regulation, oversight, and/or subsidy.[3] For simplicity, this chapter and most of the book refer to collectively provided basic goods and services as "government" goods, even if they are produced by private companies.

Our theory proceeds from an assumption that government agencies and commercial firms that provide similar or identical goods already exist; our theory does not directly explain the entry of firms or agencies into a market. We are primarily interested in explaining the citizen-consumer choice between products provided by government agencies and commercial firms. Our theory does not address a government's choice to privatize or contract public services, for example. Applied to drinking water, we seek to explain an individual's choice to drink bottled or tap water, but not a city's decision to own or privatize its water utility.

## Choice and Rationality

Ours is essentially a *rational choice* theory. That is, our claims are about decisions that individuals, commercial firm managers, public administrators, and politicians make to maximize utility, given their contexts and constraints. In the tradition of Herbert Simon (1985), we assume that people rationally pursue goals (e.g., health, financial profit, or reelection) using the alternatives available to them, subject to their informational and cognitive limits.[4] Our main aims in adopting

---

[3] In this respect, we disagree with those who argue that private production of public services necessarily weakens civic life (e.g., Lerman 2019; Warner 2009). Commercial production of basic services per se does not undermine citizenship or trust in government.

[4] We do not claim that rational choice is the only valid way to understand basic services, citizen-consumer behavior, or trust in government; for instance, interpretivist (e.g., Rosenthal 2021) and constructivist (e.g., Bevir 2013) approaches can yield important insights on these topics.

a rational choice framework are clarity and rigor. Befitting a model of citizen-consumers, our argument weaves together theories of consumer choice, agency reputation, public opinion, and political behavior. We draw on existing work in economics, psychology, public administration, and political science, which we summarize along the way as necessary to craft our argument. Exhaustive reviews of these literatures are beyond the scope of this chapter – or even the book – as the research on these subjects across disciplines is voluminous and deep. Rather, we seek to lay before the reader representations of the most relevant lines of research.

We begin with a simple model of consumer choice. Building on existing research from public administration and psychology, we argue that government agencies' reputations and citizens' experiences and identities condition choices in ways that can make consumer behavior a form of political behavior. Moving from the logic of consumer choice to a logic of citizen political participation, we argue that citizen-consumers who distrust government choose not to engage with public agencies and instead opt for commercial products. In turn, governments have less incentive to respond to the needs of a disengaged populace, which drives further declines in performance through a vicious, self-reinforcing cycle of distrust.

After tracing this logic, we turn to our empirical subject: drinking water. The chapter culminates in a series of hypotheses that apply our theory of the citizen-consumer to drinking water choice, political behavior, and governance in the United States. However, although the empirical analyses that fill the chapters of this book are about drinking water, the argument is at its core about relationships between the citizens and the state – and the legitimacy of government itself.

## Citizen-Consumer Choice

Presented with a choice between government and commercial providers of similar goods, consumers choose the same way that they choose any other products or services in a market: They weigh the goods' relative benefits and costs, and then decide how much of each to buy, subject to the constraint of resources available. The consumer's goal is to maximize her *utility*, or the happiness derived from consumption of the goods or services.

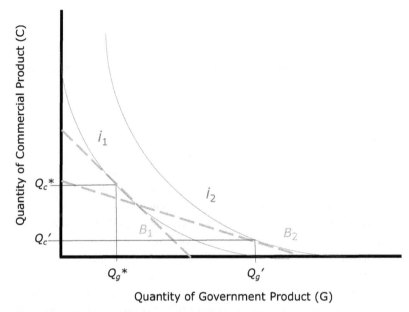

**Figure 2.1** Simple model of consumer choice with commercial and government producers.

## Basics of Consumer Choice

As depicted in Figure 2.1, the basic mechanics of consumer choice are familiar to any student of microeconomics. In Figure 2.1, the horizontal and vertical axes represent, respectively, the quantity of government ($G$) and commercial ($C$) products that the consumer purchases. The dashed diagonal lines $B_1$ and $B_2$ are the consumer's budget functions, which reflect the possible combinations of $G$ and $C$ that she might purchase, given the prices of the two goods and her available resources.[5] Sloping downward at 45 degrees, $B_1$ assumes identical unit prices of $G$ and $C$; $B_2$ is flatter, indicating that the government product is less expensive on a unit cost basis.

The curved lines $i_1$ and $i_2$ are the consumer's indifference curves, representing the combinations of $G$ and $C$ that produce the same overall utility. Indifference curves represent progressively greater utility further from the origin. The shape of these indifference curves depends

---

[5] For simplicity, we assume linear prices for both $G$ and $C$; that is, the unit price of neither good changes as the volume purchased increases.

on the consumer's marginal rate of substitution (*MRS*). Formally, *MRS* for a government good $G$ and commercial good $C$ is the ratio of marginal utility that the consumer receives from the government good ($MU_g$) to the marginal utility that she gets from the commercial good ($MU_c$):

$$MRS_{g,c} = \frac{MU_g}{MU_c} = \frac{\partial g}{\partial c}. \tag{2.1}$$

Therefore, $\frac{\partial g}{\partial c}$ is the rate at which the consumer will trade off a unit of $G$ for a unit of $C$ at various quantities of each good. A consumer's indifference curve is convex to the origin, reflecting diminishing marginal rates of substitution between the two goods.

If government and commercial prices are equal, the consumer's overall utility is greatest at the point of tangency between $B_1$ and $i_1$, depicted in Figure 2.1 as point ($Q_G^*$, $Q_C^*$). If government prices are lower, then the consumer maximizes utility at the point of tangency $B_2$ and $i^2$, or point ($Q_G'$, $Q_C'$). In this depiction, $i_2$ is further from the origin than $i_1$, so $i_2$ represents greater utility for this consumer: She will buy more $G$ and less C. Consumers will always prefer to buy more government goods than commercial goods if the government goods are less expensive, *provided that government products are perceived as qualitatively identical or superior to commercial products.* We turn to differences in perceived quality next.

### Substitutes

Many of the services that governments and commercial firms provide are substitutes: Consumers choose either one or the other, as it makes no sense to buy some of one and some of the other. For example, if a father wants to send a birthday gift to his daughter who lives in a different city, he can take his gift to a government post office or to a private shipping firm. If he has only one gift to ship, he will use either the government post office or the private shipping firm, but not some fractional amount of shipping from each. If the consumer perceives the two services as qualitatively identical – that is, they ship on the same schedule, with the same reliability, provide similar customer service, and so on – then the two providers are *perfect substitutes*. If the father with the gift to ship considers the postal service and commercial firm to be qualitatively identical, he will choose the less expensive option. The $MRS_{g,c}$ for perfect substitutes is constant, as depicted in Figure 2.2 for

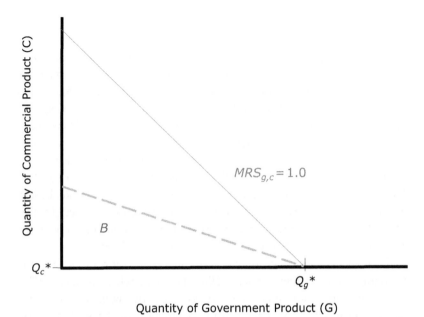

**Figure 2.2** Consumer choice with commercial and government perfect substitutes.

$G$ and $C$. If the price of government service $G$ is lower than its identical commercial service $C$, the rational consumer maximizes his utility by buying only $g$ and no $c$ at all $(Q_g^*)$.

The sustained presence of more expensive commercial alternatives to government providers implies that consumers perceive qualitative differences between government goods or services and commercial goods or services. In other words, $MRS_{g,c}$ must vary such that, for a substantial set of consumers, commercial goods and services are valued differently from government goods and services.[6] Those differences in value might stem from real differences in quality or merely from perceptions about quality.

---

[6] Of course, it is possible for commercial firms to provide products and services at lower prices than governments. The logic of consumer behavior is fairly straightforward in that case: Consumers select less expensive products and services from commercial firms because they are less expensive. Our theory is concerned with situations in which consumers opt for commercial alternatives that are more expensive than government goods and services.

**Beliefs and Branding**

Consumers' beliefs about the relative quality of goods and services are enormously important to commercial firms' success. In consumer economics, positive consumer perceptions about a company's products raise consumers' willingness to pay (Lassar, Mittal, & Sharma 1995), reduce price elasticity (Krishnamurthi & Raj 1991), and allow firms to capture larger profit margins from sales (Aaker 2009; Keller 1993). Consumers tend to choose branded products when they have preferences about quality, but little valid information about quality (Cobb-Walgren, Ruble, & Donthu 1995; Erdem & Swait 1998; Faircloth, Capella, & Alford 2001). Firm reputations communicated through branding thus evoke beliefs about a product apart from the "objective reality of the product" (Keller 1993, 8). Successful brands convey reputational information so potently that consumers may choose products of their favored brands at substantially higher prices than qualitatively identical competitors (Foxall, Oliveira-Castro, & Schrezenmaier 2004; Foxall & Schrezenmaier 2003).

A firm's reputation thus plays a key role in growing firm value (Lane & Jacobson 1995; Mahajan, Rao, & Srivastava 1994; Simon & Sullivan 1993), independent of its products' qualitative merits. Firm reputations can also be negative, driving consumers to competitors. Commercial firms thus have strong incentives to invest in, manage, and develop their brands in ways that make their products seem superior to competitors' products. For commercial firms, the payoffs for investments in reputation building are growth and profitability. For government bureaucrats, the payoff for reputation building is greater autonomy or career advancement (Krause & Douglas 2005; MacDonald & Franko 2007; Moffitt 2010; Teodoro 2011). For politicians, the reputational payoffs are support for parties and the legitimacy of the state itself (Teaford 1984). A strong, positive reputation leads citizen-consumers to choose government products and services. Where commercial firms' main competition is from government agencies, profitability and growth rest in significant part on consumers' belief that the commercial products are superior to the government's.

## Trust in Government and Consumer Choice

Unlike commercial firms, beliefs about the quality of government agencies' reputations are inexorably political. Consumer perceptions of government products and services depend to some degree on their *trust in government itself.* Apart from qualitative differences between government and commercial products is the consumer's perception that government itself is good, bad, or trustworthy (Lerman 2019). The very idea of government carries ideological implications that may shape perceptions about the quality of government services for people of different partisan affiliations (Teodoro & An 2018). For public agencies, trust in government is akin to a brand.

We take up the meaning and sources of trust in detail later in this chapter; for now, we simply adapt the basic model of consumer choice to account for a consumer's trust in government. Trust in government ($t$) modifies $MRS_{g,c}$ such that

$$MRS_{g,c} = \frac{MU_g}{MU_c^{1/t}}, \qquad (2.2)$$

where $t$ is the consumer's degree of trust in government from zero to one; a value of one indicates complete trust and a value approaching zero indicates absolute distrust. In a case where $g$ and $c$ are qualitatively identical, a consumer who trusts government completely is indifferent between the government and commercial product $\left( lim_{\,t-1}t = MRS_{g,c} = 1 \right)$. As $t$ decreases, the consumer values $g$ less relative to $c$ and is increasingly willing to trade consumption of $g$ for units of $c$. As $t$ approaches zero, the value of $c$ relative to $g$ increases exponentially, to the point that the commercial product is extremely valuable compared with its government equivalent – simply because trust in government is low. In specifying $t$ as a fractional exponent to $MU_c$, we emphasize that the effect of trust in government on consumer choice is nonlinear: Small declines in $t$ can exponentially increase the appeal of commercial products relative to government products. This analytical depiction of trust in government aligns with well-established psychological evidence that evaluations are much more strongly influenced by negative experiences than positive ones (Braumeister et al. 2001; Kanouse & Hanson 1972; Lau 1985). Negatives greatly outweigh positives in cognitive processes, even when negative experiences are few in number and small in magnitude, and positive experiences are frequent and meaningful. Experimental research demonstrates that this negativity bias occurs in citizen evaluations of government performance and that the effects of negative performance on evaluations are stronger for public agencies than for private firms (van den Bekerom, van der Voet, & Christensen 2020).

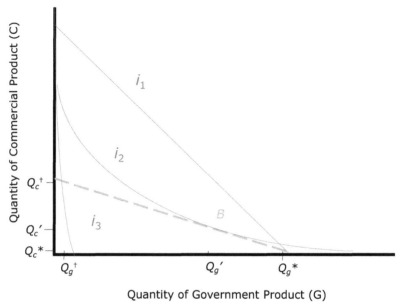

**Figure 2.3** Government and commercial product choice with varying trust in government.

The effect of trust in government (*t*) on consumer behavior is illustrated in Figure 2.3, a simple adaptation of the basic model of consumer choice presented in Figure 2.1. In this depiction, the budget function *B* retains a gradual slope, indicating that the unit price of the commercial good (*c*) is greater than the price of the government good (*g*). If *G* and *C* are qualitatively identical, and the consumer believes that the government is completely trustworthy ($t{\rightarrow}1$), then the two products are perfect substitutes and the consumer maximizes utility at the point of tangency of $i_1$ and $B$ [$Q_c^*$, $Q_g^*$]. In this case, the consumer will buy the lower-priced *g* almost exclusively and seldom opt for the more expensive *c*. If the consumer trusts government only moderately, then some amount of *c* provides greater utility than *g* alone, represented by the more convex indifference curve $i_2$. This moderately trusting consumer will buy a combination of *c* and *g* where $i_2$ touches $B$, [$Q_c'$, $Q_g'$]. As an inverse exponential function, the marginal utility of the commercial product ($MU_c$) rises sharply as trust declines.

For an entirely distrustful consumer, $t$ approaches zero, and $MRS_{g,c}$ also approaches zero, making the commercial alternative nearly infinitely preferable to the government product. The extremely distrustful consumer's indifference curve becomes nearly vertical at $i_3$; she will consume $g$ and $c$ at the point where $i_3$ meets $B$, $[Q_c^\dagger, Q_g^\dagger]$ in Figure 2.3. This highly distrustful consumer will buy the more expensive $c$ almost exclusively and only rarely consume the less expensive $g$. Importantly, holding actual product quality constant, the consumer's overall utility declines as her trust in government declines, such that the total payoff to the consumer in Figure 2.3 is $i_1 > i_2 > i_3$. This consumer loss of utility occurs because substituting more expensive commercial goods for less expensive government goods reduces the total amount of the good that she can buy, given prices and resources. This *distrust premium* is profit to the commercial firm. In cases of extreme distrust, consumers will eschew government products entirely and engage in "defensive spending" on commercial products and services because they fear and wish to avoid government itself (Dupont & Jahan 2012).

## Roots of Government (Dis)trust

To this point, we have argued that trust in government (or lack thereof) drives citizen-consumers to opt for commercial or government products that are qualitatively similar. But on its own, this claim amounts to little more than a tautology: People choose commercial products because they trust commercial firms more than they trust government agencies; we know that people distrust government because they choose expensive commercial products over cheaper government products.[7] To be useful, a theory of citizen-consumer behavior that turns on trust in government must define and account

---

[7] The tautology can be expressed mathematically. Rearranging Eq. (2.2), we see that

$$t = \frac{\ln(MU_g)}{\ln(MU_c)}$$

so that trust in government ($t$) is the ratio of log marginal utility of government products to log marginal utility of commercial products. That is, the more that citizen-consumers value government products relative to commercial products, the more they will trust the government. The opposite is also true: As the value of commercial products increases relative to the value of government products, trust in government decreases.

for variation in trust. What exactly *is* trust in government? Where does it come from? Why do some people trust government more than others do? What causes trust to increase or decrease?

Trust in government is a subject of deep and perennial interest to social scientists generally and political scientists specifically. Although the term is contested, we adopt Margaret Levi and Laura Stoker's (2000) understanding of *trust* as a relational condition between a truster and an individual, group, organization, or institution. In developing a workable definition of *trust*, Levi and Stoker argue,

> Trust is a judgment that can be conceptualized dichotomously (one either trusts or distrusts) or in a more graded fashion (one trusts or distrusts to a degree).... Trust judgments are expected to inspire courses of action. Distrust, for example, may inspire vigilance in and monitoring of a relationship, uncooperative behavior, or the severing of a relationship. (2000, 476)

Social contexts with high levels of generalized trust tend to enjoy more effective governance because trust reduces transaction costs associated with political and economic relationships (Fukuyama 1995; Hetherington 2005; Putnam 1993). Levi and Stoker further identify *morality* and *competence* as separate dimensions of trust. A morally trustworthy person or institution is committed to "act in the interests of the truster because of *moral values* that emphasize promise-keeping, caring about the truster, [and/or] incentive compatibility." A person or an institution also can enjoy trust rooted in "*competence* in the domain over which trust is being given" (2000, 476, italics added). Trust and its opposite, distrust, have both moral and performative dimensions.[8]

Much of the vast research on trust in government deals with public opinion about parties and politicians, along with the effects of trust on elections, citizen behavior, and public policy. Since our interest is in citizen-consumer choices, we draw on the narrower body of research on trust in government agencies and institutions. Studies on public administration, bureaucratic politics, and racial/ethnic identity each take up elements of trust in government and provide building blocks for our theory. Specifically, we connect trust in government to three factors: (1) people's direct *experiences* with government, (2) public

---

[8] Some public relations researchers have argued that *trust* and *distrust* are related, but separate, psychological constructs (e.g., Kang & Park 2017). We follow the political science/public administration convention by depicting *trust* and *distrust* as ends of a single continuous spectrum.

agencies' *reputations*, and (3) the degree to which people *identify* with the recipients of government benefits or with the victims of government abuse and neglect.

## Experience with Government

At its heart, democratic theory is concerned with whether governments sustain conditions that align with citizen preferences (Mill 1861). Perhaps the most immediately obvious determinant of a person's trust in government is his or her lived experience with government. People who enjoy and recognize benefits from government programs are more supportive of government and engaged in civic life generally, owing to their positive experiences with government (Mettler 2007, 2011). The relationship between trust and experiences with government may be direct or indirect. Individuals' perceptions about the trustworthiness of a government agency can follow from their own personal interactions with government agencies or officials. For example, children's classroom experiences shape their trust in schools as institutions (Torney-Purta, Barber, & Richardson 2004), and interactions with police officers affect citizen trust in courts and law enforcement agencies (Tyler & Huo 2002).

Experiences with and observations of government can also affect trust indirectly. Some of the most compelling recent empirical research on this subject is Gregg Van Ryzin's work on the connections between public agency performance and trust in government. Van Ryzin led a series of studies aimed at clarifying the links between citizens' trust in government and their perceptions of government performance and fairness. The American Consumer Satisfaction Index (ACSI) is based on an annual survey of hundreds of thousands of US consumers, and it has been a touchstone of consumer research since 1994. In 2004, Van Ryzin applied ACSI survey items on satisfaction, expectations, and preferences to local government services and found that local government ACSI results correlated strongly with several other measures of local government service quality. He also found that government ACSI scores correlate with trust in government (Van Ryzin 2004b). Refined analyses of data from New York City residents showed that citizen perceptions of local government performance predict satisfaction with local government and, in turn, trust in local government (Van Ryzin 2007). Van Ryzin also showed that experiences and/or observations about the quality of government service have effects across policy areas. That is, perceived government performance in one area (e.g., postal delivery or traffic management) can affect perceptions about government in other areas (e.g., firefighting or libraries) and thus shape an individual's trust in government indirectly (Van Ryzin 2004a, 2007).

Van Ryzin also identified two important aspects of the links between government performance, citizen satisfaction, and trust in government. The first is a distinction between public administration *outcomes* and *processes* (2011, 2015). Conventional wisdom supposes that citizens evaluate their governments chiefly, or perhaps exclusively, based on observed outcomes. In this line of thought, most people have well-formed preferences over the state of the world (e.g., safe streets, a clean environment, secure borders, educated children) but less clear preferences on the means by which government should achieve that state. Citizens are generally thought to hold weak preferences over laws and administrative processes, apart from their effects on outcomes. Similarly, research on citizen satisfaction in public administration tradition tends to proceed from the assumption (often unstated) that citizen evaluations of government are driven chiefly by outcomes, not processes. Challenging this view, Van Ryzin used a series of public opinion surveys in the United States (2015) and several other countries (2011) to demonstrate that citizen perceptions of procedural fairness, equity, respect, and honesty also contribute significantly to trust in government. It is not enough for governments to produce good outcomes; to be trustworthy, government administration also must be procedurally fair, equitable, respectful, and honest. In distinguishing between *outcome* and *process* effects and demonstrating the importance of each concept to citizens, Van Ryzin's model aligns remarkably well with the two dimensions of trust that Levi and Stoker (2000) identify: *competence* and *morality*.

Van Ryzin's second key insight is that the effects of individuals' experiences and observations on their trust in government are conditioned by their *expectations* about government (2007, 2011). According to this expectancy-disconfirmation model, "citizens form their overall satisfaction judgments by comparing their perceptions of performance to their prior expectations," argued Van Ryzin. "To the extent that perceived performance meets or exceeds expectations, citizens are satisfied, and to the extent that perceived performance falls short of their expectations, citizens grow dissatisfied" (2007, 529). A citizen's evaluation of government – especially at the ballot box – follows from these expectations: When the conditions that a person observes and experiences align with her preferences, then she is more satisfied with and supportive of the government; when the state of the world deviates substantially from her preferences, she is less satisfied and supportive of the government. This basic logic underlies the model of retrospective voting familiar to political scientists (Fiorina 1978). Van Ryzin does not address the implications of extremely negative expectations under this expectancy-disconfirmation model. If expectations of government are not just low (e.g., *I expect government to fail*) but extremely negative (e.g., *I expect government to do harm*), it could be possible for government to perform well and yet engender distrust nonetheless. Cognitively, expectations about the quality of government service inform both the perception of government performance and the degree to which government performance drives trust in government (Favero & Kim 2020). We turn, then, to the source of those expectations: government reputation.

## Government Reputation

Reputations are widely held beliefs about something or someone. Applied to commercial firms and government agencies, reputations define baseline expectations that feed Van Ryzin's expectancy-disconfirmation model. Just as a commercial firm's reputation conveys information about the trustworthiness of its products, so does a government's reputation. In *Good Enough for Government Work*, Amy Lerman (2019) argues that government in the United States suffers from a broad "reputation crisis." She writes, "Over the past several decades, a majority of citizens have come to believe that government is wasteful and inefficient, and that the public sector is incapable of offering services that are equivalent to or better than what the private market can provide" (2019, 4). Lerman's analysis of public opinion data demonstrates that, on average, Americans believe that government is poorly managed relative to the private sector; this perceived government mismanagement drives broad distrust in government.

In a series of clever experiments, Lerman (2019) shows that Americans are likely to ascribe positive experiences to private providers and negative experiences to governments, regardless of the true service provider or quality. For example, she finds that residents of Princeton, New Jersey, and Chicago, Illinois, who believe they are receiving high-quality private services are more likely to favor privat-ization, even when the services they receive are actually provided by local government (2019, 113). Lerman argues that these perceptions lead citizens to opt for private instead of public providers of goods and services.[9] Lerman mostly blames political rhetoric for government's poor reputation, observing that right-leaning politicians often stoke distrust in government for electoral purposes. To counter the govern-ment reputation crisis, Lerman looks to prominent private-sector examples of corporations such as Citigroup and Nike that repaired their damaged reputations with careful public messaging. Although she acknowledges that governments sometimes fail abjectly, her main prescription for government's reputational ailments involves calls to "think about efficiency in the public sector in a new and potentially more productive way" (2019, 240) and to "reimagine how we talk about government" (244). For Lerman, government's reputation prob-lems are principally problems of perception and communication.[10]

At the same time, a lively body of research on bureaucracy analyzes the causes and consequences of public agency reputations. Perhaps the most prominent works in this line of inquiry are Daniel Carpenter's

---

[9] Most of Lerman's experiments measure opinions and attitudes, not consumer behavior. Lerman offers anecdotes about consumer choices between public and private providers (e.g., families choosing private schools rather than public schools), but she does not establish the relationship between government distrust and consumer behavior empirically. For example, Lerman argues that "individuals with negative perceptions of government performance are also more likely to opt out of participation in public programs" (2019, 126). As evidence, Lerman uses a survey experiment on whether uninsured individuals would participate in the Affordable Care Act (ACA). In the experiment, individuals are treated with a website that emphasizes the public or private nature of the ACA. Lerman finds that uninsured individuals who hold negative views of government are more likely to enroll in insurance if they receive the private-oriented treatment. She concludes, "In the end, beliefs about government inefficiency and waste can help explain why citizens opt out of government services and programs from which they might otherwise benefit" (2019, 147). While this experiment demonstrates that an individual's partisanship and beliefs about government affect her participation in a government program, it is not really a test of opting out. In order to opt out of government service, an individual must currently receive that service. Lerman's behavioral test was conducted on *uninsured* individuals – the test measures whether individuals are likely to *opt in* to a new service, not whether they are likely to *opt out* from an existing one. Choosing to receive a new service (i.e., opting in) is different from evaluating government service and finding it to be wanting (i.e., opting out); put another way, Lerman's test subjects are not so much choosing to exit as choosing whether to enter.

[10] Lerman (2019) is mostly silent about the relationships between government performance and reputation.

studies on the development of the American administrative state (2000, 2001). In *Forging of Bureaucratic Autonomy*, Carpenter (2001) details the actions of enterprising administrators in driving society-transforming public policies through their agencies. Federal agencies extended the reach of the national government into ordinary Americans' lives immediately and tangibly through rural postal delivery, forest management, and agricultural assistance, Carpenter shows. Creating these policy regimes involved demonstrating agencies' capacity by making observable impacts on the world and honing agencies' public images. In pursuing these goals, agency leaders not only forged autonomy for themselves but also contributed to the broader legitimacy of the state.

The key to such reputation and state building is careful cultivation and management of agency reputations, as political institutions gain legitimacy when the public perceives government agencies positively. With George A. Krause, Carpenter argues that agency leaders seek to hone their performative, technical, moral, and procedural reputations (Carpenter 2010; Carpenter & Krause 2012). *Performative* reputation is the perception of how effectively and efficiently a government executes its policies. *Technical* reputation is the perception that government agencies have the skill and capacity to succeed. *Moral* reputation reflects a government's perceived compassion, flexibility, and honesty. *Procedural* reputation refers to a government's apparent fairness and consistency in following accepted rules and norms.

These four elements of agency reputation align with Van Ryzin's (2011) two drivers of trust (i.e., outcomes and process) and Levi and Stoker's (2000) two dimensions of trust (i.e., competence and morality). Table 2.1 shows how these theories relate to and complement one another. However, both Carpenter and Krause (2012) and Lerman (2019) leave aside reasons for variation in perceptions about government. Carpenter and Krause discuss the processes by which bureaucrats hone various aspects of agency reputation, but they do not address the ways that reputation building might affect perceptions differently for different citizens. Lerman (2019) demonstrates that Americans trust the private sector more than the public sector *on average*, but she does not explain why some Americans trust government more than others. Neither Carpenter and Krause (2012) nor Lerman (2019) consider the significance of social cleavages such as race, ethnicity, and socioeconomic status on government's reputation. There are good reasons to expect that trust in government – especially

**Table 2.1.** *Theories of trust in government*

| Dimensions of trust (Levi & Stoker 2000) | Morality | Competence |
|---|---|---|
| Cognitive drivers of trust (Van Ryzin 2007, 2011, 2015) | Process | Outcomes |
| Facets of agency reputation (Carpenter & Krause 2012) | Moral Procedural | Performative Technical |

its moral and procedural dimensions – is likely to vary in important ways for different populations.

### Social Identity

Since trust is relational, it follows that an individual's trust in government (or anything else) is partly a function of his own identity. Members of social groups that enjoy privileged status or sizable political influence are probably inclined to view government institutions as benevolent and competent. Individuals from historically oppressed and/or politically marginalized groups are likely to be more skeptical about or distrustful of government.

Decades of research on satisfaction with government services in the United States have found significant racial gaps in perceived government performance, with non-Hispanic white respondents expressing greater satisfaction than racial and ethnic minority respondents (Aberbach & Walker 1973; Carlson 2002; DeHoog, Lowery, & Lyons 1990; Fox & Lewis 2001; Howell 2007; Rossi, Berk, & Eidson 1974). A central challenge in understanding the relationship between race and trust in government is isolating the effects of race itself from service quality. If people of different races or ethnicities receive different basic services, then racial or ethnic disparities in trust may follow from real differences in service quality rather than racial/ ethnic identity. Seeking to disentangle the effects of race and ethnicity from objective conditions, Van Ryzin, Muzzio, and Immerwahr (2004) analyzed survey data from thousands of New York City residents across forty-two neighborhoods. They found significant racial and ethnic disparities in residents' perceptions of service quality: Black and Hispanic respondents reported much lower satisfaction across eight different city services, from libraries to fire protection to street conditions. These racial and ethnic disparities were especially strong with respect to policing. Importantly, significant racial and ethnic gaps remained in seven of the eight services after adjusting for the respondent's neighborhood. That is, objective differences in neighborhood conditions that follow from residential segregation did not fully account for racial and ethnic differences in satisfaction with government. However, these differences decline markedly after adjusting for respondents' general trust in government. Van Ryzin et al. conclude that "differences in trust of government – a fundamental aspect of one's relation to government – play a key role in accounting for the race gap in citizen satisfaction" (2004, 625).[11]

Objective conditions are thus evaluated through a lens of personal or group identity that informs trust in and expectations about government. Persistent racial and ethnic differences in citizen satisfaction and government trust make sense in light of America's troubled history and ongoing challenges with racial bias and political alienation. For members of historically oppressed minority groups, expectations about government competence and morality carry a legacy of often well-founded distrust. Deeply ingrained distrust makes minority communities quick to believe the worst about institutions generally and government specifically.

In *I Heard It through the Grapevine*, Patricia Turner (1993) argues that centuries of systemic racism have made African Americans uniquely receptive to conspiracy theories involving secretive government policies and agencies. Similarly, Black and Hispanic parents are more skeptical than white parents of child immunization programs (Shi, Weintraub, & Gust 2006). Perhaps the most notorious example of government deception and exploitation of African Americans is the Tuskegee Experiments. In 1932, the US Public Health Service conducted a study of syphilis involving hundreds of Black men in Alabama. Participants were not informed of the study's scope and purpose, and some who had the disease were not given treatment when an effective cure became available. News reporting in the 1970s exposed these abuses. Decades later, the Tuskegee study continues to undermine trust in government and medical institutions, especially among African Americans (Green et al. 1997). There is some evidence that awareness of the Tuskegee Experiments directly eroded trust in medicine among Black men, with deleterious health consequences (Alsan & Wanamaker 2018).

---

[11] Subsequent studies have yielded similar results (Li, Wenning, & Morrow-Jones 2013; Marschall & Shah 2007).

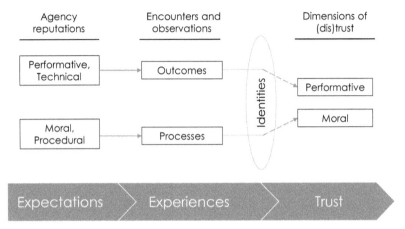

**Figure 2.4** Expectations, experiences, and trust.

Trust in government, then, is not only a function of government's reputation or people's direct experiences with government. When government succeeds or fails, the implications of those successes and failures for citizens' trust in government depend on the degree to which citizens identify with the groups who benefit or suffer due to government actions. For this reason, a moral or performative government failure anywhere can diminish trust in government everywhere, and the impact of that failure on trust will be greatest for those who identify with the victims of that failure. For members of politically marginalized groups, government failures are evidence consistent with a history of bias or antagonism between people and agencies of the state. People who share a racial, ethnic, socioeconomic, or other social identity with victims will perceive government failure elsewhere not as exceptional or distant, but rather as evidence that government is untrustworthy always and everywhere (Viscusi, Huber, & Bell 2015).

Figure 2.4 brings together these lines of research and depicts graphically the ways that expectations and experiences combine to shape citizens' trust in government. Moving from left to right, citizens bring expectations into their relationships with government. Those expectations are informed by agencies' performative, technical, moral, and procedural reputations. Citizens then experience government processes and outcomes, either directly through encounters with government itself or indirectly by observing others' interactions with government. These experiences combine with prior expectations to affect citizens' performative and moral trust in government. Experiencing a good outcome can strengthen citizens' performative trust in government, whereas observing a bad outcome can weaken performative trust. Similarly, observing positive or negative processes can shape citizens' moral trust in government.

But citizen experiences shape trust through a lens of identity. Whatever their objective experiences, members of privileged, politically powerful groups will tend to perceive government outcomes as beneficent and government processes as just, bolstering performative and moral trust accordingly. Members of politically marginalized groups will tend to perceive government outcomes as harmful and government processes as unfair, eroding performative and moral trust. In this way, two people with different identities can experience identical basic services and still come to different conclusions about government's competence and/or morality.

## A Political Theory of Citizen-Consumer Behavior

Trust in government, then, is a function of both morality and competence, grounded in an individual's direct experiences and indirect observations about the experiences of those with whom she identifies. Trust conditions the citizen-consumer's trade-off between government and commercial products when those products are substitutes. Albert Hirschman's classic *Exit, Voice, and Loyalty* (1970) advanced a simple but powerful theory about rational behavioral response to discontent. Hirschman observes that faced with products of poor or declining quality, consumers may choose either to *voice* their concerns to the unsatisfactory firm or to *exit* by choosing another firm's product.

An individual's choice of voice or exit depends on the cost of expressing discontent, his expectations about the firm's response, and the availability of alternative products. Where markets are competitive, opting for the competitor's product involves no procedural cost to the consumer and provides him with immediate, certain improvement. Exercising voice is comparatively costly, as the consumer must spend time and energy expressing himself to the unsatisfactory firm. Moreover, the consumer cannot know for certain whether or how the firm will respond to complaints about quality. Exit is thus the consumer's optimal choice in competitive markets. Firms must respond to consumer exit by improving quality, reducing prices, or abandoning the market. The same logic leads to different outcomes for a dissatisfied citizen's response to government. Since governments are monopolies by definition, exit options in most cases are expensive, few, or nonexistent. A dissatisfied citizen's primary recourse is voice. The citizen's choice to voice her dissatisfaction through lobbying, voting, and other forms of political participation depends on her expectations about government's response.

These observations about consumer and citizen behavior are not especially surprising; they are foundational tenets of economics and political science, respectively. Rather, Hirschman's key insights for politics involve the interplay of exit and voice as complementary alternatives, along with governments' responses to each behavior:

The decision whether to exit will often be taken *in the light of the prospects for the effective use of voice.* If customers are sufficiently convinced that voice will be effective, then they may well postpone *exit.* Hence, quality-elasticity of demand, and therefore exit, can be viewed as depending on the ability and willingness of the customers to take up the voice option. (1970, 37, italics in original)

Whereas competitive commercial firms are responsive primarily to consumer choices (exit), government institutions are designed to respond to political participation (voice). Persistent failures in either sector occur in those "pathological cases where an organization is in effect equipped with a reaction mechanism to which it is not responsive," argues Hirschman (1970, 122). Voice is rendered ineffective when people dissatisfied with quality "vent their feelings in one way or another, but management happens to be inured or indifferent to their particular reaction and thus does not feel compelled to correct its course" (122). Quality-conscious citizen-consumers will thus opt for exit when dissatisfied with government services, but governments are unlikely to respond by improving quality. *Loyalty* moderates the exit-versus-voice decision in Hirschman's model: Dissatisfied but loyal individuals remain passive, holding faith in their institutions and hoping that conditions will improve.[12]

---

[12] Some extensions of Hirschman's (1970) model have added *neglect* as an alternative to *exit, voice,* and *loyalty* (e.g., Lyons, Lowery, & Hoogland 1992; Peeters, Gofen, & Meza 2020). These theories depict exit and voice as active

Usefully for our purposes, the case that inspired Hirschman's magnum opus was a public enterprise that competed with commercial alternative suppliers: the Nigerian Railway Corporation (NRC). The NRC held a monopoly over Nigeria's rail freight service, so its only meaningful competitors for overland freight hauling were private trucking firms. Conventional economic logic predicts that a capitalist who enjoys a monopoly position will set inefficiently high prices in order to maximize profit. However, the NRC's prices were significantly *lower* than its private competitors. Despite its lower prices, the NRC suffered a steady decline in demand as customers opted for far more expensive private trucking due to the latter's greater reliability. As a government agency, the NRC was more attuned to political advocacy (i.e., voice) than to consumer choice (i.e., exit). As a monopoly, the NRC was insensitive to declining demand that followed its poor service. In fact, the very presence of commercial alternatives weakened the incentive for Nigerians to voice dissatisfaction with the NRC, argued Hirschman. Dissatisfied Nigerian freight customers did not believe that their complaints to government would result in improved rail service, so they opted for exit over voice.

Thousands of theoretical and empirical studies across the social sciences have taken up the dynamics of the *Exit, Voice, and Loyalty* (EVL) model in the fifty years since the publication of Hirschman's brief, brilliant book. A great deal of this research has focused on consumer economics, but studies on citizen satisfaction with government have used Hirschman's framework to analyze public service production, residential choices, and government fragmentation, for example (Dowding & John 1996; Lyons et al. 1992; Percy, Hawkins, & Maier 1995; Young 1972).

options for the dissatisfied individual, with loyalty and neglect as passive options. Although they are observationally the same, in that people take no action, loyalty and neglect emerge from different psychological processes and reflect different expectations. Loyalty implies that the dissatisfied individual expects the situation to improve eventually, whereas neglect implies resignation that poor conditions will not change. Perhaps fittingly, the idea of neglect as a fourth option emerged from psychological research on romantic relationships (Rusbult, Zembrodt, & Gunn 1982). Since our theory deals with basic services like drinking water, sanitation, and public safety, neglect is not a realistic alternative for the dissatisfied person – no one can simply stop drinking water – and so we leave it aside and focus our theory on exit and voice.

Political scientists have naturally focused their extensions of EVL on citizen-government relationships. Keith Dowding and Peter John (2012) argue that loyalty (an attitude) can be observed behaviorally as voice in the presence of dissatisfaction. That is, loyal citizen-consumers have high confidence that governments will respond positively to voice, so they are willing to exercise voice instead of exit. The cost of exit is lowest for the well-off and costliest for the poor, making exit a regressive means of achieving efficient public services. "To increase exit will be at the expense of voice," argue Dowding and John, "and that will be at the expense of the poorest and most vulnerable people in society" (2012, 141). Dowding and John's key insight is distinguishing between *individual* and *collective* voice. Individual voice involves direct communication between a citizen-consumer and a government agency regarding a specific problem or service. Complaints to elected officials or calls to a customer service telephone number about poor service are examples of individual voice. Collective voice is participation in group political action. Voting is the most obvious form of collective voice, but signing a petition, donating to a lobbying group, joining a demonstration, and running for office are also forms of collective voice. Both individual and collective voice reflect loyalty and are inversely related to exit, but the latter is conditioned by social capital, Dowding and John argue. Loyalty to community (as opposed to a service provider) can lead some citizen-consumers to opt for voice instead of exit. Individual voice can affect service quality in isolated cases, but it is most effective for the wealthy and well educated. By contrast, collective voice enhances political accountability for government writ large. Group political participation, then, is the preferable mechanism for dissatisfied citizen-consumers since it holds out the promise of improved service for all.

Turning the focus from citizens to governments, William Clark, Matt Golder, and Sona Golder's (2017) extension of the EVL framework casts governments as actors who respond strategically to citizens.[13] As in Hirschman's (1970) original model and Dowding and John's (2012) extension, Clark et al. argue that a citizen's choice of exit or voice depends on the feasibility of exit and her assessment that her voice will influence outcomes. But Clark et al. (2017) give much greater attention to governments' decisions in their interactions with

---

[13] See also Gelbach (2006).

dissatisfied citizens, modeling a world in which governments are more or less dependent on citizens. Governments will respond positively to citizen voice only when they rely on citizens in some meaningful way and those citizens have credible exit alternatives. One troubling implication of this argument is that governments may rationally ignore citizens whom they do not value or who have no exit alternative, and so may deliberately reduce the quality of goods and services offered to those who cannot exit. At the same time, governments are likely to satisfy those citizens they depend on and who might leave if dissatisfied. Therefore, the most powerful voices rarely need to speak because they are rarely dissatisfied, and the least powerful voices rarely speak knowing that their entreaties will fall on deaf ears. The result is a "central irony, perhaps tragedy, about politics," Clark et al. (2017) conclude. "Citizens who would derive the most from successfully using their voice – those whose exit options are unattractive – are unlikely to have much influence over the government" (741).

## Trust and Quality: A Self-Fulfilling Prophecy

Hirschman's (1970) classic theory and its various extensions in political science and public administration proceed from an assumption that people's perceptions of quality are independent from their perceptions of their political efficacy. That is, these arguments begin with a citizen-consumer's assessment of quality and then model the choice of exit or voice as a function of expectations about his own power and the government's likely response to his political behavior. In Hirschman's formulation, this assumption leads the most quality-conscious consumers to become discontent at the first marginal reduction in quality. These "connoisseurs" are thus the first to exit. In Dowding and John (2012), citizen satisfaction drives the exit–voice decision, modified by loyalty. In Clark et al. (2017), the citizen's perception of quality is separate from government dependency upon said citizen. But what if loyalty conditions satisfaction? In other words, what if a citizen-consumer's perception of government service quality is itself a function of her own perceived political efficacy?

Existing research demonstrates that trust in government follows from people's direct and indirect experiences with government, as well as government's general reputation for morality and competence (or lack thereof). Government's moral reputation depends to a great degree on whether its institutions are believed to be procedurally fair. For citizen-consumers who believe that government is unresponsive or even hostile to their interests, government products will always be perceived as being of poor quality because they are produced by governments that neglect or actively conspire against them. To *the politically alienated, government products are inherently untrustworthy.* Government trust and perceptions of government quality are thus endogenous and mutually reinforcing – especially when it comes to the basic services that ensure citizens' health and safety. Belief that government products are lousy is both a cause and an effect of distrust in government.

If distrust arises from government failure born of incompetence or incapacity, then the citizen-consumer may rationally respond with either exit or voice. Citizen-consumers may be dissatisfied with basic service but nonetheless maintain faith in the moral and procedural dimensions of government as an institution. In such circumstances, individual voice in the form of complaints or collective voice in the form of petitions, protests, or elections may drive governments to improve agencies that perform poorly. More likely, governments will not allow conditions to reach such an unhappy state in the presence of a potentially influential public (Clark et al. 2017).

On the other hand, if distrust stems from a *moral* failure of government, then the citizen-consumer has lost faith in government *as a political institution.* If political disaffection is a principal factor behind the perception of inferior government quality, then the rational citizen-consumer will always opt for exit and never attempt to voice her discontent. It makes little sense for a citizen-consumer to complain individually or campaign collectively to persuade a government that she believes is indifferent or hostile. Where commercial alternatives are available, the distrustful citizen-consumer will always choose them – and be willing to pay significantly higher prices for them (see Figure 2.3). Deep political alienation can lead citizen-consumers to spend "defensively" simply to avoid the government goods and services that they fear (Dupont & Jahan 2012). In the same vein, Andrew Szasz (2007) argues that as individuals lose faith in the ability of collective action to protect them from collective harm, they turn to individual consumptive behaviors as a form of protection. Through bottled water purchases, organic products, and even suburbanization, individuals choose to buy their way into a sense of security that used to

be collectively provided, Szasz argues. Rather than approach a problem collectively, individuals attempt to solve problems individually
through commercial consumption.

Whether or not government *would have* responded positively to
dissatisfied citizens' voices is irrelevant following exit. Having spent
handsomely on a commercial alternative that they believe is superior,
alienated citizen-consumers have even less reason to use their voices in
an uncertain attempt to improve government products and services
that they do not consume. Distrustful citizen-consumers who exit for
commercial providers may even *oppose* efforts to improve government
services because they perceive such efforts as costly, futile, and irrelevant to their lives.

To the extent that they are democratic, governments are attuned to
the preferences of people who are politically active, or potentially
politically active (Dahl 1961). Citizen-consumers who trust their institutions of government have reason to engage with them when dissatisfied; politicians and bureaucrats have strong incentives to respond by
providing better services and regulating responsibly. By the same
token, elected officials and public managers have little reason to heed
citizens who are disengaged from politics. Governments that operate or
regulate monopoly enterprises (as was the case with Hirschman's
Nigerian railroad example) are generally insensitive to exit.
Distrustful citizens will be apathetic or hostile toward costly efforts
to improve performance. Citizen-consumer expectations about government responsiveness are thus self-fulfilling prophecies (Kettl 2017).

## Vicious Cycle

Basic service failure, the distrust that follows from that failure, and the
citizen-consumer logic of exit and voice can set into motion a feedback
cycle. In Chapter 1, we introduced this vicious cycle of distrust in tap
water (Figure 1.10); Figure 2.5 is a generalized version of this cycle that
can apply to any basic service. Beginning at the top of Figure 2.5 and
moving clockwise, a failure of basic services causes trust in government
to decline. As trust declines, citizen-consumers will increasingly exit
from consumption of government services in favor of commercial
alternatives. The commercial firms that compete with government
profit from these exits, reaping a *distrust premium*. Increased exit
triggers reduced political participation, which in turn reduces the

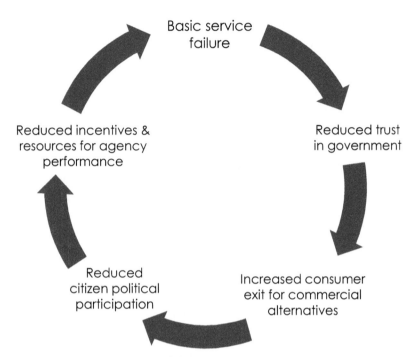

**Figure 2.5** The vicious cycle of distrust.
*Note:* This figure depicts the vicious cycle of basic service failure and distrust in government.

public resources and political incentives for excellent public services. These reduced resources and incentives then feed back into greater service failures, and the cycle continues. Figure 2.5 serves as a conceptual model to guide and tie together the chapters to come.

## *The Profits of Distrust*

The distrust premium is the marginal cost of defensive spending that citizen-consumers pay due to their distrust of government. The commercial firms that compete with governments capture this distrust premium from people who believe that governments' products and services are inferior *because they are produced by governments*.

For commercial firms that compete with government agencies, the distrust citizen-consumers feel toward government is akin to positive brand equity: Consumers willingly pay more for commercial products *because* they are commercial products and *not* government products.

A commercial firm that competes with other firms seeks to associate its products with value superior to its competitors' products. If a commercial firm's principal competitor is a government, then brand building will involve not only communicating the firm's quality and value, but also eroding trust in government. These particular appeals will include claims about government competence (e.g., *government service is lousy*) and morality (e.g., *government is unjust*). Citizen-consumers who are distrustful of government will readily pay the distrust premium.[14]

Who pays the premium? Critically, the distrust premium is not paid by every consumer equally: Since people cannot realistically abstain from consuming basic services, *the largest distrust premium will be paid by consumers who trust government the least*. We have seen that satisfaction with government services and general trust in government is lowest among politically marginalized populations. People's tendency to distrust government products and services will be inversely related to their understanding of their own political potency. The more that people identify with the victims of government failure and abuse, the more they will distrust government goods and services. Knowing that the politically marginalized will be most receptive to their claims, government's commercial competitors will focus their marketing efforts on the people who have the least willingness to voice their concerns to government. Defensive spending, then, will be most prevalent among those with the least political power. The greatest profits of distrust are reaped not from the pampered and privileged, but from the poor and powerless.

## Drinking Water and the Citizen-Consumer

Here, we trace out some implications of our general theory of the citizen-consumer for drinking water in the United States. Each implication reflects a different aspect of the theory but is consistent with the others; each is effectively a hypothesis that we evaluate empirically in the chapters to come. Taken together, these hypotheses form a coherent whole that brings life to our admittedly abstract theory of the citizen-consumer. Applying the theory to the case of drinking water

---

[14] In microeconomic terms, the distrust premium is a producer surplus to the commercial firm that takes market share from government agencies. The loss of utility to customers from paying higher prices for commercial alternatives and any ongoing lower-quality government providers is a deadweight loss to society.

helps explain some peculiarities of the American drinking water sector and offers broader lessons on the relationship between the people and the state.

As we observed in Chapter 1, governments at every level are involved in drinking water provision in the United States. Local governments are the main owners and operators of community drinking water systems, while state and federal agencies regulate drinking water safety. Where community water systems are owned and operated by investor-owned firms, state agencies regulate their pricing and quality. With the rarest of exceptions, drinking water systems operate as enterprises in the United States: whether government-owned or investor-owned, utilities provide water service to homes, businesses, and other institutions on a fee-for-service basis.

Drinking water is essential to human life, so decisions to drink from or avoid different water sources are unavoidable and carry high stakes. However, although every person needs water, people need not consume water from community water systems. Maintaining and operating a modern water system is technically complex; consequently, drinking water service quality can shape citizens' *performative* trust in government. Water service also involves interactions between citizen-consumers and utilities, chiefly in the form of periodic bills and occasional service. Utilities may be more or less transparent and fair in their decision making and interactions with the public. These procedural aspects of water service can strengthen or weaken *moral* trust in government. As we reviewed in Chapter 1, commercial alternatives to tap water abound in the United States. These characteristics, along with government's legacy and role in drinking water provision, make American drinking water an excellent subject for exploration of citizen-consumer behavior and the relationships between citizen-consumers and government.

## *Experience, Identity, and Performative Trust*

Citizen-consumer experiences with and observations of water utility performance shape their trust in government competence. When drinking water utilities fail to provide high-quality service, that failure can become an indictment of government's competence in delivering and/ or regulating public services. Recalling Table 2.1, problems with drinking water quality can damage government's performative and technical reputations (Carpenter & Krause 2012) and leave citizen-consumers dissatisfied with public policy outcomes (Van Ryzin 2011). Together, these problems erode trust in government's overall competence (Levi & Stoker 2000).

### Direct Experiences and Performative Trust
Starting from the top of Figure 2.5 (or Figure 1.10) and moving clockwise, personal experiences with drinking water quality affect trust in government directly by eroding performative trust. Citizen-consumers who experience dirty or cloudy water, service interruptions, local water main breaks, sewer overflows, or low water pressure in their own homes and businesses will associate those problems with government administration and regulation. That association – warranted or not – will reduce citizen satisfaction and trust in government's competence in providing basic services (Van Ryzin 2007). Our first expectation, then, is that *bad experiences with tap water service reduce citizen-consumer trust in government* (Hypothesis 1).

### Service Failure and Exit
Rational citizen-consumers who do not trust government's competence following tap water failures will find commercial drinking water alternatives more attractive. Continuing clockwise along the right-hand side of Figure 2.5 (or Figure 1.10), commercial firms will profit if large numbers of distrustful citizen-consumers respond to tap water failure by opting for commercial drinking water. If they do, then *commercial drinking water demand will increase where tap water failures occur* (Hypothesis 2).

## Voice, Exit, and Moral Trust

Whether experiencing government failure directly or observing and identifying with it from afar, dissatisfied citizen-consumers may either voice their concerns to public officials or exit for the commercial market. Failure seen as stemming mainly from ineptitude or limited capacity will erode citizens' trust in government's competence, and a citizen will opt for voice insofar as he believes that the government will receive and respond positively to his entreaties. However, if government's failure is viewed as a *moral* failure, then voice is never a rational response: What good will it do for a citizen to complain to a government that is evil or indifferent? Confronted with a morally untrustworthy government, the rational citizen-consumer will always choose exit options when they are available, even if they are costly. People who have been politically marginalized will be most likely to view drinking water failures as moral failures of government; therefore, they will be most likely to eschew voice in favor of exit.

### Failure, Identity, and Distrust

Citizen-consumers who observe failures in drinking water systems may lose trust in government even if they do not experience failures directly. We have argued that the effects of observed performative failure on a citizen-consumer's distrust in government depend on the degree to which she identifies with the victims of the failure (see Figure 2.4). If we are correct, then distrust is contagious, and tap water failure anywhere can damage trust in tap water everywhere. Individuals who share an affinity with the people who suffer from poor tap water quality will respond most strongly to water quality problems because tap water failures are linked to a shared history of political alienation. *When water utility failures occur, then, citizen-consumer demand for commercial water will be strongest in communities that are demographically and socioeconomically similar to the places where the failures occurred* (Hypothesis 3).

### Moral Trust and Voice

People who experience problems with their tap water might be expected to complain to their water utilities. Holding aside the possibility that some people may enjoy the act of complaining in itself, complaints to the utility imply an expectation that the utility will respond by correcting the problem. Continuing clockwise along the right-hand side and bottom of Figure 2.5 (or Figure 1.10), people who are dissatisfied about their water service but have faith in the benevolence of government as an institution may reasonably choose to voice their discontent. But people who believe that government is uncaring or malevolent as an institution will not bother complaining. The political history of the United States gives poor people and members of racial and ethnic minority communities ample reason to doubt the moral trustworthiness of government, and therefore little reason to bother complaining about their water quality. The expected result is that when encountering tap water problems, *individuals with low*

*incomes and/or members of racial and ethnic minority groups are less*
*likely to complain to their utilities about their water problems*
(Hypothesis 4).

## Moral Trust and Exit

With no reasonable hope of improving tap water through individual
complaint or collective advocacy, the unhappy tap water customer
who distrusts her government rationally opts for exit. Moreover, citizen distrust of government born of broader experiences and observations – whether connected to water or not – will influence drinking
water choices. Again working along the right-hand side of Figure 2.5,
the citizen's moral distrust of government manifests itself in consumer
behavior: *As an individual's trust in government decreases, the likelihood that he or she drinks commercial water instead of tap water
increases* (Hypothesis 5).

## Exit as Substitute for Voice

For citizen-consumers who abandon tap water for commercial alternatives, the potential payoff of voicing discontent plummets. Having
already chosen bottled or kiosk water at its premium price, it makes
little sense for the citizen-consumer to spend his limited time pestering
utility managers, elected officials, or regulators about tap water quality. Those who drink commercial water no longer rely on government
for a key basic service, so they have less at stake in politics. Citizens
who opt out of collective drinking water supplies have little reason to
support public investments in water utilities. This trade-off occurs
along the bottom of Figure 2.5. As we have seen, experiences with
and beliefs about government transcend policy areas, such that negative experiences as water customers may color citizen perceptions
about other government functions. To the extent that exit stems from
generalized moral distrust in government as an institution, the choice
to drink commercial water is likely to accompany a broader withdrawal from civic life. Thus, we expect that *as commercial water sales
increase, political participation will decrease* (Hypothesis 6).

## Trust, Voice, and Good Governance

Happily, there is hope. In choosing to focus on government failure and
adopting Hirschman's (1970) framework of response to discontent,

the discussion of drinking water to this point has been dismal. The links that we have traced between government performance, trust, consumer choice, and political participation form a feedback loop that turns failure into distrust into exit into political dysfunction and further failure. But this vicious cycle can also be virtuous. Just as distrust leads to exit and cynicism about government, trust can lead to engagement and support for better government performance. We take up this reversed, virtuous cycle at length in Chapter 8, but applied to drinking water, we can make some predictions based on our theory.

Drinking tap water is a meaningful indication of trust in government: The citizen-consumer who drinks from the tap implicitly entrusts her health to the agencies that provide and/or regulate her water system. Tap water consumption, then, is a profoundly credible signal of trust in both the competence and morality of government. Reliant on government for this critical service and trusting in government's basic capability and benevolence, tap water drinkers have good reasons to support investments in public water supplies. Support for government follows directly from this deep, implicit trust. We expect that *tap water drinkers are more likely than commercial water drinkers to support rate increases aimed at improving service* (Hypothesis 7).

Where trust in tap water prevails, so will political participation. The glad inverse of gloomy Hypothesis 6 is that tap water consumption is positively correlated with voter turnout. Voters who are personally invested in high-quality tap water will expect it from their utility managers and regulatory officials. With the political support and high expectations of tap water–drinking, civically engaged citizen-consumers, utilities will fulfill that trust with high-quality, reliable service. The ultimate evidence that governments are responsive to citizens is that discontent will be rare (Clark et al. 2017). When viewed through a virtuous lens, our expectation is that *as voter turnout increases, tap water quality also increases* (Hypothesis 8).

We take up each part of this argument with data on public opinion, consumer behavior, political participation, and water quality in the chapters that follow. Our theory suggests that trust, identity, voice, exit, and government performance are interrelated and cyclical, and so each part of our empirical analysis relates to and builds on each of the others. Trust is "both an independent and dependent variable," as Kettl put it, "a force that shapes expectations and that is the product of past experiences" (2017, 41). In the language of social science, our main variables of interest are inescapably endogenous. We do our best to isolate relationships between hypothesized causes and effects, and in Chapter 6 we explore in-depth the political mechanisms that shape the relationships between government performance and trust.

Nonetheless, our empirical case – drinking water – defies the kind of research design that would allow us to declare definitively that one thing causes another. For what we hope are obvious reasons, we cannot randomly assign contaminated tap water to see how service failure affects trust in government, or randomly disenfranchise various ethnic groups to see how political power affects tap water consumption. Scholars who cherish clever identification strategies and hold causal confidence as the highest end of social science are likely to find much of our evidence unsatisfactory. However, in the pages to come, we marshal a great deal of evidence from a wide variety of sources. We hope that the skeptical reader will find our results at least worthy of contemplation, if not compelling.

Still, an inherently cyclical phenomenon presents researchers with a challenge: where to start? The relationship between trust and voice or exit? The links between consumer behavior and political participation? The ways that political participation relates to government perform- ance? The ways that identity shapes trust, consumer behavior, and political participation? Any part of the vicious cycle in Figure 2.5 (or Figure 1.10) could be a valid point of departure. We begin our inquiry at the top of Figure 2.5 with the relationship between performance and trust. Examining the links between basic service quality, trust in gov- ernment, consumer choice, and citizen political behavior reveals important dynamics between citizens and the state generally, and practical insights into the management of US drinking water specific- ally. We start with the performance–trust link because if government's legitimacy depends on providing for people's basic needs, then restor- ing trust in the institutions of government begins with getting drinking water right.

# 3 | *(Dis)trust at the Tap*
## Experience and Performative Trust

A government is to be judged by its action upon men, and by its action upon things; by what it makes of the citizens, and what it does with them; its tendency to improve or deteriorate the people themselves, and the goodness or badness of the work it performs for them, and by means of them.

John Stuart Mill,[1] *Considerations on Representative Government*

I do not trust the water and ... I probably will never trust the water again. I've lost all trust in our government – federal, state, I have lost trust in everyone!

Nakiyah Wakes,[2] Flint resident, on the lead contamination crisis in her city

The idea of performative trust is simple but profound. Good experiences with a product or service build trust in the organization that provided it, and bad experiences reduce trust in the same way. A consumer whose car is reliable and performs well learns to trust the company that manufactured it, the dealer who sold it, and the mechanic who maintains it. A car that sputters, clunks, and requires frequent repairs makes its owner wary of the company that built it, angry at the dealer who sold it, and perhaps frustrated with the mechanic who works on it frequently.

It stands to reason that such a quality–trust relationship holds for basic services like drinking water too. In this chapter, we begin our empirical investigation with the link between performance and trust, a connection that is inexorably political. Every person who turns on a tap in the United States – to drink, cook, shower, shave, clean, brush, or flush – experiences government. Drinking water is an immediate and

---

[1] Mill (1861).
[2] Interview in documentary film, *Nor Any Drop to Drink: Flint's Water Crisis* (Taylor et al. 2018).

tangible manifestation of public infrastructure and government regulation in private life. When tap water is clean, healthy, and reliable, it builds or reinforces trust in a government's capacity to provide for its population's basic needs through effective management and regulation. It follows that dirty, contaminated, or unreliable tap water shakes people's confidence, not only in their water systems, but also in government itself.

Perhaps the most glaring, devastating illustration of the relationship between drinking water and trust in the institutions of government in recent memory is the drinking water disaster that beset Flint, Michigan, in 2014.

## The Flint Water Crisis

Any level of lead in drinking water is harmful. Lead is a toxic metal that negatively impacts human health, even at low levels. Lead exposure can cause adverse cardiovascular effects, decreased kidney function, and reproductive problems in adults. In children, lead exposure has been linked to behavior and learning problems, lower IQ and hyperactivity, slowed growth, hearing problems, and anemia. The EPA's regulatory action level for lead in drinking water is 15 ppb, but no level of lead above zero is safe in drinking water (Brown & Margolis 2012). Human exposure to lead can occur in many ways, but the most common source of lead contamination in tap water occurs with the corrosion of older pipes containing lead. In American cities, drinking water is typically carried from the water treatment facility to people via a series of pipes: water mains, service lines, and then plumbing within homes. As these pipes corrode, the rate at which lead enters the drinking water system is affected by the chemistry and temperature of the water, the amount of lead in the pipes, and the overall state and maintenance of the pipes in question.

The devastating effects of lead contamination in tap water were thrust into the national consciousness when the city of Flint, Michigan, grabbed national headlines for its drinking water disaster. The Flint water crisis began in 2014 when the city changed the utility's water source from the city of Detroit to the Flint River in an effort to save money. The change in source water altered the water chemistry in ways that changed the corrosive properties of the water flowing through Flint taps, but the city's water plant did not change its treatment procedures accordingly (Davis et al. 2016). This failure resulted in high levels of lead and other contaminants in residents' drinking water.

Far more than an engineering disaster, the Flint water crisis was a social, political, and governance crisis (Nickels 2019; Pauli 2019). The chemical processes that brought about the lead contamination were well understood, and technical solutions were available. A confluence of governance failures allowed Flint's contamination event to explode into a full-blown crisis. The Flint city council and mayor lost control of the city's finances in 2011 when Michigan Governor Rick Snyder declared a financial emergency in the city and appointed an emergency manager for the city. Financial considerations, not water quality, were the main drivers behind the decision to change the city's water supply. When confronted with the contamination event, utility operators, state officials, and federal regulators intentionally obfuscated information about their actions and the safety of Flint's drinking water. The Flint water crisis also was a glaring manifestation of racial and socioeconomic inequality. At the time of the crisis, the majority of Flint's population was African American and roughly 40 percent of its residents lived below the poverty line. The Michigan city's plight has made it an icon of environmental injustice. In the wake of the lead contamination disaster, many Flintstones (as the people of Flint like to call themselves) developed a deep and bitter distrust of government.

The Flint water crisis was an exceptionally high-profile case of governance failure, and the distrust that Flintstones harbored toward local, state, and federal government officials is understandable. But the case of Flint is only exceptional in its prominence. While the Flint water crisis is now iconic, Flint is hardly alone. News about lead and other contaminants in drinking water in American cities large and small proliferated rapidly following the Flint disaster (Siegel 2019). How does tap water quality affect people's relationships with government? Do tap water problems damage people's trust in their governments?

## Trust at the Tap beyond Flint

Chapter 2 introduced a generalized model depicting a vicious cycle relating basic service failure, reduced trust in government, increased consumer exit for commercial alternatives, reduced citizen political participation, and reduced incentives and resources for agency performance. In this chapter, we begin our investigation of this cycle as

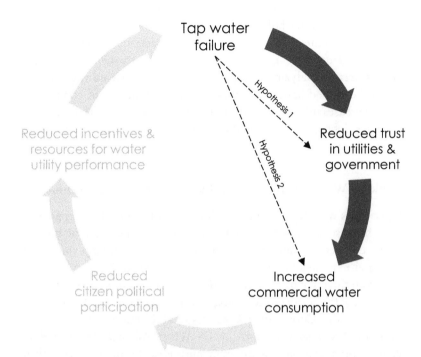

**Figure 3.1** Vicious cycle of distrust in tap water: stages investigated in Chapter 3.

*Note*: This chapter examines the relationship between tap water failure and trust in government/utilities, and the relationship between tap water failure and commercial water consumption. Subsequent chapters examine other portions of the cycle.

it applies to drinking water. Figure 3.1 displays the water-specific version of this vicious cycle that we introduced in Chapter 1, highlighting the portion of the cycle investigated in this chapter. Similar figures accompany subsequent chapters in order to highlight the portion of the cycle under investigation in each. We begin our investigation with performance, examining the relationship between tap water failure, reduced trust in utilities and government, and increased demand for commercial water.

We begin at the micro level, showing that individuals who experience problems with their own drinking water service report lower trust in all levels of government, but especially the local governments that provide this essential service. In Chapter 2, we labeled this expectation Hypothesis 1: *Bad experiences with tap water service reduce citizen-consumer trust in government.* We then turn from micro to macro by connecting tap water failure to the geography of commercial water in the United States. We labeled this expectation Hypothesis 2: *Commercial drinking water demand will increase where tap water failures occur.* Analyzing the spatial locations of private water kiosks across the United States, we show that the prevalence of commercial water increases in relation to drinking water quality: As drinking water problems increase, so does the local presence of the commercial water industry.

## Drinking Water Problems and Reduced Trust in Government

Experiences with bad tap water reduce an individual's trust in government because poor service makes citizen-consumers doubt government's competence and/or capacity. Survey data can help show how tap water experiences relate to trust in government. Here, we analyze data from three separate, nationwide surveys: the NEXUS survey from the Institute for Science, Technology, and Public Policy at Texas A&M University; the Cooperative Congressional Election Study; and the Value of Water survey from the US Water Alliance. Sponsored by separate organizations for different purposes, the three surveys were designed and administered independently. Yet all three surveys yield consistent evidence that people who experience bad tap water service trust government less than people who have not experienced bad tap water service.

### *Tap Water Problems and Trust*

The Texas A&M NEXUS survey gathered attitudinal data about health and environmental issues from a representative sample of nearly 2,000 people across the United States.[3] Conducted in the summer of 2015, the NEXUS survey was administered before the Flint water crisis captured the nation's attention late that year. Near the beginning of the NEXUS questionnaire respondents were asked to say how much they trust their government on a scale from zero to ten, where a score of zero indicates the "government is not trustworthy" and a score of ten indicates the "government is extremely trustworthy."

---

[3] Appendix A provides details on the NEXUS survey's design and administration.

The trust in government question was asked separately for local, state, and federal levels. We expect the strength of the relationship between drinking water problems and trust in various levels of government to reflect the degree of involvement of the levels of government in US water provision. Tap water problems ought to be associated with the largest decrease in trust in local government because local government is most directly involved in water provision. About 85 percent of Americans receive their tap water service from a utility that is owned and operated by a local government – usually a municipality, special district, or county agency. Similarly, we expect tap water problems to be associated with a moderate decrease in trust in state government, since state governments are typically responsible for enforcing drinking water safety regulations. Regulatory commissions also govern investor-owned water utilities in most states. State governments' involvement in drinking water provision may be more visible to citizen-consumers than federal oversight, given legal reporting mechanisms of drinking water safety laws. We expect tap water problems to be associated with the smallest decrease in trust in federal government. Although the federal government is involved in regulating drinking water, it is not directly responsible for local water provision, and many citizen-consumers may be unaware of its role in drinking water provision.

To measure drinking water problems, the questionnaire asked whether respondents had ever experienced bad-tasting tap water, cloudy tap water, low water pressure, or illness that they attributed to tap water at their current residences. Importantly, questions about water problems were presented *after* the question asking respondents to rank their trust in government. The ordering of these questions is crucial to avoid priming effects: The very act of asking about water problems might cause respondents to think differently about their governments. Asking about trust in government prior to asking about water problems helps guard against this potential bias. Questions about tap water were intentionally phrased in terms of *experiences*, rather than attitudes. That is, the survey asked about specific tap water problems that respondents might experience, rather than general thoughts about tap water.

To isolate the relationship between tap water problems and trust in government, we fitted statistical models that calculate the degree to which each type of tap water quality problem correlates with the

NEXUS survey's 0–10 trust scale. These models adjust for other factors that could cause variation in government trust, including partisanship, gender, race, ethnicity, age, income, and home ownership. We fitted separate models examining trust for each level of government.[4] Figure 3.2 shows the resulting estimates of trust in each level of government for people who reported experiencing tap water problems and those who had not.[5]

The results are remarkable. The relationship between water service problems and trust in government is consistent across all levels of government and across all types of tap water problems: Those who experienced problems are less trusting of government. The absolute effects of water problems are strongest for respondents who reported that their water tastes bad and/or caused illness. All else equal, respondents who said that their tap water tastes bad reported 11.1 percent lower trust in the federal government, 7.9 percent lower trust in state government, and 12.8 percent lower trust in local government. For people who attributed illness to their tap water (fortunately, just 3.8 percent of respondents), the gap was even greater: 20.9 percent lower for federal, 24.4 percent lower for state, and 25.0 percent lower for local government. These relationships are strongest and most statistically robust for trust in local government – consistent with the structure of water utility ownership in the United States, where municipalities and special districts operate the lion's share of water systems.

The relative effects of tap water problems and partisanship help illustrate how potent water experiences are in shaping perceptions of government. On average, people who identify as Democrats trust government at all levels more than those who identify as Republicans, as observers of American government might expect. In our models, Republicans' average trust in local government is about 0.4 points lower than Democrats' on our 0–10 scale. By comparison, the average difference in local government trust for people who report bad-tasting tap water and those who do not is 0.63. In other words,

---

[4] Appendix C reports full estimation results.
[5] Figures throughout this chapter report 90 percent confidence intervals, since the hypotheses being evaluated here are directional.

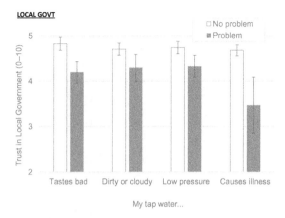

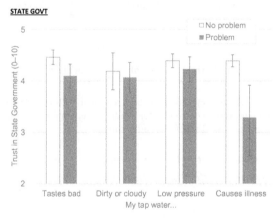

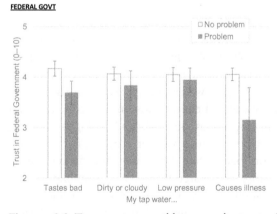

**Figure 3.2** Tap water problems and trust in local, state, and federal government.

*Note*: Estimated trust from NEXUS survey. Thin bars represent 90% confidence intervals. Produced with OLS regression, controlling for partisanship, gender, race, ethnicity, home ownership, age, and income. See Appendix C, Tables C2–C4 for full estimation.

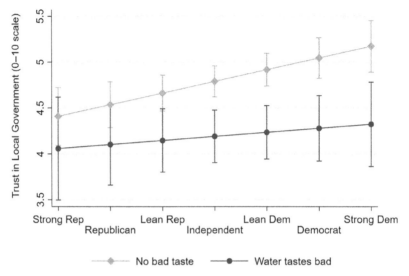

**Figure 3.3** Tap water taste and trust in local government by party identification.

*Note*: Regression analysis of NEXUS Survey data. Thin bars represent 90% confidence intervals. Produced with OLS regression, controlling for gender, race, ethnicity, home ownership, and income. See Appendix C, Table C5 for full estimation.

*the effect of tap water taste on trust in local government is comparable to – or even stronger than – the effect of partisanship on trust in local government*. Indeed, an interactive statistical model using the NEXUS survey data indicates that the negative effect of tap water taste on trust is greatest among Democrats. Figure 3.3 plots estimated trust in local government across the customary seven-point partisanship scale used in public opinion research (1 = strong Republican, 2 = Republican, 3 = Independent-leaning Republican, 4 = Independent, 5 = Independent-leaning Democrat, 6 = Democrat, 7 = strong Democrat). For people who do not report bad-tasting tap water (the lighter line in Figure 3.3), the relationship is what we would expect: Government trust is lowest among strong Republicans, slopes upward, and is highest among strong Democrats. The slope is much weaker – nearly flat, in fact – among those who report bad-tasting tap water (the darker line in Figure 3.3): People whose tap water tastes bad, Republicans and Democrats alike, have similarly low trust in local government. Put another way, *when it comes to trust in local government, bad-tasting tap water seemingly makes Democrats think about government as if they were Republicans.*

## Service Quality Satisfaction and Trust in Government

The Cooperative Congressional Election Survey (CCES) is a nationwide annual survey.[6] In election years, the CCES asks people a series of questions before and after the November elections. The total sample includes more than 50,000 individuals stratified to reflect the US population, with half of the questionnaire consisting of common content that is asked of the entire sample and the other half of the survey administered to team-based modules of 1,000 respondents. We use data from the 2018 CCES, which included questions related to trust in government and respondent satisfaction with the quality of their tap water. These questions were asked on the pre-election wave of the survey, from late September to late October. As in the NEXUS survey data, the questions related to trust in government were asked prior to the questions related to satisfaction with tap water quality, which helps guard against potential bias caused by priming. Whereas the NEXUS survey asked about experiences with tap water problems, the CCES module asked respondents about their satisfaction with the quality of their tap water.

In order to measure trust in government, respondents were asked, "How much of the time do you think you can trust each of the following to do what is right?" about local, state, and federal government. As possible answers, respondents were given the following options: "Just about all of the time," "Most of the time," "Only some of the time," and "Never." To measure satisfaction with the quality of their tap water services, the CCES later asked respondents, "Are you satisfied with the quality of your water?" and given the option of responding "yes," "no," or "neither satisfied nor unsatisfied." Respondents who answered "no" were given a follow-up question asking, "What is the primary reason for your dissatisfaction?" The possible responses were "health/safety of tap water," "taste of tap water," and "other."

We used a series of logistic regression models to investigate the relationship between the measures of tap water satisfaction and trust in government.[7] As before, we expect the relationship between tap water problems and trust in government to be strongest at the local level; we expect the effect of tap water satisfaction to be weaker for state and federal government, respectively, given the structure of US drinking water

---

[6] Appendix A provides details on the CCES's design and administration.
[7] Analysis using ordered logistic and ordinary least squares regressions yielded nearly identical results.

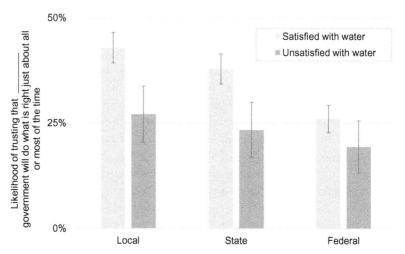

**Figure 3.4** Tap water satisfaction and trust in local, state, and federal government.

*Note*: Logistic regression analysis of CCES Survey. Thin bars represent 90% confidence intervals. Produced with logistic regression, controlling for gender, political ideology, race, ethnicity, education, and immigrant status. See Appendix C, Table C7 for full estimation.

provision. For the purpose of this analysis, we divided responses into trusting and distrusting categories: Respondents who reported trusting the government "Just about all of the time" or "Most of the time" are counted as trusting, whereas those who trust government "Only some of the time" or "Never" are counted as distrusting of government. The models also included a series of controls to account for the effects of gender, political ideology, race, ethnicity, education, and immigrant status on trust. Figure 3.4 shows the relationship between general satisfaction with tap water quality and trust in government while Figure 3.5 shows the relationship between trust in government and the reasons why individuals are dissatisfied with the quality of their water service.

Once again, the results show that poor service quality correlates with a lower level of trust in government. Figure 3.4 shows the likelihood that respondents trust that "government will do what is right" for people who are satisfied with their tap water (the lighter bars in Figure 3.4) and those who are not (the darker bars in Figure 3.4). Across all three levels of government, individuals who are not satisfied with the quality of their drinking water are more likely to report lower trust in government. Consistent with our results analyzing the NEXUS survey data, dissatisfaction with water quality most strongly affects trust in government at

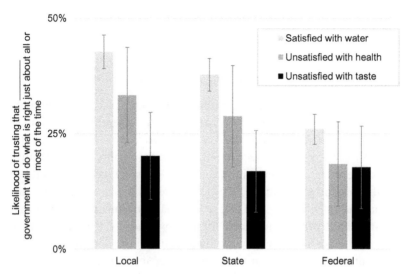

**Figure 3.5** Reasons for tap water dissatisfaction and trust in local, state, and federal government.

*Note:* Logistic regression analysis of CCES Survey. Thin bars represent 90% confidence intervals. Produced with logistic regression, controlling for gender, political ideology, race, ethnicity, education, and immigrant status. See Appendix C, Table C8 for full estimation.

the local level. The relationship between dissatisfaction with water quality and trust in government is weaker at the state level and weaker still at the federal level. Being dissatisfied with tap water quality is associated with a 16 percent decrease in the probability of trusting the local government all or most of the time, a 14 percent decrease in the probability of trusting state government, and a 7 percent decrease in the probability of trusting the federal government (although this difference is not statistically significant by conventional standards).

Analysis of the reasons for dissatisfaction with water quality (i.e., health or taste) indicates that dissatisfaction is primarily due to taste concerns. Whereas both taste and health/safety concerns are associated with lower levels of trust in government at all levels (Figure 3.5), only dissatisfaction with taste is statistically different. This result suggests that taste is perhaps the most important factor when it comes to evaluations of government on the basis of water services. Once again, the relationships are stronger for trust in local and state governments than in the federal government, where there is no statistically significant difference. Overall, the results from the CCES module provide strong and consistent support to those of the NEXUS survey, showing that when measuring perceptions of service quality, rather than specific events of service failure, a significant relationship persists.

## Community Infrastructure and Trust in Government

The relationship between drinking water and trust in government extends beyond individual taps to the quality of entire communities' water systems. Data from the US Water Alliance's Value of Water (VOW) surveys show how the public sees the quality of water infrastructure in their communities, and how those perceptions relate to confidence in government. The US Water Alliance is an advocacy organization aimed at "driving a national movement to ensure that clean, reliable water is available for all, now and in the future."[8] Much of the Alliance's advocacy work involves building political support for government investment in water and sewer infrastructure. As part of this effort, the Alliance conducts national public opinion surveys by telephone, meant to capture Americans' attitudes toward water infrastructure. The VOW survey was conducted in February–March each year from 2015 to 2021; the Alliance shared data with us from the 2018–2021 waves of its survey, with just over a thousand respondents in each wave.[9] We use the 2021 data in this chapter, because that year's survey includes questions about trust in government, trust in tap water, and questions about specific water infrastructure problems.

The VOW survey is a useful complement to the NEXUS survey and the CCES in several ways. The 2021 VOW survey analyzed here was conducted well after the Flint water crisis and its attendant political fallout, so the effects of that high-profile event are "baked in" to the results. The survey's spoken introduction framed the questionnaire in terms of "issues facing the nation," making clear that the government and public policy were the survey's subjects. Like the NEXUS survey and the CCES, the VOW survey asked respondents about their trust in government at the outset, again reducing potential bias from priming due to the order of questions.

The 2021 VOW survey's questions about trust in government were worded very similarly to the CCES items measuring trust. Respondents were asked, "How much of the time do you trust _____ to do

---

[8]  From the US Water Alliance's website: http://uswateralliance.org/about-us.
[9]  Appendix A provides details on the VOW survey's design and administration.

the right thing?" about local, state, and federal government. As possible answers, respondents were given the following options: "Always," "Most of the time," "Some of the time," and "Never." Shortly after expressing their trust in government, each respondent was asked whether he or she trusts "that the drinking water being delivered to your home is safe." Respondents could answer on a four-point scale: "Strongly yes," "Somewhat yes," "Somewhat no," or "Strongly no." The 2021 VOW survey also asked "how often you or your community experienced" water main breaks, sewage backups or overflows, and waterfronts closed due to water pollution or algae blooms. Once again, respondents were given a four-point scale for answers: "Frequently," "Occasionally," "Rarely," or "Never."

As with the NEXUS survey, we used statistical models to analyze the degree to which each type of water problem in the 2021 VOW survey correlates with trust in government at each level. These models also adjust for respondent age, race, ethnicity, gender, and party identification. As in our analyses of the NEXUS and CCES data sets, we generally expect the associations between water problems and trust in government to be strongest at the local, or community, level.

The picture that emerges parallels the findings from the NEXUS survey and the CCES: The relationship between water infrastructure problems and attitudes toward government is consistent across all levels of government and across all types of problems. People who observe problems with their communities' water are less trusting of government. For each type of problem and each level of government in Figure 3.6, individuals who never observe or experience community water problems report higher trust in government than those who experience the same kinds of water problems frequently. The relationship between sewage overflows and trust is particularly large across all levels of government. The sole exception is waterfront closure due to pollution, which is strongly associated with trust in local government but has virtually no correlation with trust in federal government.

Overall trust in the safety of tap water also strongly correlates with trust in government in the 2021 VOW survey. Figure 3.7 shows trust in local, state, and federal government by varying degrees of trust in tap water. An ordered relationship appears in Figure 3.7, with local government enjoying higher overall trust than state government and respondents reporting lowest average trust in the federal government. More importantly, trust in tap water correlates with trust in

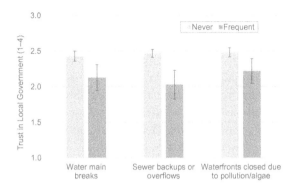

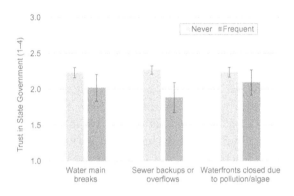

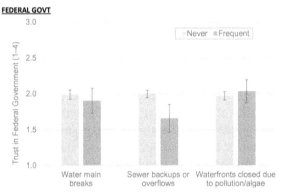

**Figure 3.6** Water/sewer system problems and trust in local, state, and federal government.

*Note*: Regression analysis of 2021 VOW survey data. Thin bars represent 90% confidence intervals. Produced with logistic regression, controlling for partisanship, age, gender, race, and ethnicity. See Appendix C, Tables C10–12 for full estimation.

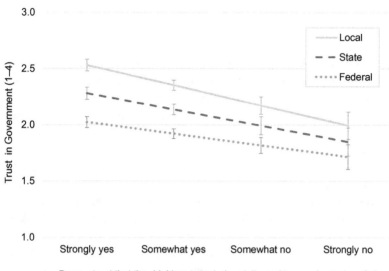

**Figure 3.7** Trust in tap water and trust in local, state, and federal government. *Note*: Regression analysis of 2021 VOW survey data. Thin bars represent 90% confidence intervals. Produced with OLS regression, controlling for partisanship, age, gender, race, and ethnicity. See Appendix C, Table C13 for full estimation.

government at all levels: As trust at the tap decreases, so does trust in government, even after adjusting for partisanship, race, ethnicity, gender, and age. Once again, these relationships are strongest at the local level, where governments operate most water utilities. In statistics, the standard deviation is a measure of a variable's spread: a way of describing how much a variable deviates from its average value. A *one standard deviation increase* means that the observed values of a variable are one "unit" above its average value. Applied to our discussion, a one standard deviation increase in trust in tap water means individuals have higher-than-average trust in their tap water; specifically, individuals trust their tap water one "unit" more than the average individual. Discussing variables in terms of standard deviations is useful for ambiguous concepts, such as trust, because standard deviations compare variables to their own average values (e.g., higher-than-average trust in tap water). We will interpret our findings using standard deviations later in this chapter and again in Chapter 4. In the present analysis, a one standard deviation increase in trust in tap water correlates with a .21 increase in trust in local government. Remarkably, this a stronger relationship than even partisanship, where a one standard deviation shift on the seven-point partisanship scale (Democrat to Republican) predicts a .18 decrease in trust in local government.

Taken together, these three surveys show that individuals who observe or experience problems with their local water and/or sewer systems are less likely to trust local, state, and federal governments. Dirty water, foul taste, service interruptions, local water or sewer main breaks, low water pressure, and other troubles with these basic systems are apparently associated with deeper pathologies of governance in the minds of citizen-consumers. These findings are consistent with qualitative evidence on the relationship between water service and trust in government. For example, Scott et al. (2005, 13) interviewed thirty-two residents of Martin County, Kentucky, following a large drinking water disaster and found that "interviewees did not trust local government to guarantee water quality ... most saw local government officials as essentially corrupt, incompetent, or both ... perhaps most significantly, no one expressed outright confidence in the government."[10] Although not all of the differences in government trust between those who do and do not experience water problems are statistically significant by conventional standards, the consistency of the disparity across levels of government and three separate, unrelated surveys lends confidence to our inferences. Ordinary but seldom scrutinized, a community's water infrastructure performance evidently shapes trust in institutions of government.

## Government Failure Predicts Consumer Behavior

Turning from attitudes to actions, we next examine the consequences of government performance failures on citizen-consumer behavior (Hypothesis 2). Does distrust of government make people more likely to turn to commercial providers? If consumer behavior follows our expectations about performative trust, then observing or experiencing local tap water problems should increase commercial water consumption, resulting in greater demand for commercial drinking water.

Throughout this book, we assess the consequences of distrust for different types of commercial drinking water: bottled water and water kiosks. We take up bottled water demand in later chapters; in this

[10] We return to the case of Martin County in Chapter 6.

chapter, we use the presence of water kiosks as a way to measure demand for commercial drinking water. Water kiosks differ from bottled water in a way that makes them especially useful for understanding citizen-consumer behavior with respect to drinking water: Kiosks are geographically defined. Customers visiting water kiosks must drive to a specific location to fill their containers. By comparison, bottled water is sold practically everywhere and requires less effort to purchase. The geographically fixed nature of kiosks means that kiosks provide a rare opportunity to study commercial water availability and demand as *a localized phenomenon.* Kiosks act as a visible signal of local citizen-consumer distrust of tap water and exit to commercial alternatives, distinctly anchored in geographic space. As San Diego, California, resident Martin Mendoza Barreto explained, he patronizes Watermill Express kiosks because he is "dissatisfied and distrustful of his tap water" (Rivard 2019).

Despite kiosks' presence throughout the United States (see Figure 1.4 in Chapter 1), very little research explains the presence of water kiosks outside of remote, rural US regions. Jepson and Brown (2014) argue that water consumers in rural South Texas *colonias* depend on water kiosks because these areas have inadequate or poor-quality tap water. These areas lack high-quality drinking water because their residents are effectively shut out of local political processes, argue Jepson and Brown (2014); kiosks are the by-product of historical, political marginalization (see also Jepson 2012).[11] With little legal or political recourse to provide or improve tap water quality, *colonias* residents purchase water from pricey kiosks. However, the presence of kiosks in major urban areas of the United States where high-quality tap water service is easily accessible raises different questions. Why do kiosks emerge where they do? Is demand for commercial kiosk water a response to poor water quality? The geographically fixed nature of kiosks allows us to examine the effects of local tap water problems on commercial water demand.

## Water Kiosks in the United States

To understand water kiosk supply (and, by implication, commercial drinking water demand), we built a data set on the location of water

---

[11] We explore the relationship between political marginalization and kiosks further in Chapter 6.

kiosks in the continental United States in 2017 (see Figure 1.4 in Chapter 1).[12] We created this data set by collecting and verifying the locations of two major kiosk companies (Watermill Express and Ice House America) using water kiosk company websites and the Google Maps platform.[13] With the help of six undergraduate researchers at Texas A&M University, we collected the complete list of Watermill Express and Ice House America kiosk locations from the respective company websites. However, both of these companies operate as franchises; kiosk location information may be difficult to update or collect across individual operators. We identified the locations of additional kiosks using Google Maps by searching for the location of these businesses.

To confirm the location of each kiosk, we tasked our student researchers with "visiting" each kiosk location in Google Street View (GSV). GSV is a feature of Google Maps that gives "the viewer the feeling of virtually being on the street and the capacity to virtually walk down that street" (Clarke et al. 2010, 1225). We took advantage of GSV's design to "travel" virtually to each kiosk location in the continental United States cheaply and efficiently. The kiosks' distinct appearance made Watermill Express and Ice House America kiosks easy to identify in Google Street View. For example, Watermill Express kiosks are hexagonal structures shaped like windmills with neon blue roofs. Ice House America kiosks are typically large, white rectangles (with penguins painted on the side) with royal blue roofs. If we were able to visually confirm a kiosk's location in GSV, it remained in the data set. If we were unable to confirm a kiosk's location visually in GSV, it was removed from our data set. In some of these cases, the kiosks in question appeared to have been recently removed (e.g., only an empty concrete plinth in the shape of a hexagon or rectangle was present at the purported location in GSV). Often, we were able to correct the location listed for a kiosk by using GSV; sometimes a kiosk would not be where the company listed its location but would be visible within a block or so. Though painstaking, this process yielded uncommonly reliable data from which we can draw inferences with confidence.

---

[12] We did not attempt to collect data on water kiosks in Alaska or Hawaii.

[13] More information about the collection and validation of the kiosk data is available in Appendix B.

Because water kiosk companies are private corporations, we do not have data on the volume of water sold or their income at each location. However, we have good reasons to believe that the number of water kiosks in an area is a meaningful proxy for measuring citizen-consumer demand for commercial water. These water kiosk companies follow a franchising business model, meaning that each company is decentralized enough to encourage response to local demand. Since water kiosks are privately owned, for-profit companies, local demand for their services must be present for them to exist profitably in an area. Entrepreneurs seeking to open a kiosk must see an economic opportunity in the local area to justify their investments, so we can interpret the presence of kiosks as a signal of consumer demand for commercial water: the more water kiosks in an area, the higher the demand for commercial water.[14] Based on these observations and our experience visiting kiosk locations using GSV, we are confident that (1) our data set contains functional kiosks and (2) kiosk presence is responsive to local customer demand for commercial water. In Chapters 5 and 6, we account for actual dollars spent on commercial water using data on bottled water sales.

To analyze the relationship between water quality problems and commercial demand, we combined our kiosk location data with the locations of water utilities in the United States serving populations of 40,000 or more.[15] We combined these data sets based on location: If a kiosk was located inside the boundaries of a utility's service area, it was joined to that utility. If more than one kiosk was located inside the boundaries of a utility's service area, we summed the total number of kiosks within the service area. Conversely, kiosks that did not fall

---

[14] Other studies have similarly used business locations of big-box stores and coffee shops to capture demand for local business and collaborative environments, respectively (e.g., Goetz & Shrestha 2009).

[15] Since this analysis includes only utilities that serve populations of at least 40,000, the question of whether our findings extend to smaller systems naturally arises. However, numerous studies show that drinking water problems are actually much more common in small systems than in large systems (e.g., Allaire, Wu, & Lall 2018; Marcillo & Krometis 2019; Scott, Moldogaziev, & Greer 2018; Teodoro & Switzer 2016). We have no reason to believe that the effects of water problems on demand for commercial drinking water in small systems will be different from their effects in large systems. Indeed, Jepson and Brown's (2014) research on rural water kiosks suggest that, if anything, our analysis of larger utilities likely *understates* the relationships between tap water quality and commercial water demand.

within the boundaries of a utility's service area are not included in this final data set. This spatial merge resulted in a data set of kiosks within 1,185 water systems service areas across the United States, ranging from zero to 144.[16] The majority (921) of utility service areas in our sample have no kiosks at all operating within their boundaries; 268 contain one or more kiosks.

Creating this data set with information on both utilities and kiosks makes it possible to compare utilities' water quality records with the number of kiosks located within their service areas, giving us a glimpse of the relationship between tap water quality and demand for commercial drinking water. We operationalize tap water quality using utilities' health-related violations of the Safe Drinking Water Act (SDWA). Health violations of the SDWA are strong indicators of water service failure generally. Passed in 1974, the SDWA regulates the safety of the US drinking water supply through a series of rules on how drinking water is treated and limits contaminants that may be present in drinking water. Health violations of the SDWA occur when a "utility's drinking water exceeds contamination limits or fails to employ the required treatment techniques" (Konisky & Teodoro 2016, 565).[17] For example, lead contamination in tap water, as in the Flint water crisis, is an SDWA health violation. Health violations of the SDWA indicate significant moments of tap water failure because these violations reflect instances when tap water is unsafe for human consumption.

Although few people are likely to monitor their drinking water utilities' regulatory compliance records religiously, we expect that consumers are at least broadly aware of significant drinking water problems in their communities thanks to the SDWA. In addition to these health-based regulations, the SDWA requires all water utilities to issue annual drinking water quality reports to their customers. Critically for our purposes, the SDWA also requires utilities to notify the public when water quality violations occur. In other words, water

---

[16] Summary statistics for all variables are provided in Appendix C, Table C.14.

[17] The SDWA also carries specific procedural and reporting requirements; failures to adhere to these requirements are management violations. Management violations occur much more frequently than health violations. We do not include management violations in the present analysis because they do not represent immediate threats to human health and they are generally not announced to the public.

utilities are required by the SDWA to broadcast serious and ongoing water quality problems to the general public. Local news media and/or government alert systems also make citizen-consumers aware of these violations and that they pose a health risk. When local drinking water becomes contaminated, the utility, local news, and/or government text alert systems communicate these violations and health risks to local residents, typically along with a boil water advisory. Although the NEXUS and VOW survey results make clear that people are aware of direct personal problems (i.e., taste, illness) they experience with their tap water, these SDWA public notification requirements make it likely that residents are aware of serious tap water problems in their communities even if they do not personally experience them. In short, consumers can be generally aware that local tap water quality problems have occurred, even if they do not know the specific type or severity of contamination and do not personally register any change in water quality.

Accordingly, we measure the quality of tap water using SDWA health violations, which reflect imminent threats to human health. Because our kiosk data were collected in spring 2017, we aggregate the total number of health violations committed by each utility from 2010 to 2016. The total number of health violations committed by utilities during this period ranges from zero to 164. This summary of heath violations measure captures a community's recent history of tap water quality – in particular, the recent total of a utility's significant tap water failures.[18]

## Tap Water Failure and Commercial Water Demand

As before, we use statistical models to isolate the relationship between tap water failure, measured as a community's SDWA health violations,

---

[18] Time series analysis, where data are compared over time, is often a preferred method of analysis because it clearly captures *when* events occurred. Applied to this kiosk analysis, a time series analysis would count the number of kiosks year over year and compare these numbers to the numbers of SDWA health violations year over year. Ideally, this would make clear that health violations occur *before* kiosks are installed. We cannot use a true time series analysis because we have data on kiosk location only for 2017 and we do not know when each kiosk was constructed. However, SDWA health violations summed from 2010 to 2016 approximate the proper theoretical order since we collected our kiosk data in 2017.

and demand for commercial drinking water, measured as the number of kiosks located in the community's water utility service area. Statistical modeling helps identify this relationship because it accounts for other explanations apart from drinking water quality that could explain kiosk presence in a community. For example, it could be that people view water from water kiosks as a luxury good, since kiosks' prices are high compared to tap water. With luxury goods, people are willing to pay more for a product they believe to be superior. If this perception of quality drives local demand for kiosks, then there should be more kiosks located in higher-income areas.

We test the relationship between drinking water quality and the number of water kiosks using a zero-inflated negative binomial regression model. This statistical procedure is appropriate when the process that causes zeroes (no kiosks) is different from the process that drives the total count in the data (number of kiosks). For instance, many states do not have a single kiosk (see Figure 1.4 in Chapter 1); it could be that utilities within states that have no kiosks experience no SDWA health violations, but this explanation is unlikely. Instead, these zeroes may reflect barriers to entry for water kiosk operators, such as state regulations or kiosk companies' franchising rules. The zero-inflated negative binomial model accounts for these alternative explanations by modeling a two-step process. First, the model estimates the likelihood that there is at least one kiosk present in a utility's service area. Second, if there is at least one kiosk present, then the model predicts how many total kiosks are present (e.g., one, two, three, four). Both stages of the model yield useful information about the relationships between water quality problems and demand for commercial water: The first (zero-inflation) stage tells us whether SDWA health violations make it more or less likely that a community has any kiosks at all, and the second (count) stage tells us how the number of SDWA health violations correlates with the number of kiosks present in that community.[19]

In addition to SDWA health violations, our models account for competing explanations for the presence of water kiosks. In the first step of the model, which predicts the likelihood that there is at least one kiosk within a utility, we include a measure of whether the community has experienced any health violations at all. A utility's first health violation may alarm citizen-consumers and have a strong effect on the appearance of the first kiosk within a utility. We also include measures

---

[19] We report the full model results in Appendix C, Table C.15.

of the local population, utility characteristics such as source water (surface water or groundwater), and whether or not the water system is operated by a government or a private company. We also adjust for the state where the utility is located to account for any state-specific quirks or company bylaws. This adjustment is especially important because SDWA implementation takes place at the state level (except in Wyoming), so SDWA enforcement may vary from state to state.

In the second stage of the model, we expect decreasing water quality to correlate positively with the demand for commercial water. In other words, a higher number of SDWA health violations should result in a higher number of total kiosks located within a utility's service area. This second stage of the analysis again includes additional variables to account for competing explanations behind demand for water kiosks. First, our estimates account for community population because a larger population implies a larger consumer market for commercial drinking water. Our estimates also control for home ownership, as renters may prefer commercial drinking water if they do not control their own premise plumbing. Race, ethnicity, and socioeconomic status are also expected to drive demand for commercial drinking water. We take up these factors in greater depth in Chapters 4–6; for present purposes, we simply adjust our estimates of kiosk counts to adjust for the percentage of Hispanic and Black residents, as well as for socioeconomic status.

Socioeconomic status reflects a series of conditions such as income, poverty, and education that combine and interact with each other. Rather than analyzing the effects of each of these variables individually, we created a single socioeconomic status variable by combining measures of the percent of the utility's population living below the poverty level, the percent of the population with a bachelor's degree, the percent of the population with a high school diploma, and the community's median income using factor analysis.[20] Education and income both relate to overall socioeconomic status. Factor analysis mathematically identifies this underlying relationship, resulting in a single variable approximating a community's overall socioeconomic status. Including socioeconomic status in our model accounts for the possibility that commercial drinking water is a luxury good; if kiosks are luxuries, then they should be located in areas with higher socioeconomic status.

---

[20] Details on the construction and interpretation of this socioeconomic status measurement are included in Appendix C and Figure C.1.

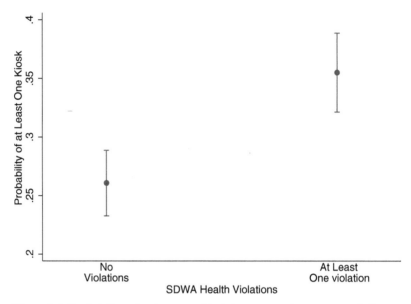

**Figure 3.8** Probability of at least one kiosk by community tap water failure.
*Note*: Estimated likelihood of at least one kiosk being in a community. Thin bars represent 90% confidence intervals. Produced with logistic regression to mimic the first stage of the zero-inflated negative binomial regression, controlling for total population (logged), source water, private utility, and state fixed effects. See Appendix C, Table C16 for full estimation.

The results are striking: As tap water quality decreases, demand for commercial water increases. Figures 3.8 and 3.9 present the relationship between SDWA health violations and the presence of at least one kiosk (the first step of the model), and Figure 3.10 presents the relationship between water quality failures and the total number kiosks (the second stage of the model). In both steps, *tap water quality failures positively predict demand for commercial drinking water in a community*. As Figure 3.8 shows, a community with at least one SDWA health violation has a 35.5 percent chance of having at least one kiosk.[21] This statistically significant effect is roughly 10 percent higher than a community with a perfect SDWA health compliance record. Put simply, water utilities that committed at least one SDWA health violation from 2010 to 2016 are significantly more likely to host at least one kiosk in 2017 than utilities that did not commit any SDWA health violations,

[21] This is the predicted probability, or the relationship between at least one SDWA health violation and the presence of at least one kiosk ($p < 0.001$).

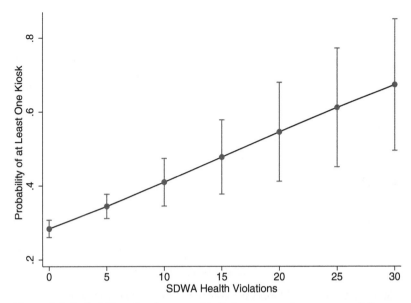

**Figure 3.9** Probability of at least one kiosk by community tap water failures.
*Note*: Estimated likelihood of at least one kiosk being in a community. Thin bars represent 90% confidence intervals. Produced with logistic regression to mimic the first stage of the zero-inflated negative binomial regression, controlling for total population (logged), source water, private utility, and state fixed effects. See Appendix C, Table C16 for full estimation.

meaning *even one serious mistake by a utility correlates with increased demand for commercial water.*

Communities that experience multiple health violations are even more likely to have at least one kiosk, as Figure 3.9 shows. If we replace our binary measure of SDWA health violations with the total number of health violations, then the impact of increasing SDWA health violations on the chance of there being at least one kiosk becomes even more apparent. For example, a community with thirty SDWA violations has a 67 percent chance of hosting at least one kiosk: more than 100 times more likely than a community with a clean record.[22]

Similarly, communities with a higher number of SDWA health violations have a higher number of kiosks. Figure 3.10 plots the estimated number of kiosks in each community as a function of its 2010–2016

---

[22] We estimated a logit model to mimic the first step of the model and replaced the binary measure of SDWA health violations with a count measure of SDWA health violations.

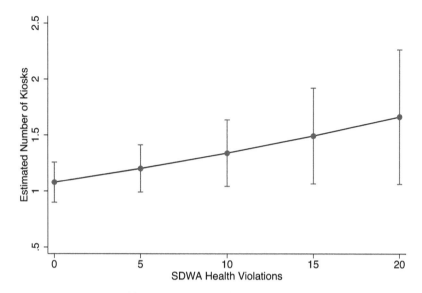

**Figure 3.10** Estimated kiosks per community by tap water failures.
*Note*: Estimated number of kiosks in a community, based on zero-inflated negative binomial regression. Thin bars represent 90% confidence intervals. Produced with zero-inflated negative binomial regression, controlling for ethnicity, race, home renters, socioeconomic status, and total population (logged). The first stage of the model controls for total population (logged), source water, private utility, and state fixed effects. See Appendix C, Table C15 for full estimation.

SDWA health violations. As the number of SDWA health violations by a water system increases, the estimated number of kiosks within its service area also increases: For each additional SDWA health violation, the estimated number of kiosks increases by .024 kiosks.[23] The strong relationship between SDWA violations and kiosk locations emerges even when accounting for competing explanations of kiosk location.

On the other hand, is it possible that drinking water kiosks simply provide a luxury good? If kiosks are luxuries, then the number of kiosks in a community should increase as its socioeconomic status increases. However, the opposite relationship appears in our analysis, as Figure 3.11 shows: As socioeconomic status (i.e., overall education and income) of its residents improves from below average to above

---

[23] This average marginal effect is statistically significant by conventional standards ($p < 0.05$). The full set of estimates is available in Appendix C, Table C.15.

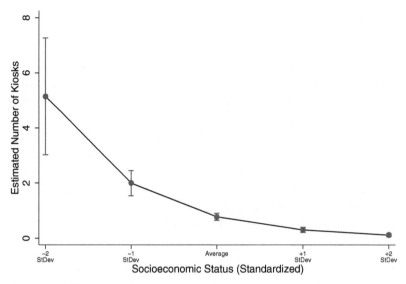

**Figure 3.11** Estimated kiosks per community by socioeconomic status.

*Note*: Estimated number of kiosks in a community, based on zero-inflated negative binomial regression. Socioeconomic status is standardized, so that one unit represents one standard deviation about a mean of zero. Thin bars represent 90% confidence intervals. Produced with zero-inflated negative binomial regression, controlling for ethnicity, race, home renters, socioeconomic status, and total population (logged). The first stage of the model controls for total population (logged), source water, private utility, and state fixed effects. See Appendix C, Table C15 for full estimation.

average, the expected number of kiosks within a community *decreases* by roughly one kiosk.[24] Because socioeconomic status is an ambiguous concept, we again use standard deviations to discuss how changes in socioeconomic status relate to the demand for commercial water. For example, Bakersfield, California, has a socioeconomic status that is two standard deviations below the average socioeconomic status in our data set and hosts nineteen kiosks. The city of Tracy, California, has average socioeconomic status and is home to two kiosks. Mountain View, California, a city with a socioeconomic status two standard deviations above the average socioeconomic status, has no kiosks at all. Far from a luxury for the affluent, it seems that people with lower incomes and/or lower levels of education are the most likely kiosk customers. This apparent relationship is startling, given kiosks' high

---

[24] This is the average marginal effect ($p < 0.01$).

price point. The locations of kiosks indicate that commercial drinking water companies profit from those with the least money to spend. We explore this proposition further in Chapter 6.

These results indicate that tap water failure increases demand for commercial water within communities: People who experience SDWA health violations apparently exit to water kiosks. Even a single SDWA health violation significantly increases the probability that local demand for commercial water will increase, and a kiosk will appear to exploit that demand. The effects of tap water problems and the distrust that follows are so strong that they drive citizen-consumers to purchase water from kiosks at a price twenty to thirty times as expensive as tap water, despite kiosks primarily locating in areas with lower-than-average income and education.

## Causes and Consequences of Performative (Dis)trust

The mosaic of data here reveals a vivid picture of performative (dis)trust in government. The quality of the water that flows from people's taps is intimately tied up with their perceptions about government's capacity to provide, regulate, and secure people's basic needs. It seems reasonable that a government's competence in providing basic services such as water supply and sanitary sewers informs citizens' trust in the institutions of the state. And indeed, data from three independent national surveys indicate that individuals who experience or observe tap water problems trust government, at all levels, less than people who have no such problems.[25]

Demonstrating that basic service failure erodes performative trust is important, but not terribly surprising. Less obvious but perhaps important is the way that citizen-consumers respond to such failures. The SDWA's public notice requirements were designed in part to raise public alarm about tap water quality failures, with the expectation that an alarmed public would clamor for better quality services from the government (McCubbins & Schwartz 1984). In Hirschman's (1970) language, Congress designed the SDWA to help citizens exercise voice in demanding safe tap water. But careful analysis of drinking water kiosks shows that, in many instances, tap water quality failures also

---

[25] We labeled this expectation Hypothesis 1 in Chapter 2.

evidently drive increased demand for commercial drinking water.[26] That is, many citizen-consumers apparently respond to water system failure not by *voicing* their concerns to government, but rather by *exiting* to the commercial market. Commercial drinking water firms reap the profits of distrust from the exit that follows tap water failure.

Our analysis of SDWA violations and commercial drinking water kiosk locations hints at a deeper dynamic too. Paradoxically, exit to commercial water demand in response to tap water quality failures seems to be greatest in low socioeconomic status communities. If water kiosk companies locate their facilities to be near their customers, then it seems that failure-driven exit from tap water to commercial water is greatest among poorer Americans. This finding aligns with a large and growing body of empirical research identifying socioeconomic, racial, and ethnic disparities in drinking water behavior (Drewnowski et al. 2013; Family et al. 2019; Hobson et al. 2007; Rosinger et al. 2018; York et al. 2011). Hirschman (1970) thought that "connoisseurs" who care most deeply about the quality of a good or service would be the first and most likely consumers to exit from an unsatisfactory provider. But it is hard to see why the poor or members of racial or ethnic minority groups would be more sensitive than others to tap water quality problems or respond differently to them – unless their responses reflect their expectations about the effectiveness of voice and exit in securing basic services.

If we are correct, then members of politically marginalized populations are more likely to respond to government failure with exit than with voice, whether they experience that failure personally or observe it from afar. Performative (dis)trust is filtered through the lens of identity, we argue. In the next three chapters, we take up the implications of identity for citizen voice and consumer exit, show how *performative* (dis)trust becomes *moral* (dis)trust, and connect citizen-consumer choices to politics.

---

[26] We labeled this expectation Hypothesis 2 in Chapter 2.

# 4 | *Hyperopia and Performative Trust*
## How Failure over There Shapes Behavior Right Here

*hyperopia* (hī̯ pə-rō ʹpē-ə). n. A condition in which visual images come to a focus behind the retina of the eye and vision is better for distant than for near objects.

Merriam-Webster (2021)

We hear on the news: "In such-and-such a state the water is contaminated." We think it's going to be that way here.

Mayra Fuentes,[1] Denver resident, on why her family does not drink<br>tap water

People need not experience poor basic services directly for such failures to erode their trust in government. In Chapter 3 we demonstrated that individuals' direct experience with drinking water problems reduces their trust in government and subsequently increases demand for commercial water products, despite the higher cost. But the consequences of drinking water problems are not geographically bound. In an age when information spreads widely and at lightning speed, regulatory or organizational failure anywhere can damage trust in government everywhere. When Americans hear about drinking water problems in other communities, they may believe their own water supplies are at risk regardless of their actual local water quality. Distrust in government is contagious.

Chapter 2 argued that the contagion of distrust and the damage it causes will be greatest where people identify with the victims of government's failure. Chapter 3 opened with the Flint water crisis, an event that roiled that southeast Michigan city. But the effects of the Flint water crisis rippled across the country in ways that changed how Americans everywhere think about their drinking water. In this chapter, we demonstrate that distrust of tap water born from water utility failures transcends political jurisdictions and geographic space. Consider, for

---

[1] Quoted in Turkowitz (2016).

example, the apparent effects of the lead contamination crisis in Flint, Michigan, on people many miles away in Providence, Rhode Island.

## A Toxic Tale of Two Cities

Lead contamination in the drinking water supply is a long-standing problem for the residents of Providence. Like many older American cities, Providence has many buildings with lead plumbing. Lead has been consistently detected in Providence's water system since testing began in 1992 – usually hovering just below the EPA's action level of 15 ppb – but it spiked to 30 ppb in 2009 and again in 2013, prompting increased scrutiny. Providence's water utility, Providence Water, applies corrosion control in its treatment process to limit the release of lead into the drinking water supply. To help monitor for lead contamination and educate the public about the issue, Providence Water began offering tap water lead-testing kits to their customers in 2014.[2] These tests were originally offered for a $10 fee, but the program was later updated to offer these voluntary lead tests at no cost to the customer. Despite the low costs of these tests, very few participated in the first two years of Providence Water's lead-testing program. From 2014 to 2016, an average of only 4.7 customers per month requested that their water be tested for lead.

In 2016, something unexpected happened. Participation in Providence Water's voluntary lead-testing program skyrocketed following the Flint water crisis. Figure 4.1 shows monthly voluntary lead testing in Providence from 2014 to 2017 (the solid black line). Prior to 2016, the overall number of lead tests conducted in Providence was low. The small peaks in Providence Water's voluntary lead-testing program during this period occurred when the utility sent lead-testing brochures during its May/June billing cycle, creating jumps in testing in June and July each year. The dashed gray line shows the monthly average Google News Index for coverage of the Flint water crisis, a measure of national public attention to Flint's plight.

As Figure 4.1 shows, Providence Water's voluntary lead-testing program began in 2014, but Providence citizen-consumers largely acted only *after* Flint put drinking water quality into the national spotlight in 2016. It seems that as Providence residents became more

---

[2] The program also offered financial assistance to qualifying customers to help replace lead-contaminated pipes.

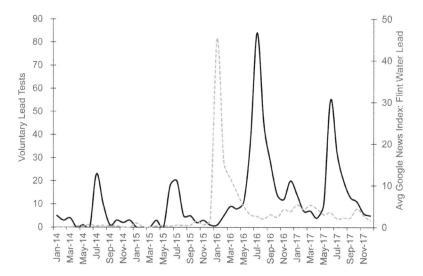

**Figure 4.1** Flint water crisis news coverage and Providence Water voluntary lead test participation, 2014–2017.

*Source*: Providence Water, Google News. The dashed gray line shows the monthly average Google News Index for coverage of the Flint Water Crisis. The solid black line shows monthly voluntary lead testing in Providence from 2014–2017. Periodic spikes in voluntary lead testing correspond to annual mailing of an informational brochure each year in May.

aware of the crisis in Flint, they became more critical of their own drinking water. Flint was not the nation's first, worst, or largest case of lead contamination in an urban water supply, but it garnered national and international public attention in ways rarely seen. The *New York Times* began reporting on Flint's water contamination in late 2015, and by early 2016 news outlets across the world were covering the city's plight in near real time. Like the 1969 Cuyahoga River fire in Cleveland, Ohio, the water crisis in Flint thrust a widespread but underappreciated problem into the national consciousness.[3] Political scientists call these *focusing events*: harmful, high-profile occurrences that suddenly put previously obscure issues onto the public policy agenda. Historically, racial and ethnic minority communities with low socioeconomic status have had a higher likelihood of living with

---

[3] In 1969, the Cuyahoga River caught fire in Cleveland, Ohio, due to extensive pollution in its waters. The Cuyahoga River fire spawned an increased public awareness of environmental degradation and subsequent focus on environmental conservation efforts during the 1970s.

drinking water quality problems (Switzer & Teodoro 2018); the Flint water crisis thus took on special significance for poor and nonwhite Americans who could see in Flint a reflection of their own lives.

Providencians could likely see a great deal to identify with in the saga of the Flint water crisis. Like Flint, Providence is a "Rust Belt" city with older housing stock and high poverty.[4] Two-thirds of Providence's population is nonwhite: The Rhode Island capital is 16.0 percent Black and 43.0 percent Hispanic (compared with 8.5 and 16.3 percent statewide, respectively). Like Flint, Providence's city government faced deep financial challenges, flirting with municipal bankruptcy and living each day with the looming specter of state takeover that could accompany a financial emergency. Even though lead contamination in Providence was significant – at least one test site yielded lead contamination greater than 200 ppb, far higher than the lead levels that sparked outrage in Flint – many residents of Providence evidently reconsidered the safety of their own tap water only after the Flint water crisis.

Providence's response to Flint's water crisis illustrates important dynamics in the relationships between citizen-consumers and their governments. The Flint water crisis made Americans everywhere reconsider what comes out of their own taps, and increased participation in Providence Water's lead-testing program reflected this broader awakening. This toxic tale of two cities raises new questions about how people perceive basic services and the governments that are supposed to protect and serve them, even when they personally do not experience basic service failure. Applied to drinking water, how does the quality of a faraway drinking water system affect perceptions of the local drinking water? People who do not experience tap water failure personally may still feel a loss of trust in government to the extent that they identify with the people who *did* experience that failure. Faraway water events can affect an individual's perception of water and behavior in her own community, just as the Flint water crisis apparently affected citizen-consumer behavior in Providence.

## Hyperopia at the Tap

To this point, we have analyzed direct experiences with basic government services and how these experiences relate to trust and consumer

---

[4] At 27 percent, Providence's poverty rate was the highest among major cities in the northeastern United States in 2019.

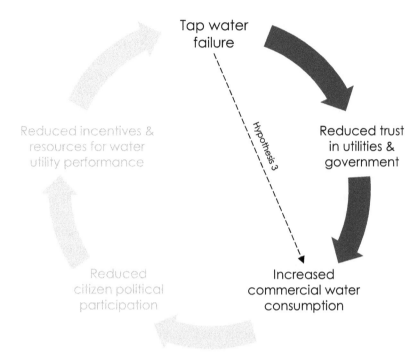

**Figure 4.2** Vicious cycle of distrust in tap water: stages investigated in Chapter 4.

*Note*: This chapter examines the relationship between indirect tap water failure and commercial water consumption. Subsequent chapters examine other portions of the cycle.

behavior. As we demonstrated in Chapter 3, when a citizen-consumer personally experiences problems with her water service or observes them in her own community, her trust in government declines and commercial drinking water becomes more appealing. But what about drinking water problems elsewhere? Why would water contamination in Michigan change citizen-consumer behavior in Rhode Island?

We argue that government failure in one place affects citizen-consumer behavior in another place to the extent that residents in one place identify with the victims of government failure in another. In Chapter 2, we labeled this expectation Hypothesis 3: *When water utility failures occur, then, citizen-consumer demand for commercial water will be strongest in communities that are demographically and socioeconomically similar to the places where the failures occurred.* Figure 4.2 displays the water-specific version of the vicious cycle introduced in Chapter 1 and highlights the portion of the cycle that

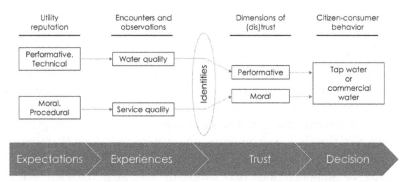

**Figure 4.3** Expectations, experiences, trust, and drinking water choice.

relates to Hypothesis 3. Whereas the previous chapter focused on direct experiences with basic service failure, we now turn our attention to indirect experiences with basic service failure as understood through the lens of identity.

Chapter 2 argued that expectations and experiences shape citizens' trust in government. These expectations and experiences are filtered through the lens of a citizen's identity (see Figure 2.5). Figure 4.3 applies our theory about citizen-consumer identity to drinking water. Moving from left to right, citizen-consumers bring expectations into their relationships with a tap water provider, or utility. Those expectations are informed by a utility's performative, technical, moral, and procedural reputations. Citizens then experience utility processes (i.e., service) and outcomes (i.e., drinking water quality), either directly or indirectly by observing others' experiences with tap water. Our focus in this chapter is on these indirect observations. Observing bad outcomes or negative processes can weaken performative trust and shape citizens' moral trust in government, particularly when citizens identify with the victims of these failures. When citizens lack moral trust in government, they are more likely to exit and purchase commercial water and less likely to voice their concerns to a utility or regulatory agency.

Prior research suggests that commercial water purchasing is driven by local perceptions informed by water quality elsewhere. McSpirit and Reid (2011) demonstrated that bottled water purchasing is primarily driven by perceptions of tap water quality, which are influenced by indirect factors such as general concerns over the health implications of poor water quality, awareness of larger-scale drinking water quality issues within the watershed, and trust in the local water treatment facility. Economists Diane Dupont and Nowshin Jahan's (2012) theory of "defensive spending" on bottled water was inspired by a high-profile drinking water failure event in Walkerton, Ontario. In April 2000, *Escherichia coli* contamination in Walkerton's drinking water system killed seven people and sickened more than 4,000 residents. Demand for bottled water increased across Canada in the wake of the Walkerton disaster, with significant bottled water sales growth in communities hundreds or thousands of miles away from Walkerton. Similarly, Asher Rosinger and Sera Young (2020) found that bottled water consumption increased nationally following the Flint water crisis, particularly in Black communities.

We investigate the role of identity in commercial water demand using spatial statistical analysis to show how distrust can spill across political jurisdictions, so that tap water problems in one community correlate with demand for commercial water in other communities. We find that the strength of this spillover of distrust from one place to another depends on communities' social similarity. Commercial water emerges most readily as a response to other communities' tap water problems when communities are demographically and/or socioeconomically alike. Applied to Flint and Providence, our theory suggests that Providencians saw themselves reflected in the Flintstones and changed their behavior based on the massive government failure that affected *people like them*. Accordingly, we argue that poor-quality drinking water in one place increases the demand for commercial water in another place, especially when residents identify with those experiencing poor-quality drinking water. This kind of indirect concern for drinking water quality is reflected in Denver resident Mayra Fuentes's explanation of her family's bottled water consumption quoted in this chapter's epigraph (Turkowitz 2016). Testing this proposition requires seeing whether and how commercial drinking water demand relates to tap water failure in neighboring communities. If the psychological effects of tap water contamination spill across utility service areas and into similar communities, then *tap water failure anywhere can stoke distrust everywhere.*

## Who Is My Neighbor?

Testing this claim about the contagion of distrust requires thinking carefully about space, proximity, and what it means to be "similar."

How we define similar, or "neighboring," communities is central to our analysis. The term "neighbor" is often used in social science research to describe a spatial unit that has a relationship with another spatial unit: If two units are related, they are neighbors; if two units are not related, they are not neighbors. The relationship between units can be defined based upon many different dimensions. Most commonly and intuitively, space can be related in terms of physical distance: California is physical neighbors with the state of Arizona, but not with New York. Hawaii is an island chain with no physically proximate neighbors. Less obviously but no less importantly, the relationship between spatial units can also be defined based on nonphysical qualities (Beck, Gleditsch, & Beardsley 2006). For instance, units can be related in terms of shared ideology: California and Arizona may not be neighbors in terms of median political ideology, but California and New York could be seen as ideological neighbors insofar as both states have tended to elect Democratic politicians in statewide races over the past thirty years. Hawaii could be considered cultural neighbors with other Pacific Islands, despite its physical isolation as an island.

Separated by four states and 632 miles, Providence and Flint are not physical neighbors. However, these two communities are similar demographically and socioeconomically. The social similarity between these cities' residents is crucial in understanding how government failure in Flint affected residents of Providence. Applied to our example, Providencians looked to the crisis in Flint, identified with its residents suffering from poor water quality because Providencians are demographically and socioeconomically similar to Flintstones, and changed their own behaviors because of this contagious distrust.

## Measuring Identity: Physical Proximity and Shared Demographics

To understand how distrust spills over between similar communities, we analyzed the relationship between tap water failure in one community and demand for commercial water in neighboring communities. As in Chapter 3, we measure tap water failure using Safe Drinking Water Act (SDWA) health violations and demand for commercial water using the prevalence of commercial water kiosks.

In order to test the role of identity in these distrust spillovers, we define neighbors as a function of physical proximity or demographic similarity. Residents of neighboring communities may worry that a basic service failure in a physically proximate community may also affect them. The first law of geography is that while all things are related, "near things are more related than distant things" (Tobler 1970). Water utilities that are physically close to one another could (1) both provide poor-quality tap water as a function of their proximity (e.g., by suffering from a common contamination) or (2) share a *perception* that drinking water in the entire area is not safe to drink. In the latter case, individuals may hear about nearby water problems via the local news media, government alert systems, or word of mouth and thus lose confidence in their own drinking water supply.

On the other hand, identity can also be a function of demographic similarity. Demographic neighbors may worry that a problem in a demographically similar community may also affect them. A citizen-consumer who hears that people like him have suffered due to government failure may believe that the government is also likely to fail him, regardless of the actual quality of the services that he receives. That certainly seemed to be the case following the Flint water crisis, when bottled water purchasing increased nationwide (Rosinger & Young 2020) and lead-testing requests in Providence increased sharply (Figure 4.1).

To capture our two identity mechanisms – geographic proximity and demographic similarity – we define which water systems are "neighbors" in different ways. First, we define neighbors based on physical proximity: Communities located within 195 miles of each other are neighbors. We selected a threshold of 195 miles because it roughly captures a three-hour driving radius: communities that are located reasonably close to one another, as well as any nearby major cities. Defining neighbors within this finite distance also subsumes the range of local news broadcasts, which are likely to report local SDWA violations. Within this 195-mile radius, communities that are closer are expected to have more influence than communities that are farther away. We measure physical proximity in terms of *inverse distance*, meaning a neighbor who is one mile away is expected to have more influence than a neighbor who is 194 miles away.

Second, we define neighbors based on demographic similarity. Communities with populations that are more demographically similar are considered "closer" to each other while community populations that are demographically dissimilar are "farther" away from each other. This way of measuring demographic similarity is analogous to how we measure inverse physical distance: If a neighbor who is one mile away matters more than a neighbor who is 194 miles away, then a neighbor who is 99 percent alike matters more than a neighbor who is only 1 percent alike. Calculating this "social distance" reflects an expectation that demographically similar neighbors will have more influence than neighbors who are less demographically similar. We calculate three separate measures of communities' demographic similarity along three dimensions: percent Black population, percent Hispanic population, and socioeconomic status.

## The Direct and Indirect Effects of Tap Water Failure

Whether we define identity in terms of physical distance or demographic similarity, we can test these neighboring community influences using a special family of statistical models called *spatial econometric models*.[5] Spatial econometric models articulate the theoretical effects of neighboring units on other units. These models make it possible to estimate the effects of spatial processes like spillovers and common shocks (Anselin 1988).[6] Here, these statistical models allow us to calculate how distrust in government spills over between communities and increases demand for private products. In the case of commercial water, these statistical models allow us to calculate the effect of tap water failure in a community's neighbors on demand for commercial drinking water within that community. Pairing these models with our different concepts of identity allows us to test which types of neighbors affect each other.

We expect that *when tap water failures occur, the citizen-consumer reaction will be strongest in communities that are demographically and socioeconomically similar to the places where the failures occurred.* To test this argument, we analyze the correlation between local demand for commercial drinking water and tap water failure committed by *neighboring* utilities, using the same data that we used in Chapter 3. As in Chapter 3, the outcome we are interested in explaining is demand for commercial drinking water, measured as the total number of kiosks within a community. And as before, we need to account for competing explanations for kiosks within the analysis.

---

[5] See Appendix C for a larger discussion of spatial regression methodology.
[6] For more background on spatial econometric models, see Anselin (1988), Ward and Gleditsch (2008), Franzese and Hays (2008), and Elhorst (2014), among others.

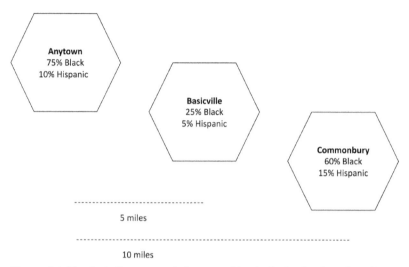

**Figure 4.4** Physical distance and demographic similarity in three imaginary communities.

*Note*: Anytown, Basicville, and Commonbury are imaginary communities. This figure illustrates that the connection between places, or which places are "neighbors," can be defined using different criteria. For instance, we can define which of the three communities are neighbors based on the physical distance between them or the demographic similarity of their populations.

The most reasonable competing explanation is that a utility's own tap water failures explain kiosk location, not a utility's neighbors' tap water failures. We saw in Chapter 3 that a community's own SDWA health violations affect the total number of kiosks located within that community; this within-community effect is called the *direct effect*. We need to account for the direct effect of a community's own water system failures (measured as SDWA health violations) in order to test whether its neighbors' water system failures affect its total number of kiosks. This cross-community effect is called the *indirect effect*. To account for both the direct and indirect effects of SDWA health violations, we include a community's own SDWA health violations *and* its neighbors' SDWA health violations in each model.

To illustrate, consider three imaginary water systems serving "Anytown," "Basicville," and "Commonbury." Though these three communities are located near each other, their demographics vary considerably (Figure 4.4). Anytown's population is 75% Black and 10% Hispanic, Basicville's population is 25% Black and 5% Hispanic, and Commonbury's population is 60% Black and 15%

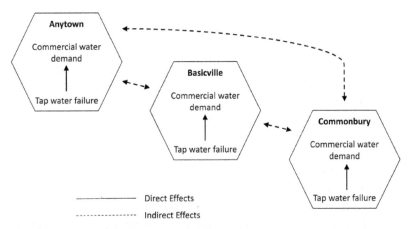

**Figure 4.5** Illustration of direct and indirect effects.
*Note:* The direct effect, or the effect of a community's own tap water failure on its commercial water demand, occurs within each community and is represented by the solid arrows. The indirect effect, or the effect of a neighbor's tap water failure on a community's commercial water demand, occurs between communities and is represented by the dotted arrows.

Hispanic. Anytown and Basicville are located five miles apart, Basicville and Commonbury are located five miles apart, and Anytown and Commonbury are located ten miles apart. We can define the degree to which each of these three imaginary communities is neighbors with each other using our two criteria: physical proximity and demographic similarity. In the case of physical proximity, we define neighborly connections as the inverse distance between utilities. As such, the connection between Anytown and Basicville is 1/5, whereas the connection between Anytown and Commonbury is 1/10. Inverse distances mathematically give more weight to neighbors that are closer physically, which is clear in our example of the three imaginary communities: Basicville has more influence over Anytown than Commonbury does. Demographically, we define neighborly connections in terms of their demographic similarity. When neighbors are defined based on demographics, Anytown and Commonbury become more closely related than Anytown and Basicville because Anytown and Commonbury are more demographically similar. Importantly, demographic similarity connects Anytown and Commonbury in a way that physical proximity does not.

We observe the direct effect of tap water failure on demand for commercial drinking water within each community. In Anytown, Basicville, and Commonbury, the direct effect of a community's own tap water failure on commercial water demand within its boundaries is illustrated by the solid arrows within communities (Figure 4.5). In this case, people living within Anytown directly experience or observe Anytown's tap water failure (i.e., SDWA health violations), exit to the private sector, and increase their demand for commercial water within their own community as a result. We analyzed this phenomenon, wherein a community's own tap water failure influences demand for commercial drinking water within itself, in Chapter 3.

In this chapter, we are concerned with the *indirect effects* that occur across communities (the dotted arrows in Figure 4.5). For example, Basicville's SDWA health violations might affect the demand for commercial drinking water in Anytown's service area: People in Anytown observe Basicville's SDWA violations, get nervous due to Basicville's physical proximity, and so practice defensive spending by exiting to the private sector and buying water from kiosks. Similarly, we are interested in whether Commonbury's SDWA health violations affect commercial water demand in Anytown due to these communities' demographic similarities (Figure 4.4). Even though the two cities are farther apart geographically, people in Anytown observe Commonbury's SDWA health violations, identify with the demographically similar residents of Commonbury, and spend defensively against similar possible failures within their own community. Accordingly, we analyze the indirect effect of a community's neighbors' SDWA health violations on the prevalence of water kiosks within a community.

We test these expectations about indirect effects due to physical proximity and demographic similarity with a set of statistical models.[7] As in Chapter 3, we estimate a series of zero-inflated negative binomial regressions to estimate the impact of SDWA health violations on kiosks. As before, the first step of the model predicts the likelihood that there is at least one kiosk in the community, and it accounts for whether a community has experienced at least one SDWA health violation, the size of the population served by the community water system, whether the system uses a groundwater source, and whether the water system is investor owned. We also include a variable for each state in this step of the model to capture any state-to-state differences in SDWA administration. Estimating this first step accounts for common alternative explanations for kiosks, such as state-based regulations or kiosk company franchising rules. The second step of the model predicts the total number of kiosks within a community and adjusts for the

---

[7] Appendix C reports the full results of models discussed in this chapter.

characteristics of the local population: percent Hispanic population, percent Black population, percent renters, total population, and socio-economic status of the population served by the utility. Accounting for local demographics is important, given the documented relationship between race, ethnicity, socioeconomic status, and SDWA health violations (Switzer & Teodoro 2018).[8] However, the most obvious alternative explanation for the indirect effect of neighbors' tap water failure is the direct effect of a community's own tap water failure. Thus, the second step of the model continues to include a measure of a community's own SDWA health violations. As before, we are mainly interested in the results from this second step of the model: demand for commercial drinking water, reflected in the proliferation of kiosks.

To assess the effect of SDWA health violations in a community's neighbors on its own kiosk count (the indirect effect in Figure 4.4), we include an additional variable in the second step of the model – a measure of neighbors' SDWA health violations, weighted by our various definitions of identity: physical proximity and demographic similarity.[9] In addition to physical proximity, we define neighbors by demographic similarity based on socioeconomic status, the percentage of the Black population, and the percentage of the Hispanic population. We test each of these variables in its

[8] It may strike some readers that the well-known relationship between SDWA health violations and race, ethnicity, and socioeconomic status may drive our results. To test whether SDWA health violations cluster according to our definitions of space (i.e., by physical proximity or by racial, ethnic, and socioeconomic similarity), we conducted Moran's I tests for spatial autocorrelation on the SDWA health violations variable. For all definitions of space, we failed to reject the null hypothesis of an i.i.d. error. In other words, SDWA health violations do not cluster spatially in our data terms of physical proximity or demographic similarity. Additionally, when spatial clustering in an outcome (e.g., kiosks) is solely attributed to spatial clustering in a predictor (e.g., race, ethnicity, or socioeconomic status), then specifying a nonspatial model is appropriate (Cook, An, & Favero 2019). Given SDWA health violations are not spatially clustered *and* we account for the direct influence of demographics in the model, we are confident that the indirect relationships discussed in this chapter exist in addition to the direct relationship between demographics and SDWA health violations. See Appendix C, Table C.17 for Moran's I test results.

[9] A spatially lagged covariate (i.e., the variable measuring neighbors' tap water failure) is exogenous, meaning we can include it in our zero-inflated negative binomial model and treat it like any other predictor (Elhorst 2014; Whitten, Williams, & Wimpy 2021). In the case of a negative binomial regression, we calculate the spatial effect by transforming the estimate on the spatial lag. The inclusion of this spatially lagged covariate technically categorizes the model we estimate as an SLX spatial model (Vega & Elhorst 2015). See Appendix C for an expanded discussion on our spatial model specification.

own model. Overall, we expect kiosks to be more numerous in communities that are physically proximate or demographically similar to communities that experience SDWA health violations.

We start by analyzing neighbors based on physical distance. Applied to our example in Figure 4.4 where Anytown and Basicville are close physical neighbors, we expect that as the number of health violations in Basicville increases, the number of water kiosks in Anytown will increase. In the next series of models, we include a measure of neighbors' health violations in which neighbors are based on demographic similarity. Applied to our example in Figure 4.4 where Anytown and Commonbury are close demographic neighbors, we expect that as the number of SDWA health violations in Commonbury increases, the number of water kiosks in Anytown will increase.

## Results: Contagious Defensive Spending

The results of all this modeling provide extraordinary evidence that the effects of service failures on demand for expensive commercial alternatives spill over from one community to another. We find that SDWA violations in a community's neighbors increase the number of local kiosks, even after accounting for a community's own drinking water compliance. In other words, *the demand for commercial drinking water in a community depends not only on local water quality, but also on water quality problems in demographically similar – but not necessarily physically proximate – communities.* What's more, such defensive spending apparently is more contagious among socially similar communities, not physically proximate communities.

### Physical Proximity
When we define neighbors based on physical proximity, SDWA health violations in a community's neighbors have little effect on the number of local kiosks. Consistent with our analysis in Chapter 3, a local SDWA health violation (i.e., the direct effect) increases the kiosk count by 0.024 kiosks.[10] But the indirect effect of physically neighboring utilities is negligible. Recall that physical neighbors are communities within 195 miles of each other, and communities that are nearby

---

[10] See Appendix C, Table C.18 for full estimation results. This is the average marginal effect ($p < 0.05$). This finding is similar to the effect of a utility's own health violations on kiosk count, as we discussed in Chapter 3.

within that 195-mile radius matter more than utilities that are far away. For each additional SDWA health violation that occurs in a community's physical neighbors, the predicted number of kiosks within that utility actually decreases by 0.14 kiosks (this indirect effect is not statistically significant from zero, however).[11] Although a community's own health violations correlate with an increase in demand for commercial water, demand for commercial water is not significantly affected by a utility's neighbors' health violations when those neighbors are defined in terms of physical proximity.

**Demographic Similarity**
Instead, we find that health violations in neighboring communities correlate with local kiosk count when "neighbors" are demographically similar. When neighbors are defined in terms of demographic similarity (i.e., similarity in socioeconomic status, percent Black population, or percent Hispanic population), our theory predicts that service problems in other communities will drive demand for commercial alternatives locally. Communities that are more demographically alike affect each other more than communities that are less alike.[12] We find these indirect effects persist even after accounting for the direct effects of a community's SDWA compliance on its own commercial water demand. In many cases, these indirect effects are substantively larger than the direct effect of a community's own tap water failure!

When identity is defined as socioeconomic similarity, SDWA health violations in neighboring communities have a strong correlation with local commercial water demand. Figure 4.6 shows the change in the estimated number of local water kiosks, given a one standard deviation increase in direct and indirect SDWA violations. To compare the direct and indirect effects, we rely on changes in a community's own SDWA health violations and socioeconomic neighbors' SDWA health violations, measured in standard deviation units. Recall from Chapter 3 that the standard deviation is a measure of a variable's spread: a way of

---

[11] This is the average marginal effect of the spatial lag (i.e., the indirect effect; $p = 0.352$).

[12] First, we calculated the difference between communities' populations along each demographic variable of interest. Larger values indicated communities are less alike, while smaller values indicated communities are more alike. Next, we calculated the inverse social distance for each demographic measure (i.e., socioeconomic status, percent Black, and percent Hispanic) using double-power distance weights: $[1 - (d_{ij}/d_{max})^2]^2$. When $d_{ij} = d_{max}$, the distance between unit $i$ and unit $j$ collapses to 0.

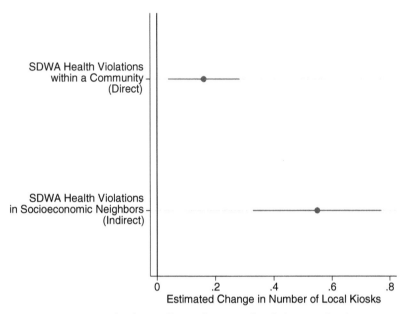

**Figure 4.6** Direct and indirect effects of water utility failures on local commercial drinking water demand in socioeconomically similar communities.

*Note*: Estimated change in the number of kiosks in a community, given a one standard deviation increase in local and neighbors' SDWA health violations. A one standard deviation increase means that the community's own SDWA health violations and the observed number of neighbors' SDWA health violations are one "unit" above their average respective values. The x-axis represents the change in the estimated number of kiosks given this one standard deviation increase. Thin bars represent 90% confidence intervals. Produced with zero-inflated negative binomial regression, controlling for a community's own SDWA health violations, ethnicity, race, home renters, socioeconomic status, and total population (logged). The first stage of the model controls for total population (logged), source water, private utility, and state fixed effects. See Appendix C, Table C19 for full results.

describing how widely a variable deviates from its average value. Discussing variables in terms of standard deviations is useful for ambiguous concepts, such as weighted neighbors' SDWA health violations, because standard deviations compare variables to their own average values. Relying on standard deviations is also useful when comparing the size of changes; by relying on standard deviations, we can compare the magnitude of the direct and indirect effects with confidence. Figure 4.6 plots the change in the estimated number of local kiosks when SDWA health violations in a community or in its neighbors increase to a higher-than-average number.

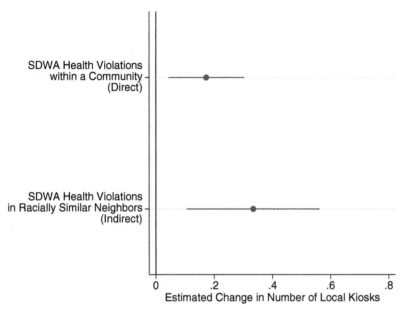

**Figure 4.7** Direct and indirect effects of water utility failures on local commercial drinking water demand (defined by similarity in percent Black population). *Note*: Estimated change in the number of kiosks in a community, given a one standard deviation increase in local and neighbors' SDWA health violations. A one standard deviation increase means that a community's own SDWA health violations and the observed number of neighbors' SDWA health violations are one "unit" above their average respective values. The x-axis represents the change in the estimated number of kiosks given this one standard deviation increase. Thin bars represent 90% confidence intervals. Produced with zero-inflated negative binomial regression, controlling for a community's own SDWA health violations, ethnicity, race, home renters, socioeconomic status, and total population (logged). The first stage of the model controls for total population (logged), source water, private utility, and state fixed effects. See Appendix C, Table C20 for full results.

The positive value of SDWA health violations within a community in Figure 4.6 indicates that as a community's own violations increase by one standard deviation, the estimated number of local kiosks increases by 0.16.[13] This result is unsurprising and consistent with our findings in Chapter 3. But the positive value of socioeconomic "neighbors'" health violations in Figure 4.6 is also positive and even stronger. When health violations in socioeconomic neighbors increase by one standard deviation, the estimated number of local kiosks

[13] This is the standardized average marginal effect ($p < 0.05$).

increases by 0.55 – roughly half a kiosk.[14] That is, the behavioral effects of tap water problems in socioeconomically similar communities elsewhere apparently can be stronger than the effects of local tap water problems. And though "roughly half a kiosk" may seem like a small change, the average number of kiosks located within communities where kiosks are present is five kiosks. An increase of half a kiosk represents an 11 percent increase in kiosks, compared to a 3 percent increase in kiosks caused by a community's own violations.

A similar picture emerges when "neighbors" are defined as the similarity between communities' percent Black population. As depicted in Figure 4.7, as the number of health violations in a community's racial "neighbors" increases by one standard deviation, the estimated number of kiosks increases by 0.33.[15] As was the case with socioeconomic similarity, SDWA health violations correlate strongly with kiosks in neighboring communities when the communities in question are similar in racial composition. This indirect effect is strong even when accounting for the most obvious alternative explanation: a community's own water quality problems. When a community's own SDWA health violations increase by one standard deviation, the estimated number of local kiosks increases by 0.17.[16] These changes represent respective increases in kiosks of 7 and 3 percent. As before, the indirect effect of SDWA health violations is substantively larger than the direct effect: The correlation between neighbors' health violations and local kiosks is roughly double the correlation between a community's own health violations and its kiosks.

When identity is defined as communities' similarity based on percent Hispanic population, once again we find that SDWA health violations in a community's ethnically similar "neighbors" correlate with an increase in the estimated number of local kiosks (Figure 4.8), though this indirect effect falls short of statistical significance by traditional standards.[17] As in Chapter 3, when a community's own SDWA violations increase by one standard deviation, the number of local kiosks

---

[14] This is the standardized average marginal effect of the average indirect effect ($p < 0.001$).

[15] This is the standardized average marginal effect of the average indirect effect ($p < 0.05$).

[16] This is the standardized average marginal effect ($p < 0.05$).

[17] The standardized average marginal effect of the average indirect effect is 0.15 kiosks ($p = 0.233$).

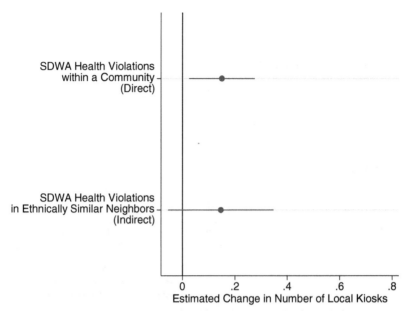

**Figure 4.8** Direct and indirect effects of water utility failures on local commercial drinking water demand (defined by similarity in percent Hispanic population).

*Note:* Estimated change in the number of kiosks in a community, given a one standard deviation increase in local and neighbors' SDWA health violations. A one standard deviation increase means that the observed number of a community's own SDWA health violations and neighbors' SDWA health violations are one "unit" above their average respective values. The x-axis represents the change in the estimated number of kiosks given this one standard deviation increase. Thin bars represent 90% confidence intervals. Produced with zero-inflated negative binomial regression, controlling for a community's own SDWA health violations, ethnicity, race, home renters, socioeconomic status, and total population (logged). The first stage of the model controls for total population (logged), source water, private utility, and state fixed effects. See Appendix C, Table C21 for full results.

increases by 0.15.[18] This increase in kiosks associated with a community's own SDWA health violations is consistent with the increase observed in our other models.

Figure 4.9 layers the indirect and direct effects presented in Figures 4.6–4.8 onto the same plot. When viewed together, the direct and indirect consequences of drinking water problems on commercial water demand are clear. Accounting for all three types of neighbors

---

[18] This is the standardized average marginal effect ($p < 0.05$).

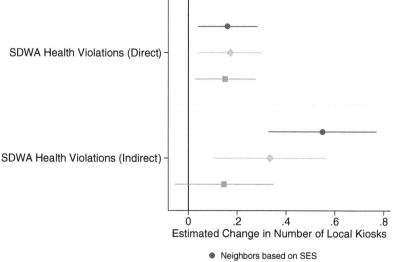

**Figure 4.9** Direct and indirect effects of water utility failures on local commercial drinking water demand (all similarity definitions).

*Note*: Composite of results presented in Figures 4.6–4.8. Each line type presents results from calculations using a different demographic similarity neighbor definition. The x-axis represents the change in the estimated number of kiosks. Thin bars represent 90% confidence intervals. Produced with zero-inflated negative binomial regression, controlling for a community's own SDWA health violations, ethnicity, race, home renters, socioeconomic status, and total population (logged). The first stage of the model controls for total population (logged), source water, private utility, and state fixed effects. See Appendix C, Tables C19–21 for full results.

based on demographic similarity, the direct correlations are strong and consistent, as indicated by the clustered, direct plotted values in the upper half of Figure 4.9. These direct effects are consistent with our findings in Chapter 3.[19] However, the indirect effect of tap water failures (i.e., SDWA health violations in a community's neighbors) when demographic neighbors are defined based on socioeconomic status and the percent Black population are substantively *at least twice as large* as the direct effect (i.e., a community's own SDWA health

[19] Each individual SDWA health violation within a community correlates with an average increase of .025 kiosks; this statistically significant direct effect is consistent with our findings in Chapter 3.

violations). Indeed, the results consistently indicate that the average *indirect* effects of tap water problems in socioeconomically and racially similar communities elsewhere can be greater than the *direct* effects of local tap water problems on local water kiosks. Demand for commercial drinking water is apparently hyperopic: Consumers seem to respond to problems elsewhere more strongly than they respond to conditions within their local communities.

These findings suggest that identity amplifies the effect of tap water failures on demand for commercial drinking water. Even when people do not personally experience poor-quality tap water themselves, many will still exit to the commercial sector when they identify with people who experience poor-quality tap water. Interestingly, the effects are heterogeneous among different concepts of identity. It is clear, however, that *the effects of identity are strongest when identity is defined by social similarity, not in terms of geographic proximity*.

Basic service failures' impact on citizen-consumer behavior evidently transcends geographic space and is not limited to the places where failures happen. Tap water failures anywhere appear to drive consumer behavior wherever people identify with the victims of those basic service failures. When SDWA health violations occur, their effect on commercial water consumption transcends operational boundaries and political jurisdictions.

## Calculating Flint's Impact

We opened this chapter with a surprising story about how the water crisis in Flint, Michigan, apparently changed citizen-consumer behavior in Providence, Rhode Island – a city hundreds of miles away. But though they are distant in space, Providence and Flint are much more closely linked in terms of demographics and socioeconomics. Our analysis gives us reason to expect that the two Rust Belt cities' social similarity makes citizen-consumer responses in one sensitive to conditions in the other. In the case of drinking water, the effects of drinking water quality problems on commercial water demand can ripple across socially similar communities nationwide.

The models we fitted allow us to calculate the indirect effect of tap water failures in Flint on commercial water demand in Providence.[20] These effects are displayed in Figure 4.10, which shows how a single

---

[20] See Appendix C, Table C.22 and accompanying discussion.

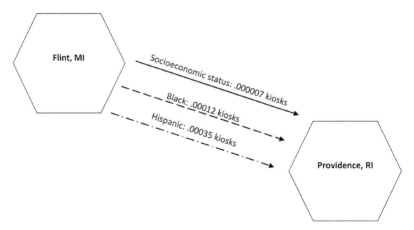

**Figure 4.10** Indirect effects of water utility failures in Flint on commercial drinking water demand in Providence, based on different measures of social similarity.
*Note*: Figure shows the indirect effects of a single SDWA health violation in Flint, Michigan on the predicted number of kiosks appearing in Providence. Each arrow represents a dimension of demographic similarity across the two communities. See Appendix C, Table C22 and accompanying discussion for details on how these effects were calculated.

SDWA health violation in Flint affects commercial water demand in Providence as a function of the two cities' socioeconomic, racial, and ethnic similarities. Each dimension of similarity is associated with a different indirect, cross-community effect. When we define neighbors based simply on physical distance, Flint and Providence are not connected to one another at all in our analysis because they are more than 195 miles apart. Therefore, a health violation in Flint has no indirect effect on kiosks in Providence as a function of physical distance.

When we define the connection between Flint and Providence in terms of demographic similarity, health violations in Flint indirectly raise commercial water demand in Providence. As seen in Figure 4.10, our models indicate that when the connection between Flint and Providence is defined based on similarity in socioeconomic status, a single health violation in Flint increases the number of kiosks in Providence by 0.000007 kiosks. Similarly, when the connection between Flint and Providence is defined based on similarity in percent Black population between the two cities, a single health violation in Flint increases the number of kiosks in Providence by 0.00012 kiosks. When the connection between Flint and Providence is defined based on percent Hispanic population, a single health violation in Flint increases the number of

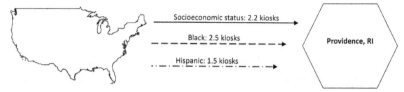

**Figure 4.11** Aggregate indirect effects of water utility failures in Providence's neighbors on commercial drinking water demand in Providence, based on different measures of social similarity.

*Note*: Figure shows the aggregated indirect effects of SDWA health violation in other U.S. utilities on the predicted number of kiosks appearing in Providence. Only the continental U.S. is represented, as our analysis does not include Alaska or Hawaii. Each arrow represents a dimension of demographic similarity linking Providence to its neighboring communities. See Appendix C, Table C23 and accompanying discussion for details on how these effects were calculated.

kiosks in Providence by 0.00035 kiosks. Importantly, these changes in Providence's kiosks occur after a single SDWA health violation in Flint, a city located 632 miles away. These indirect effects persist even when accounting for Providence's own SDWA health violations.

With effects measured in tiny fractions of a kiosk, it might be tempting to dismiss these indirect racial, ethnic, and socioeconomic impacts of Flint's water quality on Providence's commercial water demand as trivial. However, Flint and Providence are just one pair of water systems. In addition to Flint, Providence's hundreds of other "neighbors" (as defined by similarity in socioeconomic status, race, or ethnicity) simultaneously exert indirect effects of basic service failure upon Providence. The total indirect effects are much larger when the impacts of all these neighbors are aggregated, as Figure 4.11 illustrates. When SDWA health violations occur in Providence's socioeconomic neighbors, the accumulation of these violations increases the number of kiosks in Providence by 2.2 kiosks.[21] Similarly, when the connection between Providence and its neighbors is defined based on similarity in percent Black population, neighbors' health violations increase the estimated number of kiosks in Providence by 2.5 kiosks. When the connection between Providence and its neighbors is defined based on percent Hispanic population, neighbors' health violations increase the estimated number of kiosks in Providence by 1.5 kiosks. Although the change in kiosks produced by a single health violation in a single neighbor is small (Figure 4.10), health

[21] See Appendix C, Table C.23 and accompanying discussion.

violations in many neighbors compound (Figure 4.11) to produce marked hyperopic effects.

Furthermore, these identities compound: Providencians may identify with victims of government failure via socioeconomic status *and* race *and* ethnicity simultaneously across thousands of other cities. These multiple mechanisms of identity may work simultaneously or in tandem, rather than in isolation from one another (as we have analyzed them here). Combined, the indirect effects of neighbors' health violations correlate with a significant increase in demand for commercial water in Providence. Indeed, in some communities, local demand for commercial drinking water may depend more on tap water quality elsewhere than on local quality. For poor and nonwhite Americans, water service failure anywhere contributes to defensive spending everywhere.

## Contagious Exit

The effect of poor service quality on demand for commercial alternatives apparently transcends political borders. Apart from and in addition to their own experiences, citizen-consumers may seek commercial alternatives and spend defensively when they identify with victims of government failure in other communities. In the case of drinking water, the quality of tap water in a distant community can affect local commercial water demand in demographically and socioeconomically similar places.

Discontent does not necessarily imply distrust. A person who is concerned about service quality *here* due to problems *over there* could either express his concern to officials here or opt for service from a commercial firm. The proliferation of kiosks and meteoric growth of bottled water indicate that plenty of citizen-consumers choose to exit to the commercial market rather than voicing their discontent to government regulators and providers. Taken together, the negligible effects of physical proximity and the powerful effects of demographic and socioeconomic similarity on the demand for commercial drinking water hint that the exit/voice decision turns in large part on identity. That racial, ethnic, and socioeconomic factors predict commercial water demand even after accounting for local tap water quality suggests that responses to discontent vary across social groups. In the next chapter, we examine who voices their discontent to government, who exits for commercial firms, and what those choices tell us about politics.

# 5 | *Speaking Up or Opting Out*
## Moral Trust, Voice, and Exit

That is my personal mission, to make sure that this gets changed, so what happened to my family and my community never happens to anyone else again.

LeeAnne Walters,[1] Flint water crisis whistleblower

My husband Don and I became passionate about providing safe drinking water back in the 1980s. At that time our local monthly water bill warned pregnant woman [sic] and infants under the age of six months to not drink the water. ... We would regularly attend neighborhood meetings where the government warned us not to drink our tap water. Because of these issues, Don and I developed a miniature water purification kiosk in Brighton in 1984.

Lani Dolifka,[2] Founder and CEO of Watermill Express

Although tap water in the United States is largely safe to consume, there are unfortunately many for whom it is not. Millions of people do not have safe and consistent access to drinking water services (Meehan et al. 2020), and new threats to drinking water quality lurk constantly (Siegel 2019). Since drinking water is a basic service for which the government is responsible, either directly or through regulation, drinking water failure is a government failure. In Chapter 3, we showed how problems with tap water erode trust in government and correlate with increased demand for commercial water. Chapter 4 showed that the effects of tap water problems transcend political and geographic boundaries in ways that make distrust contagious. In this chapter, we

---

[1] YouTube video accompanying receipt of 2018 Goldman Environmental Prize (www.youtube.com/watch?v=hpFNG8DDTrs). See also Goldman Environmental Prize (2018a, 2018b).
[2] Dolifka (2017a).

take up the consequences of that distrust for citizen-consumer behavior, political participation, and bottled water consumption.

When experiencing unsatisfactory basic services, citizen-consumers may choose either to *voice* their concerns to government or to *exit* by buying those services from a commercial firm. As we explained in Chapter 2, an individual's choice between voice or exit depends on her expectations about the government's response to her concerns, along with the availability and perceived quality of commercial alternatives. Any basic service failure erodes citizen-consumer belief that government can produce satisfactory outcomes – what we call *performative* trust. Voicing discontent may be a rational response for citizen-consumers whose performative trust in government is shaken by basic service failure. But rational citizen-consumers who believe that government is *morally* untrustworthy will always opt for exit and never attempt to voice discontent. A citizen-consumer would be crazy to complain to an agency or lobby a government that he believes is indifferent or hostile toward him. Therefore, the morally distrustful citizen-consumer will choose commercial alternatives when they are available, and be willing to pay significantly higher prices for them, because he believes that voicing his concerns to government is not a viable alternative. Voice and exit are thus substitutes, and the voice/exit choices that people make reflect trade-offs in the ways that individuals perceive themselves politically as citizens and economically as consumers.

## Two Women's Responses to Tap Water Failures

The voice/exit dichotomy can be seen starkly in the stories of two women who confronted government failure: LeeAnne Walters and Lani Dolifka.

### *Voice: LeeAnne Walters*

Prior to 2014, LeeAnne Walters was a stay-at-home mother living in Flint, Michigan. But when the city of Flint began to use the Flint River as the main source of water for the water system, the effects on her family were immediate and terrifying. Her three-year-old twins both developed rashes, she and her daughter began losing their hair, and her older son fell ill (Lurie 2016). Walters attempted to inform the city government of these problems but did not receive a response for months. Finally, the city tested the water from her taps and found that the water far exceeded the 15 ppb action level against lead contamination set by the Environmental Protection Agency (EPA). Although city officials told her that the problem was isolated to her home, Walter's frequent attendance at city council meetings told her otherwise: She was far from alone. Other Flint residents were experiencing similar health problems. Understandably alarmed, Walters continued to exercise her voice in a number of avenues. She contacted Miguel Del Toral, a regional manager at the EPA, but his warnings to the Michigan Department of Environmental Quality were ignored (Fonger 2018; Lurie 2016). Finally, she enlisted the help of Virginia Tech University researcher Marc Edwards. Edwards's team collected more than 800 water samples from homes around the city, showing that the lead contamination issue in Flint was widespread. This citizen-initiated research helped bring national attention to the Flint water crisis and the subsequent actions to remedy Flint's drinking water problems.

When confronted with a catastrophic government failure, Walters used every avenue available to exercise her voice and doggedly persisted until she was heard. After her own experience in Flint, Walters set her sights on a national goal, partnering with Edwards and other researchers at Virginia Tech to use science in order to "address infrastructure inequality, water contamination, waterborne diseases and a lack of trust, occurring in economically-disadvantaged rural towns and post-industrial cities across the U.S." (Virginia Tech University 2020). Her personal experience of government failure inspired Walters to attempt to fix the problem, not just in her hometown, but nationwide. Walters had hearty company, as the water crisis spurred a cadre of activists in Flint who mobilized to demand a solution to the city's water woes (Pauli 2019). It is easy to imagine even more tragic alternative outcomes to the Flint water crisis had Walters and other activists chosen exit instead of voice when faced with devastating government failure. Instead, the city's water crisis sparked a democratic reawakening in Flint, along with an attendant opening of political channels for Flintstones at state and federal levels. "We're protagonists in our own liberation struggle," said Flint community organizer Nayyirah Shariff (Pauli 2019, 223).

## Exit: Lani Dolifka

Lani Dolifka's story starts similarly to LeeAnne Walters's, with government failure and tap water contamination. As she put it,

> I've experienced poor water quality in my own lifetime. I used to live near a designated Superfund site where 600 documented chemicals were discovered in the local groundwater. We were told not to drink our tap water and had to rely on alternative sources for our water (Dolifka 2017b).[3]

Dolifka says that she regularly attended local meetings where she was warned by the government to avoid drinking the tap water (Dolifka 2017a).

Unlike Walters, Dolifka's primary response to experiencing drinking water contamination was not to exercise her voice to the officials who governed her water utility or the regulatory agencies responsible for its oversight. Instead, she chose to exit from basic public services –both as a consumer and as a commercial producer. Dolifka and her husband developed a vending machine to sell filtered tap water as a commercial good. Much as LeeAnne Walters was not satisfied with exercising her voice in Flint alone and sought to build a national movement for safer drinking water, Dolifka decided to share the opportunity to exit with others by expanding her water-vending business. She and her husband founded Watermill Express, one of the water kiosk companies in our data set. Dolifka credits her passion for clean water as the impetus behind the spread of Watermill Express kiosks across the country (Dolifka 2017a). We examine Watermill Express's growth and marketing further in Chapter 6; for Lani Dolifka, distrust evidently has been quite profitable.

## Voice and Exit in Response to Tap Water Failure

These two women's stories illustrate the very different ways that individuals can respond to basic service failure. As presented in the generalized model in Chapter 2, the citizen-consumer's choice of voice or exit in response to government failure reflects his or her relationship with government. In this chapter, we explore some of the ways these responses can manifest. Figure 5.1 shows the specific part of the vicious cycle of distrust that we examine in this chapter.

---

[3] Superfund sites are areas where hazardous waste has been dumped or mismanaged in some form. They are regulated under the Comprehensive Environmental Response, Compensation, and Liability Act (CERCLA).

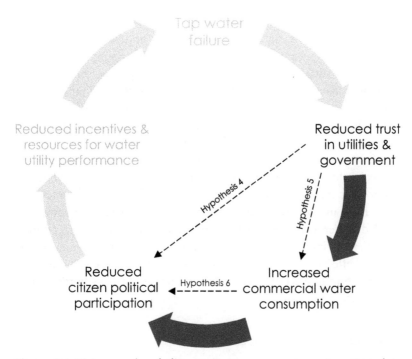

**Figure 5.1** Vicious cycle of distrust in tap water: stages investigated in Chapter 5.

*Note*: This chapter examines the relationships between trust in government, commercial water consumption, and political participation. Earlier and subsequent chapters examine other portions of the cycle.

We begin by showing that marginalized groups may be less likely to exercise voice when faced with tap water failure. The political history of the United States gives individuals from historically marginalized groups ample reason to be morally distrustful toward government – a topic explored in greater depth in Chapter 6. Distrustful individuals should be less likely to use voice in response to tap water problems, owing to their moral distrust of government. This logic underlies Hypothesis 4: *Individuals with low incomes and/or members of racial and ethnic minority groups are less likely to complain to their utilities about their water problems.* In this chapter, we test this hypothesis empirically, showing that poor and minority individuals are less likely to complain to officials when they experience tap water problems.

We then turn to the relationship between moral trust and exit for commercial services with an evaluation of Hypothesis 5: *As an individual's trust in government decreases, the likelihood that he or she drinks commercial water instead of tap water increases.* This hypothesis forms part of the core logic of the argument expressed in Chapter 2. The evidence presented in this chapter supports the claim that as individuals' distrust in the government grows, they are more likely to consume commercial water products instead of tap water.

Finally, we explore the downstream political effects of a citizenry that exits from public services by examining the relationship between commercial water use and political participation. Citizen-consumer exit from a service as basic as drinking water may foretell a wider exit from civic life. This logic of exit is behind Hypothesis 6: *As commercial water sales increase, political participation will decrease.* We test this hypothesis in two ways. First, at the individual level, we show that bottled water drinkers are less politically active, pursuing political activities at significantly lower rates. Then we explore the aggregate political effects of exit to commercial water consumption, finding that participation in elections across the country declines as bottled water consumption increases.

## Choosing Voice: Who Speaks Up?

Democratic governance is rooted in the idea that governments respond to citizen preferences. People who respond to government failure by voicing their displeasure must believe that government is morally decent enough to respond positively to their concerns. But people who believe that government is uncaring or malevolent as an institution will not bother complaining – to voice concerns to an antagonistic government is pointless at best and, at worst, potentially damaging. Voicing discontent is an act of moral trust.

The political history of the United States gives people with few economic resources and members of racial and ethnic minority communities good reasons to question government's benevolence. As we discussed in Chapter 2, persistent racial, ethnic, and socioeconomic differences in government trust make sense in light of institutional biases that have too often systematically excluded some segments of the population from governance – a topic we explore more deeply in Chapter 6. With little confidence in the basic morality of the governments charged with their protection, members of minority groups may see little value in voicing concerns about service conditions. Although indifference to and alienation from government are hardly unique to low-income and/or minority communities, we expect socioeconomic and demographic disparities in the use of voice when encountering basic service failures.

Applied to water, disparities in moral trust will be observable as differences in who complains to officials in response to tap water problems. To analyze complaints about tap water quality, we turn again to the Texas A&M NEXUS survey.[4] In Chapter 3, we used the NEXUS survey to show that experiences with bad-tasting tap water, cloudy tap water, low water pressure, or waterborne illness are correlated with lower trust in government. Participants who reported that they had experienced tap water problems in their current residences were then asked, "Did you contact your water utility to address any of the problems you experienced?" Here, we analyze patterns of responses to this question. If we are correct, then members of racial and ethnic minorities will be less likely to complain to their utilities when they experience water problems compared with whites. Moreover, we expect these demographic disparities to be greatest for the poor, with differences diminishing as incomes increase.

Of course, tap water problems do not occur at random. Research on Safe Drinking Water Act (SDWA) compliance demonstrates that tap water regulatory violations correlate significantly with communities' socioeconomic status (SES) and racial and ethnic composition. Race and ethnicity matter most in predicting a utility's tap water quality where people are poor. Specifically, communities' Black and Hispanic populations most strongly predict SDWA violations where socioeconomic indicators are low (Switzer & Teodoro 2017, 2018). Further, Switzer and Teodoro (2017, 2018) find an ordered relationship: Among low-SES communities, SDWA health violations are most strongly correlated with the percentage Hispanic population, followed by percentage Black population. In other words, race and ethnicity both correlate with SDWA compliance in low-SES communities, but Hispanic ethnicity is a markedly stronger predictor.

These patterns of SDWA compliance present an analytical challenge for understanding complaints about tap water: Someone who does not experience tap water problems is unlikely to complain about her tap water! If tap water problems correlate with race, ethnicity, and/or SES,

---

[4] See Chapter 3 and Appendix A for full methodological details about the NEXUS survey.

then racial, ethnic, and socioeconomic patterns of complaints to the government about tap water problems might have nothing to do with moral trust and everything to do with the incidence of tap water quality problems. Indeed, as we observed in Chapter 2, the ultimate evidence that governments are responsive to politically powerful citizens is that discontent will be rare among the powerful (Clark, Golder, & Golder 2017).

Since existing research gives us good reason to think that race, ethnicity, and SES correlate with tap water problems, an analysis of voice must account for systematic biases in the distribution of tap water problems. To address this problem, we use a two-stage statistical analysis (Heckman 1979). We begin by estimating the likelihood that a NEXUS respondent has experienced tap water quality problems. The results of that analysis allow us to adjust our estimates of complaints in ways that account for systematic racial, ethnic, and socioeconomic biases in the incidence of tap water problems.

## *Trouble at the Tap*

Do tap water problems correlate with race, ethnicity, and/or SES at the household level? Recall that the NEXUS survey asked respondents whether they experienced bad-tasting tap water, cloudy tap water, low water pressure, or illness that they attributed to tap water at their current residences. Only respondents who answered "yes" to one or more of these were asked whether they complained about their problems to their water utilities. In the first stage of analysis, we used a probit regression to model the likelihood that NEXUS survey respondents experienced one or more tap water quality problems as a function of respondents' income, race, and ethnicity.

Although tap water quality problems do not vary significantly by race and ethnicity among NEXUS survey respondents, the relationship between income and the likelihood of experiencing water quality problems is strong and pronounced. Figure 5.2 shows the estimated likelihood of experiencing one or more tap water quality problems by income.

Two aspects of this first-stage analysis are noteworthy. First, as income increases, the likelihood of experiencing water quality problems decreases sharply. At the 2015 federal poverty–level annual income for a three-person family ($20,090), the likelihood of experiencing a tap water quality problem is 53 percent. A household at the 95th percentile of annual income in 2015 ($214,463) has only a

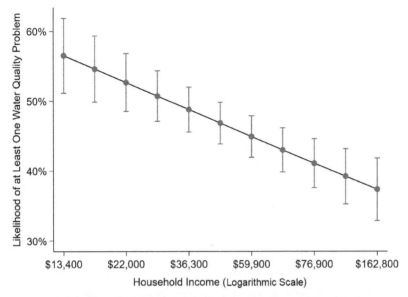

**Figure 5.2** Likelihood of experiencing tap water quality problems by income. *Note*: Probit regression analysis of NEXUS Survey predicting at least one water quality problem, as a function of income (logged), race, and ethnicity. Thin bars represent 95% confidence intervals. See Appendix C, Table C24 for full estimation.

35 percent likelihood of having ever experienced a tap water quality problem. This finding is consistent with the voluminous literature on environmental justice, which has long found environmental issues to be more common among populations with lower SES, with some studies specifically finding higher contaminant levels in the drinking water of poor communities (Balazs et al. 2011; Balazs & Ray 2014; Ringquist 2005). Second, our analysis indicates that tap water service failures are remarkably common even among very high-income households: More than one in three respondents with very high incomes reported experiencing a tap water failure of some kind in their current residence.

## Race, Ethnicity, Income, and Voice

Who complains to authorities when they experience basic service failures? Does the use of voice in response to discontent vary by race, ethnicity, and income? The results from the first stage of our analysis allow us to test whether different groups of people are more or less likely to complain to their utilities about tap water problems, after

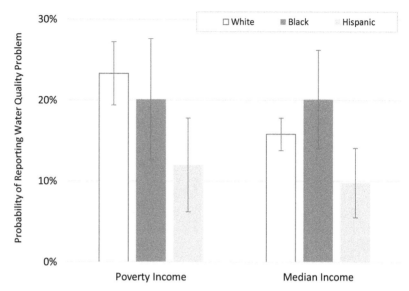

**Figure 5.3** Probability of reporting tap water quality problems to utility.

*Note*: Probit regression analysis of NEXUS Survey with Heckman (1979) selection adjustment. Model estimates probability of reporting a water quality problem as a function of income (logged), race, ethnicity, and the interaction of income with race/ethnicity. Models include controls for home ownership, party identification, and an indicator for whether the respondent is responsible for paying a water bill. Thin bars represent 90% confidence intervals. See Appendix C, Table C24 for full estimation.

accounting for the probability of experiencing a problem in the first place. Our second-stage statistical model estimates the probability of complaining to authorities as a function of race, ethnicity, and income.[5] In addition to adjusting for the probability of experiencing tap water problems, our model accounts for other factors that could cause variation in reporting tap water problems, including partisanship, home ownership, and whether the respondent receives a bill directly from her water utility. Figure 5.3 shows the resulting estimated probabilities of complaining for white, Black, and Hispanic respondents with incomes at the 2015 federal poverty level ($20,090) and the median income level ($56,516).

Two findings are noteworthy here. First, the probability of complaining about tap water problems is generally low. Only about one-

---

[5] Our models also included multiplicative interaction terms for income with race and ethnicity. A Wald test of independent equations indicates that the two-stage Heckman estimation procedure significantly improves fit ($X^2 = 26.4$, $p < 0.001$). See Appendix C, Table C.24 for full estimation results.

third of respondents who experienced a tap water problem reported the problem(s) to their utilities. Voice, it seems, is the last-place option as a response to experiencing tap water problems.

Second, and importantly for our present purposes, a marked ethnic disparity in the probability of reporting tap water quality problems emerges from this analysis, especially at low income levels. An ordered relationship appears at the 2015 poverty income level: White individuals are most likely to complain to their utilities about tap water problems (23 percent), followed by Blacks (20 percent), with Hispanics least likely to complain (12 percent). The ethnic disparity is large and statistically significant, with whites nearly twice as likely as Hispanics to complain to their utilities. These disparities are muted somewhat as income increases. For respondents at the median income level, the probability of complaints by whites falls to 16 percent. The probability of white complaints is still higher than Hispanic complaints, but with a statistically weaker difference. Interestingly, income does not moderate tap water quality complaints by Blacks: The probability of a Black respondent complaining is virtually identical when comparing respondents with poverty-level income versus median income levels. This result is broadly consistent with research on racial and ethnic disparities in political participation (Anoll 2018; Leighley & Vedlitz 1999). Hispanics are consistently less likely than whites to complain about bad tap water service, with the greatest disparities among the poor. Silence, it seems, has an ethnic accent.

## Choosing Exit: Moral Distrust and Commercial Water Consumption

Myriad research has shown that in addition to being less likely to report water issues, historically marginalized groups are also more likely to choose bottled water as a primary source of drinking water. As we discussed in Chapter 1, numerous studies have shown that Black and Hispanic individuals are more likely to express concern with their tap water and choose commercial alternatives (Hobson et al. 2007; Hu et al. 2011; Pierce & Gonzalez 2017; Rosinger et al. 2018). Often studies examining the relationship between race or ethnicity and bottled water consumption couch their findings in the language of distrust or provide anecdotes about trust and drinking water, but the direct links between trust in government and drinking water behavior remain little explored.

We suggest that there is a direct relationship between moral distrust of government and choosing commercial services. When individuals do not believe that the government is acting in good faith, the decision to exit from public services is simple. If the government is not just failing in terms of performance but failing *morally*, then voice becomes a useless option and exit is the only rational choice. Consequently, we expect that people who trust government are more likely to drink tap water, and those who distrust government are more likely to drink commercial water.[6]

We again use survey data to test the relationship between bottled water consumption and trust in government. For these analyses, we use data from the Cooperative Congressional Election Survey (CCES) module introduced in Chapter 3. The survey includes questions about respondents' trust in different levels of government, as well as questions regarding their household water consumption.

## Bottled Water Consumption and Trust

The 2018 CCES includes questions about trust in government at different levels. Respondents were asked, "How much of the time do you think you can trust each of the following to do what is right?" about local, state, and federal government. They were given the options "Just about all of the time," "Most of the time," "Only some of the time," and "Never." These questions capture moral trust since they are not asking about the government's ability to provide quality services, but rather about how much respondents trust the government to *do what is right*, targeting respondents' beliefs about the morality of government.[7]

In order to measure citizen-consumer behavior, respondents to the survey were asked, "Some people drink water directly from the tap in their homes, some drink water that has been filtered with some device at home, and others buy bottled water to drink at home. Where do you get most of your drinking water?" We are primarily interested in whether individuals consume bottled water. While the distinction between plain and filtered tap water is interesting, in-home filtration is used mainly for aesthetic purposes (i.e., to improve taste or odor, rather than protect health). Home filtration systems still rely on government-provided or -regulated tap water, suggesting that it is not a replacement for tap water, but rather an augmentation of or complement to tap water (Lanz & Provins 2016). Therefore, we are primarily

---

[6] In Chapter 2, we labeled this expectation Hypothesis 5.
[7] See Chapter 3 and Appendix A for full methodological details for the CCES survey.

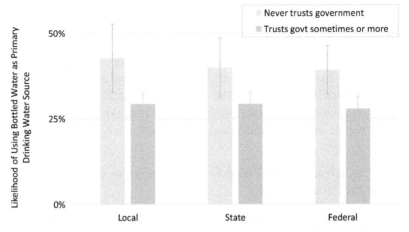

**Figure 5.4** Likelihood of bottled water use as a function of distrust in government.

*Note*: Logistic regression analysis of CCES Survey. Models estimate likelihood of using bottled water as primary drinking water source as a function of trust in government, with controls for ideology, race, ethnicity, income, gender, and age. Thin bars represent 90% confidence intervals. See Appendix C, Table C25 for full estimation.

interested in how bottled water drinkers think about government, compared with tap water drinkers. A total of 29.8 percent of CCES respondents said that they used bottled water as their primary source of drinking water. To avoid priming effects, the question about trust in government was asked prior to the question on bottled water consumption. We use logistic regression models to investigate the relationship between trust and bottled water consumption. Since we are interested in moral distrust, we looked at the effect of an individual's never trusting a level of government to do what is right on bottled water consumption, controlling for political ideology, race, ethnicity, gender, income, and age.

The results of the multivariate models show a consistent relationship between trust in government and bottled water consumption across all three levels of government.[8] These results can be seen in Figure 5.4. On average, individuals who never trust the federal government to do what is right are estimated to have a 13.4 percent higher chance of using bottled water as their primary form of drinking water than individuals who trust the federal government.

---

[8] As previously discussed in Chapter 3, we expect distrust at all levels of government to affect commercial water consumption, given local, state, and federal government all play roles in the provision of drinking water.

Individuals who do not trust state government have a 10.6 percent higher chance of using bottled water than individuals who trust state government. Similarly, an individual who never trusts her local government has an 11.4 percent chance of using bottled water than an individual who trusts her local government. In all cases, moral distrust in government is associated with exit from government-provided and -regulated water to commercial, bottled water. Distrust in government apparently leads people away from public services and toward commercial goods.

### Exit as Substitute for Voice: Does Commercial Water Depress Political Participation?

Across two separate and independent surveys (i.e., Nexus and CCES), we find strong evidence that voice is less likely to be used among groups that have been politically marginalized *and* that distrust in government is associated with exit from publicly provided goods toward commercially provided alternatives. The negative impact of government failure does not end there, however. As discussed in Chapter 2, individuals who choose to exit from government-provided services have little reason to engage in further forms of political participation. If individuals choose to exit from publicly provided services due to a moral distrust of government, then the choice of commercial products may be associated with actions that demonstrate a general withdrawal from civic life. If we are correct, then commercial water use will have a depressing effect on political participation; for the morally distrustful citizen-consumer, consumer exit is a substitute for civic voice.

### *Commercial Water Consumption and Political Participation*

We begin our investigation of the relationship between exit to commercial water and political participation with CCES survey questions related to political participation, or what Dowding and John (2012) call "collective voice." Specifically, the CCES asks respondents a series of questions about their political activities in the past year.[9] Each respondent was asked whether he or she

- Attended local political meetings (e.g., school board or city council);
- Put up a political sign (e.g., a lawn sign or bumper sticker);

---

[9] The CCES also asks respondents whether they had donated blood in the past year, but we exclude that question from the analysis since it is not an explicitly political act.

- Worked for a candidate or campaign;
- Attended a political protest, march, or demonstration;
- Contacted a public official; or
- Donated money to a candidate campaign or political organization.

In order to test the relationship between bottled water consumption and political participation, we created an index of political participation that is the total number of activities each respondent selected.[10] The index ranges from zero for individuals who did not report participating in any of the listed activities to six for those who did all of them. We used statistical analysis to isolate the relationship between drinking water choices and political behavior while accounting for a number of other factors that could influence levels of political activity, such as political ideology, race, ethnicity, income, gender, and age.

We find that individuals who consume bottled water as their primary source of drinking water at home have lower average levels of political participation. As Figure 5.5 shows, individuals who consume bottled water engaged in just .54 political activities in the year prior to the survey, compared to .88 political activities reported by those who drink tap water – a remarkable 63 percent difference in political activity.[11]

If exit from public services could mark a general withdrawal from civic life, it is useful to look at whether individuals engaged in any form of political participation at all. Figure 5.6 shows the results of a logistic regression that investigates whether bottled water consumption relates to an individual's likelihood of doing any one of the six political acts we previously combined into an index. Individuals who use tap water as their primary source of household drinking water have an estimated 40 percent likelihood of having taken at least one political action in the past year, compared to just 27 percent for bottled water drinkers. It appears that exit from a government-provided public service can mean more than simply spending money on a commercial alternative; exit to the private market is associated with a broader exit from the political world.

---

[10] Both Cronbach's alpha and factor analysis point to the validity of this index of political participation. Cronbach's alpha is .75. The factor analysis results in a single factor with an eigenvalue of 2.00, with all six variables loading positively onto the single factor.

[11] The "tap water" category includes respondents who consume filtered or unfiltered tap water. Analysis including a dummy variable indicating filtered water use showed no statistical difference between unfiltered tap water users and filtered tap water users.

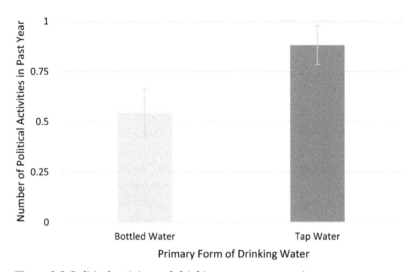

Figure 5.5 Political activity and drinking water consumption.
Note: OLS regression analysis of CCES Survey, estimating political participation as a
function of primary drinking water source, with controls for ideology, race, ethnicity,
income, gender, and age. Thin bars represent 90% confidence intervals. See Appendix C,
Table C26 for full estimation.

## The Political Costs of Exit: Bottled Water and Voting

Do these individual consumer choices carry wider implications for
citizen political participation? If people who exit from tap water consumption are also likely to exit from political life, what are the implications for participatory democracy? The relationship between bottled
water sales and voter turnout in the United States reveals something
deeper about citizens' relationship with the market and the state, and
the broader social costs of consumer exit from government.

To measure bottled water consumption at an aggregate level, we use
data from Simply Analytics. Simply Analytics is a data aggregation
company that provides data on political, social, and other types of
variables from many different data sources in a single place. The data
we use on bottled water consumption comes specifically from the US
Consumer Expenditure Database (CEX) from the US Bureau of Labor
Statistics. Here, we analyze estimated consumer expenditures on
bottled water within each county in the United States from 2011 to
2018. To account for vast differences in population and urbanization
across US counties, we adjust these measures using the number of

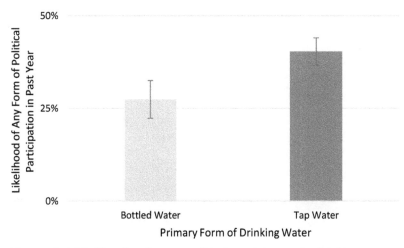

**Figure 5.6** Likelihood of any political activity and drinking water consumption.

*Note*: Logistic regression analysis of CCES Survey, estimating likelihood of at least one political act as a function of primary drinking water source, with controls for ideology, race, ethnicity, income, gender, and age. Thin bars represent 90% confidence intervals. See Appendix C, Table C26 for full estimation.

occupied housing units from the American Community Survey (ACS) five-year estimates to develop a measure of average annual household spending on bottled water in each county.

Given our expectation that exit to the commercial sector holds consequences for other aspects of civic life, we are interested in how increasing levels of bottled water spending at the county level relates to turnout in elections. We obtained the total number of votes cast at the county level in each general gubernatorial election in the United States between 2011 and 2017 from CQ Press's Voting and Elections Collection. Gubernatorial elections are staggered, meaning that different state elections for governor take place every year. Adjusting for citizen population over the age of eighteen from the ACS yields a measure of county-level turnout of voting-age citizens.

Once again, we use statistical modeling to analyze the relationship between bottled water consumption and county-level turnout in gubernatorial elections. We analyze gubernatorial elections rather than presidential or congressional elections because federal elections are dominated by national issues and generate greater average voter participation. Gubernatorial elections typically see lower average participation,

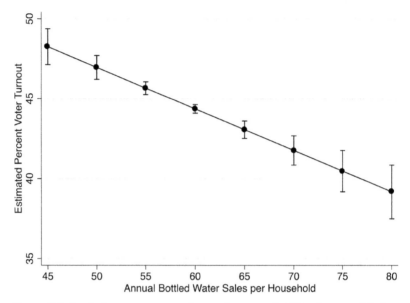

**Figure 5.7** Bottled water consumption and turnout in US gubernatorial elections, 2011–2017.

*Note*: OLS regression analysis of voter turnout in county-level gubernatorial elections as a function of primary drinking water source, controlling for percent Black population, percent Hispanic population, socioeconomic status, unemployment, percent home ownership, and percent Democratic vote share. Thin bars represent 90% confidence intervals. See Appendix C, Table C28 for full estimation.

experience greater variation in turnout, and can turn on more immediate, local issues. Crucially for our purposes, tap water regulation occurs at the state level, typically through agencies that are headed by officials appointed by the governor.[12] Our models control for a number of variables that are typically associated with voter participation in the United States, including race, ethnicity, socioeconomic status, and the percent of the major party vote in the county cast for the Democratic candidate for governor. We also included year fixed effects in order to account for the large differences in turnout from year to year – particularly for

---

[12] Ideally, we would analyze local government voter turnout since local governments provide the lion's share of drinking water utility. Unfortunately, the highly fragmented US local governance complex makes such an analysis virtually impossible. At the time of this writing, no national data set with aggregated US local election participation exists.

gubernatorial elections that coincided with the presidential election years of 2012 and 2016, which saw unusually high voter turnout.

Figure 5.7 shows the results of our analysis. There is a strong, significantly negative relationship between bottled water consumption and turnout in gubernatorial elections. As bottled water consumption in a county increases, voter turnout in gubernatorial elections decreases. For a county where households spend an average of $50 a year on bottled water, the estimated turnout in gubernatorial elections is 47 percent. In counties where annual household bottled water sales average $80, however, the estimated turnout in gubernatorial elections falls to 39 percent, an 8 percent difference. This difference is small in percentage terms, but stark in electoral terms. In 2018, the average margin of victory in gubernatorial elections was just 4.7 percent. The 2018 midterm elections had a turnout of 49 percent, the highest turnout in over a century, whereas the 2014 turnout of 37 percent was the lowest in 72 years (Stewart 2018). A $30 difference in annual household bottled water sales is associated with roughly the same gap between historically high turnout and historically low turnout.

This finding suggests that the distrust in government that drives exit to commercial services and diminishes civic participation at the individual level apparently carries a much greater cost to democracy writ large. As commercial water consumption increases, individuals are less likely to participate in the most basic of democratic acts: exercising the right to vote.

## When Voice Is Silenced

Representative democracy is well suited to respond to the exercise of citizen voice, not exit; democratic institutions are designed for responsiveness (Hirschman 1970). Where basic services are involved, there can be dire consequences to silencing the power of voice.

### The Cost of Silence

In describing the Flint water crisis, journalist Laura Bliss (2016) focused on people, not pipes, with the title "How Democracy Died in Flint." While the story of the failure of the water system in Flint is a multifaceted story of environmental injustice, technical failure, and local economic decline, at its core it is a story of blunting the ability of citizens to respond to government failure. The silencing began with the signing of an expansion of Michigan's emergency manager law in 2011. This law was overturned the following year via referendum, but Governor Rick Snyder signed a similar law immediately after his loss at the ballot box in defiance of voters' will. The emergency manager law allowed for the state government to take control of local government, essentially eliminating the link between local decision making and the citizens impacted by those decisions. Local opposition in Flint to the emergency manager law was high (Hughes 2021; Nickels, Clark, & Wood 2020), but Flint, long struggling financially, was put under the control of state-appointed emergency managers. These emergency managers, unaccountable to local political officials or the citizens they ostensibly served, made the ill-fated decision to change the source water in Flint and sparked a crisis. Bliss (2016) poses the tragic counterfactual that the Flint water crisis raises for democratic governance:

Faced with mounting debts, and without a state emergency manager in place, would Flint officials have made the same outrageously bad decision? Maybe – but at least they would have had to listen to citizens' concerns and outrage, or else suffer the political consequences. State emergency managers have no real responsibility to city officials or the citizens they are meant to represent, other than to slash budgets.

The switch of Flint's source water may have occurred regardless of the presence of the emergency manager, but the abdication of democratic responsiveness that followed almost certainly would not have occurred. Citizens like LeeAnne Walters who complained were systematically ignored by government officials at state and federal levels. Failures of the EPA and Michigan Department of Environmental Quality to respond to concerns compounded the original sins of the emergency managers, but ultimately *local* government is best equipped to respond to basic service concerns (Mill 1861; Tocqueville 1835). The Flint water crisis began with the institutional destruction of the instruments of voice in local government. The exercise of citizen voice is powerful in a democracy; silencing it can be disastrous.

## The Profits of Exit

Meanwhile, exit from tap water to commercial drinking water has been lucrative for Watermill Express founder Lani Dolifka. Since its founding in 1984, the kiosk company has grown steadily and boasted more than 1,300 locations around the United States at the time of this writing. In May 2021, private equity firm Brentwood Associates purchased a majority stake in Watermill Express from Lani and Don Dolifka. "Watermill Express is a perfect fit within our strategy of investing in high-growth, world-class consumer businesses," declared Brentwood partner Rahul Aggarwal in a press release announcing the acquisition (Brentwood Associates 2021). The acquisition price for Watermill Express was not disclosed publicly, but Brentwood Associates' website reports that its investment parameters are "$20–200 million." For the Dolifkas, distrust in government has been profitable indeed.

## Basic Service Failure and Democratic Decline

The analyses of survey and turnout data here show a remarkable relationship between distrust in government, the choice between voice and exit, and participation in democratic governance. Individuals who have historically experienced political marginalization are less likely to voice their concerns when problems arise, people who distrust the government are more likely to abandon public services, and the aggregate exit to commercial goods has a negative impact on civic participation. None of these patterns are surprising given the logic of distrust outlined in Chapter 2, but they are distressing nonetheless.

Perhaps most concerning are the consequences for democracy of citizen-consumer exit to commercial goods. If individuals no longer trust that government is capable of, or indeed morally inclined to, providing basic services, there is little incentive for further engagement in public life for ordinary citizens. If exit is the most rational choice when government fails, there is little incentive for governments to improve conditions for the politically marginalized. The profits of distrust through exit accrue to the commercial enterprises that compete with government; the losses of voice accumulate as a broader decline of civic life.

These analyses reveal how marginalization and distrust can lead to the choice of exit over voice, with deeper impacts on democratic action. In the next chapter, we trace the institutional roots of political marginalization and citizen-consumer choice by examining how institutional discrimination connects to disparities in commercial water use.

# 6 | Geographies of Alienation
## The Institutional Roots of Distrust

When the water that we use to make our coffee and bathe our children is poisoned by "policy," it is marked with the failures of our social institutions, and with the social injustices that force some more than others to bear the brunt of those failures.

Benjamin Pauli,[1] *Flint Fights Back*

Geography is destiny.

Thomas Sugrue,[2] *The Origins of the Urban Crisis*

Neither distrust in government nor dissatisfaction with basic services is equally distributed across people, places, or time. To this point, we have demonstrated that basic service failures such as drinking water problems are associated with distrust in government. A citizen-consumer who experiences basic service problems can complain to the government if she believes that the service failure is a matter of competence, but her choice to use voice is conditioned by her moral trust in government and an expectation that the government will respond positively to her complaints. Some citizen-consumers may have sound reason to doubt government's good intentions, and so not everyone is equally willing to voice their dissatisfaction to government. Citizen-consumers who suffer from discriminatory or negligent political institutions have legitimate reasons to distrust those institutions.

In Chapter 5, we showed that low-income Black and Hispanic people are less likely than higher-income, white, and non-Hispanic people to voice their discontent about tap water. We have also seen that distrust can drive citizen-consumers to exit to the commercial market and purchase more expensive substitutes for tap water. Individual and aggregate data on political participation and bottled

---

[1] Pauli (2019, 255).    [2] Sugrue (2005, xl).

water consumption indicate that many Americans who are dissatisfied with their tap water indeed choose exit over voice. These patterns of distrust and citizen-consumer behavior are particularly pernicious because those with relatively fewer resources are more likely to exit to the expensive commercial sector. If widespread distrust "imposes a kind of a tax" on activities within a society, as political scientist Francis Fukuyama (1995, 255) argued, then distrust is a profoundly regressive kind of tax: The costs of distrust in government fall most heavily upon politically alienated populations. Unlike real taxes, however, the profits of distrust accrue not to government, but to the commercial enterprises that provide exit alternatives to politically alienated citizen-consumers.

Historically, certain American political institutions and public policies have systematically discriminated against groups of people on the basis of race, ethnicity, and socioeconomic status. In some cases, this discrimination has been overt, targeting and defining specific geographic areas. This physical legacy of discrimination produces politically marginalized communities living in *geographies of alienation:* areas where many citizen-consumers have sound reasons to distrust government. The consequences of past discrimination in geographies of alienation emerge today in unexpected ways. Consider, for example, the relationship between early twentieth-century discriminatory lending practices and twenty-first-century water kiosk location.

## The Enduring Legacy of Biased Political Institutions

Between 1935 and 1940, a federal agency called the Home Owners' Loan Corporation (HOLC) rated the mortgage lending risk of neighborhoods within more than 200 cities across the United States. Using input from local lenders, developers, and real estate professionals, the HOLC produced "Residential Security" maps denoting ratings based on levels of risk for lending across neighborhoods within cities.[3] Among other criteria, HOLC ratings were based on the socioeconomic status, races, and ethnicities of residents. Figure 6.1 provides HOLC maps of Phoenix, Arizona, and Houston, Texas.

---

[3] The HOLC maps were unearthed in the US National Archives by historian Kenneth Jackson during the 1970s.

On HOLC-produced maps, areas rated "A" were "Best" for lending and outlined in green, areas rated "B" were "Still Desirable" and outlined in blue, and areas rated "C" were "Definitely Declining" and outlined in yellow. Areas rated "D" were considered "Hazardous" for residential lending and outlined in red. Residents of

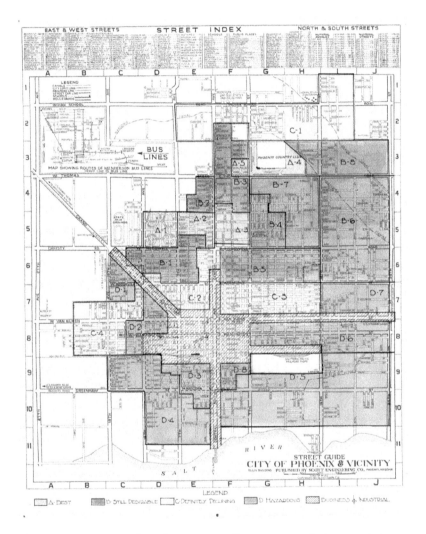

**Figure 6.1** HOLC residential security (redlining) maps of Phoenix, Arizona and Houston, Texas.

*Note*: Scans of HOLC maps provided by Mapping Inequality. Images are in the public domain.

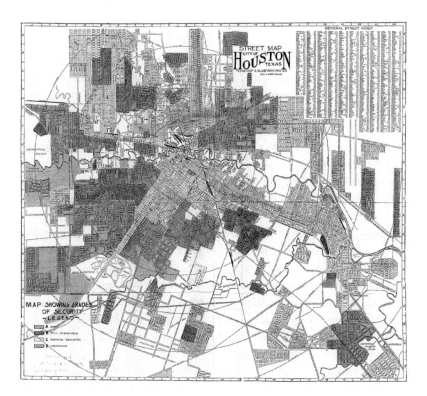

**Figure 6.1** (*cont.*)

areas with D ratings were typically denied home loans because these areas were deemed too risky for investment. These denials made it nearly impossible for residents of D-rated areas to become home-owners. As notes from the HOLC assessors reveal, areas were usually given a D rating *because* these areas had majority Black or immigrant residents.[4] Conversely, A-rated areas were typically affluent and/or native-born white neighborhoods.

Today, this discriminatory practice is known as *redlining*.[5] The legacy of this state-sanctioned racial and ethnic discrimination still

---

[4] In addition to scans of the original HOLC maps and their digitized spatial data, the *Mapping Inequality* project (Nelson et al. 2020) provides records of the HOLC's Assessment Notes: the criteria assessors used to assign areas A, B, C, or D ratings. Learn more at https://dsl.richmond.edu/panorama/redlining/.

[5] The Fair Housing Act of 1968 outlawed redlining and segregation in housing.

reverberates in the early twenty-first century.[6] Comparing HOLC maps and current demographic data, Mitchell and Franco (2016) demonstrate that HOLC ratings contribute to present-day racial segregation, income inequality, and gentrification. Their analysis shows that HOLC ratings produced a "persistent pattern of both economic and racial residential exclusion ... [and] the segregated and exclusionary structures of the past still exist in many U.S. cities" (Mitchell & Franco 2016, 6). Today, areas assigned lower HOLC grades decades ago exhibit lower home values (Howell & Korver-Glenn 2020), and redlining has been linked to high unemployment rates (Zenou & Boccard 2000) and wealth gaps between Black and white communities (Massey & Denton 1993).

People living in areas that were assigned low HOLC ratings long ago have solid reasons to distrust government because the government intentionally discriminated against them on the basis of their race, ethnicity, and socioeconomic status. This history of legally sanctioned political alienation gives these communities reason to doubt that the government will care or act if they voice their concerns today. In other words, residents in these communities have a well-founded *moral distrust* in government.

One consequence of this moral distrust is present-day demand for commercial drinking water in historically redlined areas. If we are correct, then the legacy of political alienation will reverberate today in distrust of and subsequent exit from government services. Figure 6.2 shows the total number of commercial water kiosks by neighborhood HOLC ratings within cities that received these ratings.[7] Of the 8,868 neighborhoods with HOLC ratings that we analyzed, water kiosks in 2017 are primarily located in areas that received a C or D rating in the 1930s. Amazingly, the ratings assigned by the HOLC in the 1930s

---

[6] Debates on the impacts of redlining on lending continue in academic research. For example, Amy Hillier (2003) suggests that the HOLC maps themselves did not greatly influence lending practices after their creation because the maps merely reflected discriminatory practices that were already in place at the time of the maps' creation.

[7] The redlining data come from the *Mapping Inequality* project. We downloaded their collective spatial data containing shapefiles on HOLC-rated cities across the United States. The *Mapping Inequality* project released digitized HOLC maps from more than 150 cities in 2016. We spatially merged these data with our own data on kiosk locations in the United States, allowing us to compare how many kiosks are located within areas evaluated by the HOLC. Kiosks not located within an HOLC-rated area are not included.

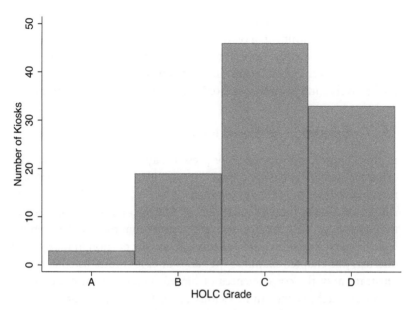

**Figure 6.2** Total kiosks located in HOLC-rated neighborhoods.
*Note:* Histogram summarizing the number of kiosks in 2017 located within areas graded A, B, C, or D by HOLC in the 1930s.

correlate with the locations of water kiosks ninety years later.[8] The relationship between modern-day kiosk location and historical HOLC ratings suggests that the effects of discriminatory public policy linger in unexpected ways.

As the relationship between redlining in the 1930s and kiosk locations in 2017 shows, the seeds of political alienation planted by unjust policies have flourished into twenty-first-century local demand for commercial water. Kiosks and bottled water proliferate in places with legacies of discriminatory policies and political institutions, where residents do not trust government's basic morality. Defensive spending on commercial drinking water within geographies of alienation is not foolish or unreasonable, even in communities with excellent tap water, because segments of the population in these places have suffered systemic political bias or neglect. The preference for commercial products instead of government products among these marginalized citizen-consumers is not simply a "cultural" expression. Rather, distrust in tap

[8] The Spearman correlation between the number of kiosks and HOLC grades is 0.629 ($p < 0.001$). Only areas with HOLC ratings were included in the analysis.

water is a rational response to expectations about the performance and morality of government. For the politically alienated, government is morally untrustworthy and exit to commercial alternatives is a rational response – even when government products are less expensive or qualitatively indistinguishable from their commercial competitors.

## The Consequences of Biased Political Institutions

In this chapter, we explore how present-day patterns of commercial drinking water behavior relate to specific histories of political marginalization in different regions of the country: Blacks in the American South, rural populations in Appalachia, and Hispanics in the Southwest. This chapter deviates in style from the previous empirical chapters. Rather than investigating a specific portion of the cycle of distrust, this chapter examines the series of case studies listed above to illustrate how the consequences of biased political institutions reverberate throughout the entire vicious cycle. Focusing on three specific regions and populations within the United States isolates particular legacies of political alienation, helping clarify the connection between moral distrust of government and citizen-consumer behavior. Each case we explore connects past political alienation or neglect born of institutional bias to modern-day commercial water consumption.

Figure 6.3 depicts the way that consequences of biased institutions cascade throughout the entire vicious cycle, generating exit to the private sector. Biased institutions create discriminatory public policies that demobilize segments of the population through intentional alienation or neglect. These policies reduce citizen-consumer political participation, reducing incentives and resources for government to provide basic services. This reduction in government accountability leads to additional basic service failure, further reducing citizen-consumer trust in government institutions. When citizen-consumers experience service failure and lack moral trust in government institutions, they are more likely to exit to the private sector, thereby increasing commercial water consumption. In this chapter, we do not test specific hypotheses. Rather, we seek to demonstrate that racial, ethnic, and poor populations living in *geographies of alienation* – areas historically targeted by discriminatory practices and policies – choose exit and purchase extreme quantities of commercial bottled and kiosk water today.

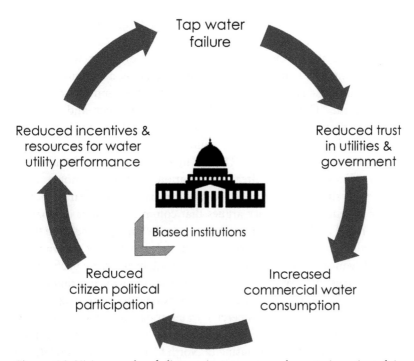

**Figure 6.3** Vicious cycle of distrust in tap water: elements investigated in Chapter 6.

*Note*: This chapter examines three case studies that illustrate the entire vicious cycle. Biased political institutions are depicted at the center of the circle to highlight their impact on the entire cycle. Biased institutions demobilize specific segments of the population in ways that shift incentives, resources, and accountability for government. These consequences cascade throughout the entire theoretical model in a vicious cycle. Subsequent chapters examine other portions of the cycle.

## Alienation or Culture?

It is tempting, perhaps, to dismiss racial, ethnic, and socioeconomic disparities in commercial drinking water consumption as cultural curiosities that will disappear as immigrants assimilate into American society. But simple cultural explanations cannot explain preferences for bottled or kiosk water among American-born citizens of different races or ethnicities, levels of education, and income who all receive tap water from the same utility or system. It may be similarly tempting to blame racial, ethnic, and socioeconomic disparities in commercial drinking water consumption on the clever marketing practices of for-profit water companies, which frequently target racial and ethnic groups in their advertising (Arumugam 2011; Sharp & Walker 2002).

We argue that preferences for commercial drinking water along racial, ethnic, and socioeconomic lines emerge as a function of citizen-consumers' beliefs about the competence and morality of government. "Cultural" beliefs about the competence and morality of governance institutions do not emerge *ex nihilo*, and profitable commercial water firms do not stumble at random upon successful marketing strategies. In its 2021 Securities and Exchange Commission (SEC) filings, Primo Water Corporation specifically notes their marketing strategy is grounded in stoking distrust and fear of public water systems.[9] Our theory argues that commercial water companies target racial and ethnic minority customers in large part *because* these politically marginalized people are predisposed to distrust government: Like alchemists seeking to turn lead into gold, firms create profits from latent distrust born of basic service failures and historic discrimination. We show that in the case of commercial water, political geography is destiny – demand for commercial water today is greatest in places marked by past political discrimination. We begin by examining how modern bottled water purchasing in North Carolina counties relates to voter protections put in place by the 1965 Voting Rights Act.

## Southern Black Communities and the 1965 Voting Rights Act

Ratified in 1870 in the wake of the Civil War, the Fifteenth Amendment aimed to guarantee the right to vote to Black Americans, including freed enslaved persons. In reality, Black voters faced many official barriers to voting immediately following the end of Reconstruction and into the mid-twentieth century: poll taxes, literacy tests and tests of "good citizenship," identification requirements, and personal vouchers from other registered voters. Beyond these formal institutional barriers, Black citizens faced physical intimidation when attempting to participate in politics. As a result, Assistant Attorney General Burke Marshall of the US Department of Justice (DOJ) Civil Rights Division reported in 1962 that

---

[9] Primo Water Corporation, 2021 Proxy Statement, *Securities and Exchange Commission Schedule* 14A, p. 5.

[R]acial denials of the right to vote occur in sections of eight states. In five of those states Negroes constitute more than a quarter of the adult population, but very few of these Negroes are registered to vote. For example, in Mississippi only five per cent [sic] are registered; in Alabama only fourteen per cent are registered; in South Carolina, sixteen per cent are registered; in Georgia, twenty-six per cent are registered; and in Louisiana, twenty-nine per cent are registered. Registration among adult whites invariably exceeds fifty per cent. In eleven counties where Negroes are in the majority none is registered. In ninety-seven counties fewer than five per cent of the adult Negroes are on the rolls. Indeed, in most counties with sizable Negro populations the Negro voter totals are significantly below the statewide percentage of eligible Negroes registered and neither figure approaches the white voter percentage. (Marshall 1962, 455)

In general, places with voter identification laws have lower racial and ethnic minority voter turnout (Hajnal, Lejevardi, & Nielson 2017). Marshall attributed low Black voter turnout to formal institutional bias: "In our experience Negro non-voting results almost exclusively from racial discrimination by state officials and fear among Negroes engendered by the attitudes and actions of white persons – including some office-holders" (Marshall 1962, 455).

The American Civil Rights Movement was in large part a response to this disenfranchisement and the broader social and economic inequalities that accompanied Black political alienation in the United States. The movement produced a series of landmark federal laws in the 1960s barring racial and ethnic discrimination, including the 1965 Voting Rights Act (VRA). The VRA's enactment was a pivotal moment in American political history. "The Voting Rights Act dismantled the legal foundations of white supremacy in the southern United States," Nicole Willcoxon observed, "and its vigorous enforcement enfranchised millions of black and poor white voters" (2017, 1). By the end of 1965, an additional 250,000 Black Americans registered to vote (National Archives, n.d.).

Section 5 of the VRA provided additional voting protections to specific areas of the country by requiring external review by the US Department of Justice (DOJ) of any proposed changes to local elections or voting procedures.[10] Section 5 applied only to places that required

---

[10] For descriptive examples of how states attempted to change electoral laws over time and the implementation of Section 5, see McCrary (2005).

voters to pass a test or other device to vote, *and* where less than half of
eligible voters were registered or voted during the 1964 presidential
election. In effect, the VRA used this formula to evaluate whether an
area required additional federal oversight to ensure voter
protections.[11] Political jurisdictions that met the criteria for these
discriminatory voter practices were "covered" by the VRA's Section
5, making the implementation of the VRA particularly potent in these
areas. In 1965, the entire states of Alabama, Georgia, Louisiana,
Mississippi, South Carolina, and Virginia were covered by Section 5:
Every suggested change to state and local electoral rules in these places
was subject to DOJ clearance.[12] Places covered by the VRA experienced increased Black voter registration (Valelly 2009), higher Black
voter turnout (Cascio & Washington 2014; Filer, Kenney, & Morton
1991), and a larger number of Black candidates elected to office
(Grofman & Handley 1991; Handley, Grofman, & Arden 1998; Sass
& Mehay 1995). Schuit and Rogowski (2016) show that areas covered
by the VRA had higher levels of political competition than uncovered
areas; subsequently, elected officials in covered areas were more likely
to vote in favor of civil rights causes. Following the removal of literacy
tests, state government funding increased in counties with higher Black
populations within covered states (Cascio & Washington 2014).
Clearly, the VRA had significant impacts on Black voter empowerment
and how Black political interests manifested within government.

While Section 5 of the 1965 Voting Rights Act originally covered
most states as a whole or not at all, one state entered partial Section
5 coverage at the outset: North Carolina.[13] The DOJ applied Section
5 at the county level in North Carolina, with some counties covered and
others not covered by Section 5. North Carolina had a statewide literacy
test and 52 percent statewide voter turnout in the 1964 presidential
election, meaning it only met half of the required formula conditions for
Section 5 coverage. As a compromise, counties with less than 50 percent
voter turnout in the 1964 presidential election were covered under the
VRA (Willcoxon 2017). Of the 100 counties in North Carolina,

[11] This formula is found in Section 4(b) of the 1965 Voting Rights Act. This
preclearance formula remained in effect until the 2013 Supreme Court case
*Shelby County* v. *Holder,* which ruled Section 4(b) of the VRA unconstitutional.
[12] Section 5 coverage later expanded to include other states and areas within states.
We discuss some of these states later in the chapter when reviewing the political
marginalization of Hispanics in the southwestern United States.
[13] After 1965, other states entered partial coverage under Section 5 of the VRA.

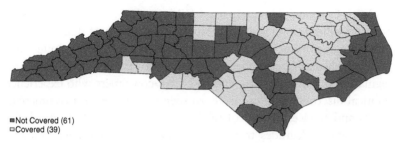

■Not Covered (61)
□Covered (39)

**Figure 6.4** Counties in North Carolina covered/not covered by Section 5 of the 1965 Voting Rights Act.
*Note*: Though North Carolina had a statewide literacy test for voting prior to 1965, its statewide voter turnout in the 1964 presidential election was 52%. Therefore, the state only met half of the requirements for coverage under Section 5 of the VRA. Consequently, counties with less than 50% voter turnout (light gray) became covered. Counties with more than 50% voter turnout (dark gray) did not receive additional Section 5 protections.

39 counties were covered by Section 5 of the 1965 Voting Rights Act and 61 counties were not covered (Figure 6.4).[14]

In North Carolina, Section 5 coverage in 1965 eventually led to significantly higher Black voter turnout and registration in counties that were covered than in counties that were not covered (Willcoxon 2017). Similarly, Section 5 VRA coverage had notable effects on Black voter empowerment and political representation in the Tar Heel State. For example, two cities in North Carolina – Reidsville and Greenville – attempted to change their electoral laws in the 1970s. These cities are located in counties covered by Section 5 (Rockingham County and Pitt County, respectively). The DOJ blocked the proposed changes following Section 5 review, expressing concern that the proposed changes would reduce the number of Black representatives in government in these places (McCrary 2005). Hypothetically, had Reidsville and Greenville been located in uncovered counties, the review of these changes by the DOJ would not have been required and these changes would have proceeded, potentially reducing Black representation in government. The DOJ maintained Section 5 protections in North Carolina until 2013, with far-reaching political effects. Nicole Willcoxon (2017) demonstrates that counties in North Carolina covered by Section 5 in 1965 had higher Black voter registration and Black voter turnout compared with uncovered North Carolina counties.

---

[14] One additional county in North Carolina was covered beginning in 1975.

North Carolina's unique partial VRA Section 5 coverage provides an extraordinary opportunity to analyze the effects of discriminatory political institutions on citizen-consumer behavior. We argue that political alienation engenders distrust of government provision and regulation of basic services, and so citizen-consumers who experience political discrimination are likely to spend defensively on commercial goods and services instead of relying on government. If political disfranchisement degrades trust in government as our theory predicts, then we expect that VRA protection shapes citizen-consumer behavior at the ballot box and grocery store alike. We expect that North Carolina counties that were covered by Section 5 of the VRA will have lower bottled water sales today than counties that were not covered by the VRA. In other words, counties that were not covered by the VRA in 1965 will have higher bottled water sales today than counties that were covered because Black citizen-consumers in uncovered counties did not receive as many protections under the VRA.

As in other chapters, we use statistical models to isolate the relationship between whether a North Carolina county was covered by Section 5 and bottled water sales by accounting for other drivers of bottled water consumption.[15] Ideally, we would use survey or expenditure data to match individuals' races and locations to consumer behavior across North Carolina counties. As a next-best alternative, we examine total bottled water sales per capita in each county in 2017 and account for 2016 measures of socioeconomic status, percent renters, percent Black population, and the total population.[16] This approach does not allow us to know the races of the individuals who are buying bottled water; we only know the total bottled water consumption in each county, as well as the county's overall demographic composition. However, in this case, the "ecological problem" of drawing inferences about individuals based on collective aggregated data stacks the inferential deck against our expectations. If marked differences in bottled water consumption emerge across counties covered and not covered by Section 5 after controlling for other relevant factors, then the differences we observe probably *understate* the real disparities associated with racial discrimination.

Figure 6.5 shows the resulting estimated bottled water sales per capita in North Carolina counties that were covered and not covered

---

[15] Full model results and descriptive statistics of the data are available in Appendix C.

[16] This analysis employs OLS regression. We repeated this analysis without including a measure of the 2016 percent Black population, and the results remain the same. For full results, see Appendix C, Table C.30.

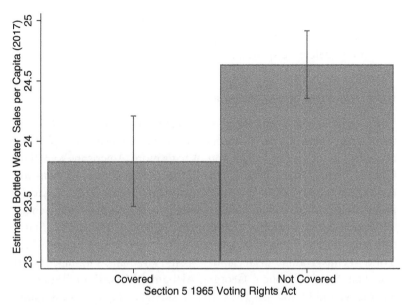

**Figure 6.5** Estimated North Carolina bottled water sales per capita by VRA Section 5 county coverage.

*Note*: Estimated 2017 bottled water sales per capita based on whether a North Carolina county was covered by Section 5 of the VRA in 1965. Thin bars represent 90% confidence intervals. Produced with OLS regression, controlling for 2016 socioeconomic status, percent renters, percent Black, and total population (logged). See Appendix C, Table C30 for full estimation.

under VRA Section 5. Counties that were not covered by Section 5 in 1965 have significantly higher bottled water sales per capita in 2017. On average, people living in counties not covered by the VRA spend $0.80 more on bottled water annually than individuals living in covered counties.[17] Although a difference of less than a dollar per year might seem trivial, across the Tar Heel State this difference amounts to a roughly $5.3 million increase in annual revenue for the bottled water industry associated with a lack of Section 5 coverage in certain counties.[18] And though $0.80 per year may not seem a heavy burden to an individual, recall that this distrust premium – *which translates into $5.3 million of additional revenue each year* – is paid for disproportionately by populations already burdened by past discrimination. As in

---

[17] OLS regression coefficient, $p < 0.05$.

[18] To calculate this number, we multiplied the marginal effect of the lack of Section 5 county coverage on bottled water sales per capita ($0.80) by the total population living in uncovered counties in 2017.

our comparison of HOLC grades and kiosks, echoes of discriminatory institutions embedded in local politics more than fifty years earlier resonate in defensive spending today.

## Rural Communities in Appalachia

The geographies of alienation in the United States are defined by more than race; Americans may also find themselves politically marginalized according to income and education. What's more, Americans sometimes find themselves isolated politically by institutional sins of *omission*, rather than commission. We next examine an area where a legacy of political neglect created another geography of alienation: Appalachia.

Appalachia is a predominantly rural region of the United States, officially consisting of 420 counties in parts of thirteen states: New York, Pennsylvania, Maryland, West Virginia, Virginia, North Carolina, South Carolina, Georgia, Alabama, Mississippi, Tennessee, Kentucky, and Ohio.[19] In 1964, the President's Appalachian Regional Commission (PARC) report described Appalachia as "a region apart – both geographically and statistically" (PARC 1964, xv) from the rest of the United States. Prior to the 1960s, Appalachia was largely isolated from the rest of the country due to its mountainous terrain, limited accessibility, lack of public infrastructure, and extreme poverty. For instance, the US Interstate Highway System in the 1950s largely avoided construction in Appalachia. Compared to the rest of the United States, Appalachia lagged on key social indicators such as education, income, and employment. In 1965, the Appalachian Regional Development Act (ARDA) established the Appalachian Regional Commission (ARC), a joint effort between levels of US government to introduce "Appalachia and its people into fully active membership in the American society" (PARC 1964, 65).

The root of the social differences between Appalachia and the rest of the United States is a history of political abandonment of the region. The PARC attributed conditions in Appalachia to a "legacy of neglect" (PARC 1964, 19). For example, the PARC report observed that federal investment in Appalachia lagged behind the rest of the country relative to its population and needs. This inattention, combined with its limited

---

[19] West Virginia is the only state where the state is entirely within the US government's official demarcation of the Appalachian region.

tax base, contributed to Appalachia's overall economic distress. When investigating the conditions within Appalachia, the PARC (1964) report found

a record of insufficiency – a history of traditional acts *not* performed, of American patterns *not* fulfilled. This sets Appalachia apart from the rest of the Nation more clearly than the diverse record of what actually was performed and fulfilled in eastern Kentucky or in central Pennsylvania, in western Virginia or northernmost Georgia. The sins of commission in Appalachia are numerous and as opaque as history; what was *omitted* – the traditional pattern of growth thwarted by this neglect – is, on the other hand, transparent and may be simply stated. (16, italics added)

The 1964 PARC report and subsequent ARDA were, in part, an effort to address an area and people that government had ignored.

The origins of Appalachian political neglect can be traced to the earliest days of the United States. Between 1717 and 1775, a quarter million Scotch-Irish immigrants made their way to the United States, the majority of whom settled in Appalachia (Hirschman, Brown, & Maclaran 2007). These immigrants were met with hostility by New Englanders, who viewed them as "unruly and unsavory" (Hirschman, Brown, & Maclaran 2007, 8). For their part, the Scotch-Irish settlers distrusted British colonial governments that were dominated by English landlords, and instead brought with them clan-based communalism from Scotland and Northern Ireland to Appalachia (Hirschman, Brown, & Maclaran 2007, x–xi). Colonial authorities were happy to settle Scotch-Irish immigrants along the hilly frontier "as a buffer against the Native American inhabitants, because these new colonists proved as adept at fighting Indians as they had the Irish Catholics" (Hirschman, Brown, & Maclaran 2007, 8). The Scotch-Irish immigrants thus formed a thousand-mile border defense of the nascent United States' western frontier (Tucker 2015, x).

Over the centuries, the political neglect and sacrifice of Appalachia evolved into systemic political discrimination. By the 1900s, the Scotch-Irish of the Appalachian region became associated with rural poverty and social pathology generally. Common ethnic slurs associated with the region's poor, white population – "hillbillies," "rednecks," "crackers" – speak to the depth of derision heaped on Appalachians (Ireland 2014). Media portrayals of Appalachia often focus on the dreariest areas of the region and portray the people in the region as backward (Bowler 1985). Senator Barry Goldwater reportedly said in 1964 that the people of Appalachia were poor because they were lazy. In his ethnographic research in Appalachia, Lewin (2017) found that many in the region feel that the rest of the country, including the government, looks at them as "hillbillies" and disparages their way of life. This feeling of marginalization, Lewin argues, is part of the reason Appalachians are reluctant to embrace clean energy production (Lewin 2017).

These stereotypes endure today, with lasting impact on Appalachians' relationship with government. Given the tenor of the conversation in both government and popular media around the time of the creation of the ARC in 1965, a commission meant to *help* Appalachia, this feeling of marginalization is understandable. Major investments in the region did little to close the gap between Appalachia and the rest of the country. Although conditions in the region have improved, Appalachia still lags behind the rest of the United States on a number of key indicators (ARC 2015). Today, 42 percent of the population living in Appalachia lives in rural areas, compared to a national rate of 20 percent. Historically, Appalachians have had lower high school graduation rates and per capita income, along with higher unemployment and poverty rates, than the rest of the United States. Whereas the Appalachian unemployment rate has largely converged on the national unemployment rate, the gaps in education and income between the rest of the United States and Appalachia remain.

Describing the economic relationship between Appalachia and the rest of the United States, researchers Jennifer Wies, Alisha Mays, Shalean Collins, and Sera Young described the region as a *sacrifice zone*: an area whose natural resources and human capital are exploited for gain elsewhere (2020). Coal and timber extracted from the region were used to build industries in cities far away, with the profits from that natural resource extraction flowing to nonresident corporations that had purchased land and extraction rights in Appalachian communities (PARC 1964). Used as a military buffer in the colonial era and then exploited for their natural resources, the people of Appalachia have ample reason to be wary of government.

## Water in Appalachia

Appalachians' drinking water behavior reflects this general distrust. Many Appalachians who have access to municipal water in their homes prefer to drink water from streams (Arcipowski et al. 2017; Krometis et al. 2019;

Patton, Krometis, & Sarver 2020), mine water (i.e., water that floods abandoned mines), or water from private wells (Wies et al. 2020).[20] And despite the region's high poverty rates, many Appalachians prefer to drink expensive bottled water (McSpirit & Reid 2011).

In light of the region's legacy of political neglect, it is little surprise that many Appalachians prefer alternative water sources to tap water. Based on observations of communities in eastern Kentucky, Wies et al. conclude, "Beyond access, individuals we spoke with were concerned about water quality, with natural sources [e.g., wells, mine water, collected rain water] considered to be 'purer' and 'cleaner' than tap water" (2020, 72). In a similar vein, Krometis et al. (2019) find nearly half (48 percent) of regular spring drinkers in five Appalachian states have access to municipal water but prefer untreated spring water for quality, health, and taste reasons.[21] Tellingly, the survey participants wrote open-ended responses to Krometis et al. (2019, 52), suggesting they prefer spring water because they do not trust municipal tap water:[22]

---

[20] Access to potable tap water is a serious challenge for many in Appalachia as well. According to the Appalachian Regional Commission, 3.2 percent of Appalachian homes lacked complete plumbing (defined as hot and cold tap water indoors, with at least one bath or shower fixture) in 2015, compared with 2 percent nationally (2015, 64–65). "Sparse population density and rugged terrain make the cost of providing basic services prohibitive" Arcipowski et al. (2017) observe, and where utility mains exist, the cost to the individual household of connecting to the system is often beyond residents' means to pay. Contamination from mining and other industries also makes water treatment to potable standards expensive (Hughes et al. 2005; Wies et al. 2020). Without access to tap water service, Appalachians often turn to bottled water, sugary drinks, or roadside springs and other natural sources of water. Although problems of access and affordability are important, our analytical interest is in citizen-consumer trust of government services and regulation, and so our focus falls to the 73.5 percent of Appalachian households that receive potable water service at home from a utility.

[21] Studies that test the water quality of popular water collection stream sites frequently detect *E. coli*, a bacteria for which no level is safe for human consumption (e.g., Arcipowski et al. 2017; Krometis et al. 2019).

[22] Krometis et al. (2019, 58) note that their findings may not generalize to all of Appalachia. Their survey was administered through questionnaires left at spring sites with prepaid postage return ($N = 35$). However, their results are consistent with those of similar studies of Appalachian drinking water behavior (e.g., Arcipowski et al. 2017; Patton, Krometis, & Sarver 2020).

Too many times we don't get notified if there is a boil advisory.

They have also been cited with chemical violations (not enough or too much) and we don't hear about them til after the fact.

City water is toxic.

I have had the honor of being raised on well and spring water.... I love good mountain spring water and believe it's better than any nasty, chlorine tasting city water.

In a different survey of Appalachians who collect water from springs but have access to municipal water, Patton, Krometis, and Sarver (2020) find that 82.6 percent of respondents do not trust their tap water; of these, 21.1 percent of respondents cited distrust of their public drinking water system. In short, many Appalachian residents simply do not trust their tap water.

Distrust in Appalachian water utilities is not wholly unfounded, given the region's lack of water infrastructure and history of environmental disasters. In 2014, ten thousand gallons of chemicals used in coal processing spilled into the Elk River in Charleston, West Virginia. Following the spill, nine water systems in southern West Virginia were "under boil water advisories for longer than five years" (Wright, Coyne, & Born 2018). One report estimates that $17 billion is needed to update West Virginia's water and sewer systems alone (Lilly, Todd, & Douglas 2019). In 2000, a Martin County, Kentucky, coal company spilled 300 million gallons of coal mining chemical by-products into the local water supply. This spill and its mismanaged cleanup damaged local trust in water quality, the water district, and government officials (Unrine 2020, 5). Many Martin County residents blamed government for the disaster, believing that the federal agencies responsible for regulating mining were lax, and seeing "local government officials as essentially corrupt, incompetent, or both" (Scott et al. 2005, 13).

As in other geographies of alienation, government distrust pushes individuals to purchase costly commercial water. McSpirit and Reid (2011) find that Appalachians living in two West Virginia counties are more likely to purchase expensive bottled water products when they do not trust their water treatment facility to meet quality standards. Studying water quality in Martin County, Kentucky, Unrine (2020) found that 96 percent of study participants primarily rely on bottled water for drinking water – only 12.4 percent of study participants drank municipal water. A 2020 article in *The*

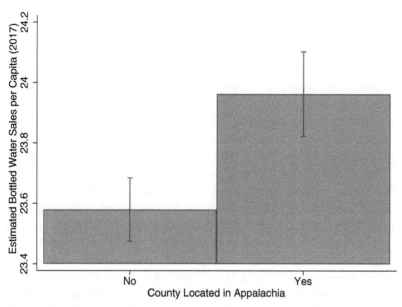

**Figure 6.6** Estimated bottled water sales in Appalachian and non-Appalachian counties.
*Note*: Estimated 2017 bottled water sales per capita on whether a county is in Appalachia, as defined by the ARC, in thirteen states. Thin bars represent 90% confidence intervals. Produced with OLS regression, controlling for 2016 socioeconomic status, percent renters, percent Black, and total population (logged). See Appendix C, Table C32 for full estimation.

*Guardian* about drinking water in Martin County, Kentucky, attributes distrust in government to "years of mismanagement" (Lakhani 2020). "In Martin County nobody drinks the tap water unless they have to," said one resident, "you can't trust it, and you can't trust the water department."

Appalachian distrust of tap water exists even when utilities apparently perform well. A 2017 study in Morgantown, West Virginia, by Jonas Levêque and Robert Burns studied resident perceptions of tap water and bottled water purchasing behavior. All participants in their study received their municipal water from the same utility: Morgantown Utility Board (Levêque & Burns 2017, 453). Notably, the Morgantown Utility Board has never committed a health violation of the Safe Drinking Water Act. Despite Morgantown's excellent regulatory record, 37 percent of survey respondents reported they drink bottled water. The same study found that bottled water consumption decreased as respondent education increased. In another survey of Morgantown residents, Levêque and Burns (2018) find that individuals with higher incomes perceived tap water provided by Morgantown Utility Board to have fewer health risks.

Consistent with these patterns of (dis)trust, our analysis of bottled water sales revenue finds that bottled water sales in Appalachian counties are higher than in non-Appalachian counties within the same states (Figure 6.6). We estimate statistical models on counties within the thirteen states containing counties located in Appalachia, adjusting for alternative drivers of bottled water consumption such as socio-economic status, percent Black population, percent Hispanic population, percent renters, and the total population (logged) in a county.[23] We find that residents of Appalachian counties spend an average of $0.38 more per person annually on bottled water, compared with same-state residents of non-Appalachian counties.[24] As in our analysis of North Carolina, an additional $0.38 per person seems small, until we consider that this increased Appalachian spending on commercial water aggregates to a total of $*9.5 million in annual revenue for the bottled water industry* – disproportionately reaped from citizen-consumers with limited resources. The region's poorest residents are the most likely to purchase bottled water.

## Hispanic Communities in the Southwest

Drinking water kiosks are physical monuments to political distrust. As discussed in Chapter 1, these free-standing, automated vending machines provide "purified" drinking water to customers who fill their own containers, usually priced at 20–35 times more than tap water on a volumetric basis. Drinking water vendors are common in the developing world, where access to potable water is scarce and public water utilities are unreliable. And indeed, kiosks are common in isolated, rural regions of the United States that lack access to reliable tap water (Garcia & Hernandez 2011; Jepson 2012; Jepson & Vandewalle 2016). However, kiosks also flourish in major US cities that enjoy high-quality drinking water utility service. American cities have seen a proliferation of private drinking water kiosks, especially in the southern and the southwestern United States (see Figures 1.4–1.7 in Chapter 1).

Water kiosks are disproportionately located in areas where individuals have been politically marginalized. Geographer Wendy Jepson

---

[23] Full model results and descriptive statistics of the data are available in Appendix C.
[24] OLS regression, $p < 0.001$.

argues that water kiosks proliferate in South Texas *colonias* – the unincorporated, industrial settlements along the US–Mexico border – because the region's governments provide inadequate or poor-quality drinking water (2012). Jepson traces the region's poor water quality to the political marginalization of the area's low-income, Hispanic population (Jepson 2012; Jepson & Brown 2014). Specifically, these communities were purposefully shut out of the political processes that govern local services: Residents of southwestern *colonias* are unable to advocate effectively to improve drinking water quality. As such, kiosks fulfill a real need for safe, clean drinking water. In another study, Jepson and Vandewalle (2016) examine factors that make *colonias* residents more or less water vulnerable. Surprisingly, they find that income does not predict water vulnerability; rather, immigration status matters most when determining access to potable water. Jepson and Vandewalle (2016, 79) suspect that immigration status drives water vulnerability because "precarious immigration status might 'spill over' into other insecurities, including household water insecurity." As such, kiosks allow people to "manage chronic problems of water access and quality without directly addressing problems with the water supply corporations or municipal services" (Jepson & Vandewalle 2016, 79). Kiosks thus mark places where individuals would rather purchase expensive commercial water than voice their concerns to water utilities, regulators, or government officials.

The political marginalization of Hispanic communities in the Southwest is not an exclusively or even primarily rural phenomenon; racial and ethnic biases are woven into the institutional fabric of the region's governments. In *Morning Glories*, Amy Bridges (1999) traces the institutional development of cities in the southwestern United States, demonstrating that the municipal reform movement that came to define the region's local governments was developed in large part to marginalize non-Anglo people. In the early twentieth century, southwestern state constitutions established or reinforced racial segregation and disenfranchisement of Black, American Indian, and Hispanic citizens. Reformers leveraged state laws to erode Hispanic political influence through changes to municipal charters in cities such as Albuquerque, Austin, Houston, Phoenix, San Antonio, and San Diego. Specifically, Anglo politicians used state laws and municipal charters to entrench nonpartisanship, city manager executives, citywide at-large elections, and limited taxation as signal features of local governance. These reforms limited popular participation and stifled

dissent generally, and they curtailed Hispanic representation specifically. Consequently, "Every city policy – hiring of municipal employees,
planning and annexation, housing, *utilities*, and education – reinforced
racial division and hierarchy," argues Bridges (1999, 20, italics added).

   This systematic ethnic political marginalization occurred simultaneously with southwestern municipal reformers' efforts to develop,
consolidate, and take control of urban infrastructure. Railroads, street
lighting, electricity, sewers, flood control works, and especially water
supplies were central to southwestern cities' political development in
the late nineteenth and early twentieth centuries (Bridges 1999). In
much of the Southwest, water is a scarce, valuable, and thus inescapably political resource. Development and control of water infrastructure was therefore caught up in the development of biased political
institutions in the American Southwest.

   In 1972, the US Justice Department extended Voting Rights Act
protections to several southwestern local governments, especially in
Arizona and Texas, citing their histories of institutionalized bias
against Hispanic citizens (Garcia 1986). As a direct consequence,
municipal charters were amended in Houston (1979) and Phoenix
(1982) to provide for city council elections by geographic districts,
along with other rules to protect ethnic minority voting. Hispanic
representation in local and state government has increased significantly
across Arizona, Texas, and the southwest region since then. However,
the legacy of Hispanic political marginalization resounds in drinking
water behavior among the region's Hispanic residents.

   As we observed in Chapter 1, commercial water companies stoke
distrust in municipal water as part of their marketing strategy; water
kiosk companies are no exception. Visitors to the Watermill Express
website are greeted with a description of the company's kiosks as
"Your local source for safe drinking water." In 2017, the Watermill
Express website featured a news blog that published stories highlighting problems with the public water supply, such as "New Report Finds
Chromium-6 in US Drinking Water" and "Studies Show Public Water
Supply Is Still Unsafe for Millions of Americans." Claims of superior
water safety in their product abound in Watermill Express advertising.

   Hispanic customers appear to be particularly frequent targets of the
kiosk industry's messaging. An Environmental Working Group study
described kiosk companies' deliberate, systematic targeting of immigrant
communities and Hispanic populations generally as "cynical and

exploitative" (Sharp & Walker 2002, 10). The Watermill Express website predominantly features images of Hispanic faces under its "Social Impact" page, and its page that displays positive customer testimonials about kiosk water is entitled in Spanish, "¡Qué Bueno!" The company also sponsors children's essay contests with small cash prizes in the South Texas cities of Laredo, McAllen, and Corpus Christi.

For a population understandably prone to distrust in government institutions, this combination of water quality alarms and ethnic appeals is a powerful marketing brew for kiosk companies. In 2017, Watermill Express was named the top US franchising company in the vending section of the food and retail sales category by *Entrepreneur Magazine* (Watermill Express 2017). A 2019 article in *The Guardian* on the proliferation of water kiosks in California opened with a description of two Hispanic men buying water from a Watermill Express location in San Diego:

"The water that comes from the tap, I don't trust it, and it doesn't taste good," Miguel Martinez said on a recent afternoon, as he filled his bottle from the kiosk. Martinez lives in San Diego's nearby Shelltown neighborhood, an area located minutes from downtown where many immigrant families have landed.

"Good water right here," his friend says, patting the machine...

"I never drink tap water," Eddie, a different customer who declined to give his last name, said in Spanish. He got used to buying bottled water 15 years ago when he lived in Mexico and never went back to tap water.

Eddie, who works in construction, said when he is at home he drinks sealed water bottles he buys from the store, but he keeps the three-gallon jugs he fills up at the kiosks when he goes to work.

"Even if they say the tap water is safe, how do we [know] it's true?" (Koran 2019)

The *Guardian* article goes on to observe that kiosks are virtually unregulated and that their claims of superior quality and taste are dubious.[25] Crucially, Miguel's and Eddie's explanations for preferring expensive kiosk water concern the distrust of both the tap water *and* the institutions charged with ensuring drinking water safety. Marketing designed to leverage institutional distrust is likely to find fertile soil

---

[25] The *Guardian* article also reported that schools and homes in some rural California communities recently experienced drinking water contamination (Koran 2019).

among Hispanics in a region with a history of ethnic political bias and disenfranchisement. In light of this political legacy, distrust of tap water and preference for commercial alternatives are rational responses.

## Water Kiosks in Houston and Phoenix

The histories of institutional bias that drew VRA Section 5 scrutiny to Texas and Arizona make these two states' largest cities – Houston and Phoenix – useful places to observe how political alienation shapes the demographics of drinking water behavior. As in earlier chapters, we fitted statistical models that estimate the number of kiosks in each census tract in Houston and Phoenix as a function of the neighborhood's ethnic composition, after accounting for population and socioeconomic factors.[26] Analyzing kiosk locations within these two southwestern cities illuminates the relationship between kiosk location and neighborhood demographics, while ensuring that tap water quality is reasonably constant throughout the city since single utilities provide the water in these cities.

The fourth largest city in the United States and among the most ethnically and socioeconomically diverse cities in America, Houston boasts an excellent municipal drinking water utility. Houston Public Works has an exceptionally resilient, hurricane-resistant water supply, and it has had perfect Safe Drinking Water Act health compliance since 1988 (as far back as EPA records go). The City of Phoenix's Water Services Department serves the fifth largest US city, similarly diverse, and boasts an excellent regulatory compliance record, with just a single health violation over the past thirty years.[27] If water quality drives the location of kiosks, then kiosks should be spread more or less evenly across these two cities. If, however, kiosk location correlates strongly with neighborhood ethnic composition, then distrust in tap water likely stems in part from distrust in government rooted in ethnic political alienation.

Figure 6.7 depicts the estimated relationship between the total number of kiosks located within a census tract and the percent of the population in a census tract in Houston that identifies as Hispanic,

---

[26] Full model results and descriptive statistics of the data are available in Appendix C.
[27] In 2014, the Phoenix Water Services Department was cited for a total coliform rule violation.

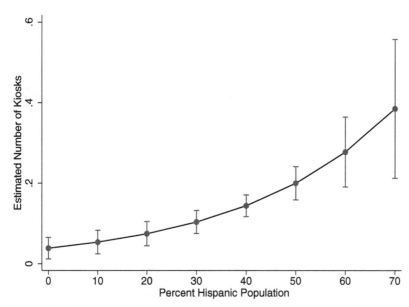

Figure 6.7 Estimated kiosks per census tract in Houston by percent Hispanic.
Note: Estimated kiosk count per census tract in Houston, TX. Thin bars represent 90% confidence intervals. Produced with negative binomial regression, controlling for socioeconomic status, percent renters, percent Black, and total population (logged). See Appendix C, Table C34 for full estimation.

after adjusting for tract population, percent renters, percent Black, and socioeconomic status. Results indicate that ethnicity strongly predicts kiosk location within Houston: As the share of the Hispanic population increases by 1 percent in a census tract, the estimated number of kiosks in that tract increases by 0.007 kiosks, or about 3 percent.[28]

Analysis of kiosk locations in Phoenix yields similar results. Figure 6.8 shows the estimated relationship between the percent Hispanic population and kiosk locations by census tract (after adjusting for the same factors as before), this time in Phoenix. As in Houston, commercial water demand correlates strongly with neighborhood ethnic composition in Phoenix.[29] These results affirm

---

[28] This is the average marginal effect ($p < 0.01$).

[29] The estimated total number of water kiosks in a census tract in Phoenix increases by 0.005 kiosks as the percent Hispanic population increases by 1 percent. This is the average marginal effect ($p < 0.05$). Given the average number of kiosks located in Phoenix census tracts, a 0.005 increase in kiosks represents a 2 percent increase.

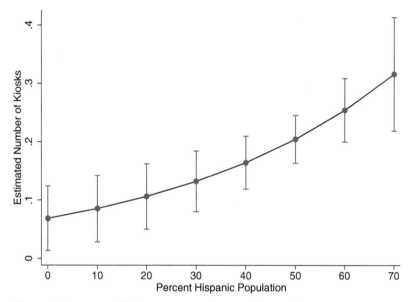

**Figure 6.8** Estimated kiosks per census tract in Phoenix by percent Hispanic.
*Note*: Estimated kiosk count per census tract in Houston, TX. Thin bars represent 90% confidence intervals. Produced with negative binomial regression, controlling for socioeconomic status, percent renters, percent Black, and total population (logged). See Appendix C, Table C36 for full estimation.

statistically the apparent spatial patterns in Chapter 1's Figure 1.6. Notably, in both of these cities with excellent drinking water records, kiosks are most likely to locate within predominantly Hispanic neighborhoods.

## Beyond Houston and Phoenix

The relationship between kiosks and ethnicity persists when we expand our analysis to examine the location of kiosks across multiple southwestern states. Figure 6.9 compares the total number of kiosks to the percent Hispanic population in counties in Arizona, California, Colorado, Oklahoma, Nevada, New Mexico, Texas, and Utah. These results account for alternative explanations of kiosk presence, such as socioeconomic status, percent Black population, percent renters, population, and the possible unique effects of each state. Since we are examining southwestern states, we also include a measure of population density; counties with higher population density may be more

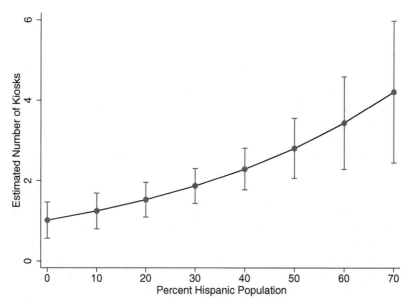

**Figure 6.9** Estimated kiosks per county in southwestern states by percent Hispanic.

*Note*: Estimated kiosk count per census tract in Houston, TX. Thin bars represent 90% confidence intervals. Produced with negative binomial regression, controlling for socioeconomic status, percent renters, percent Black, and total population (logged). See Appendix C, Table C38 for full estimation.

likely to have kiosks than remote counties. Across the Southwest, as the share of the Hispanic population increases by 1 percent in a county, the estimated number of kiosks in that county increases by 0.05 kiosks, or about 7 percent.[30]

## Political Institutions and Moral Trust

Governance institutions embed values and biases into political systems. When institutions systematically discriminate against segments of their populations in ways that muffle political voice (Figure 6.3), the victims of that discrimination learn to distrust government's morality. With voices muted or systematically excluded from politics, alienated citizen-consumers have little reason to expect high-quality basic services, or that government will respond favorably to their petitions or

[30] This is the average marginal effect ($p < 0.05$).

complaints. Steeped in distrust born of political alienation, citizen-consumers will readily pay a premium to commercial firms that can provide basic services instead of governments. Commercial water products such as bottled water and kiosks proliferate in places where residents have been shut out of political processes.

The geographies of alienation analyzed in this chapter are familiar to most observers of American history and government. The biases of the Jim Crow South, the institutionalized neglect of rural Appalachia, and the municipal charters that systematically marginalized Hispanic Americans through much of the twentieth century are now formally gone; in 1965, federal laws – the Voting Rights Act and the Appalachian Regional Development Act – sought to redress the institutional biases that plagued these regions. The stench of this past discrimination lingers, however, leaving a deficit of moral trust in government among people who suffered from disenfranchisement, neglect, or oppression.

We have seen that the traces of discriminatory institutions formally dismantled decades ago are reflected in citizen-consumer choices today. Analyses of commercial water consumption in this chapter show that bottled water and kiosks flourish in areas of the United States where portions of the population have been politically alienated; which populations are politically alienated varies by region across this diverse country. Distrustful of government and all that it regulates or produces, alienated citizens become solely consumers, willingly paying a distrust premium to protect themselves. For the commercial firms that provide exit avenues, the distrust premium is a wellspring of profit. Little wonder, then, that commercial drinking water companies target their marketing efforts at racial and ethnic minority customers (Arumugam 2011). Having opted for consumer exit over citizen voice, alienated citizen-consumers give government officials little reason to do better. With the voice of discontent silenced, public services stagnate or decline, and the erosion of trust in the institutions of government continues.

# 7 | *When Trust Pays*

## The Virtuous Cycle of Trust, Participation, and Service Quality

Even if citizens do not like or trust government itself – and it is easy to make "big government" the target for virtually any grievance – citizens do notice the services they receive, discriminate among them, and draw their conclusions about trust based on the nature of their relationship.

Donald F. Kettl,[1] *From Ideas to Results, from Results to Trust*

I honestly only read half of my little sheet that they sent out (on the water bond). I thought, "You know what, I live in Columbia, I'm going to live here forever. I'll help them out." So I voted "yes" on that. It sounded like my bill would essentially double. I don't pay that much for water right now, and I drink it every day.

Amanda Johnson,[2] Missouri voter

Like many places in the United States, Columbia, Missouri, needed water infrastructure improvements in 2018. The city's water treatment plant was forty years old and outdated. The plant's aging equipment had caused the capacity of the water treatment plant to drop from 32 million gallons a day to 24 million gallons a day, and a growing population was projected to double peak daily water demands by 2040 (Feldkamp & Hall 2018). In response, in May 2018 the Columbia City Council approved an ordinance to hold a special election on a ballot referendum for a $42.8 million water bond. If passed, the bond would pay for necessary upgrades to the water treatment and distribution system (Garrett 2018). However, the bond would also result in an 11 percent average rate increase. In holding a special election, the decision between improvements and costs was in the hands of Columbia voters.

The water bond passed overwhelmingly: An astounding 82 percent of voters approved the measure. "I'm not surprised it passed," said Kee

---

[1] Kettl (2019, 765–766).  [2] Feldkamp (2018).

Groshong, co-chair of a foundation that supported the bond, but "I'm a little surprised at how high the margin is" (Feldkamp 2018). In response to potential problems with water infrastructure in the city, the citizen-consumers of Columbia were clearly willing to pay more for higher-quality government services. Remarkably, the most prominent organized political opposition to the bond was not opposition to the rate increase, but rather from people who believed that the bond did not go far enough to address Columbia's water problems.[3] A group called COMO (Columbia, Missouri) Safe Water Coalition, formed in 2016 and devoted to improving water quality in Columbia, believed that the bond would be improved by including "more advanced water-treatment technology" (Feldkamp & Hall 2018).[4]

Importantly, Columbia's water bond also passed in the absence of a crisis or looming disaster. The city's old water treatment plant was antiquated but serviceable in the short term. Columbia voters were not reacting to failure, but rather supporting a system that had earned the public's trust over decades. Columbia's water utility enjoyed a decade of perfect Safe Drinking Water Act compliance before the bond referendum. The utility had only committed three SDWA violations in its entire history. With its citizen-consumers willing to pay for system improvements, the utility's strong compliance record is likely to continue.

## The Virtuous Cycle

To this point in the book, we have largely told a story about the negative relationships between government performance, citizen trust in government, and exit from government-provided or -regulated services. We have seen how legacies of political marginalization influence present-day citizen-consumer behavior, and how the choice of consumer products instead of public services can lead individuals to detach themselves from the political process. We have recognized how failure of government in one place can lead to distrust of government services elsewhere. Illustrations of this vicious cycle appear in each of the first six chapters of this book; the reader could be forgiven for thinking that the relationship between citizen-consumers and government is

---

[3] Local media coverage of the water bond did not make mention of much organized opposition to the bond itself, but it made frequent mention of the COMO Safe Water Coalition.

[4] Though wishing for more, COMO Safe Water Coalition ultimately supported the passage of the bond.

fundamentally negative – a feedback loop in which government fails and citizens exit from public services, leaving little incentive for government to improve infrastructure.

But a more virtuous relationship can exist between the state and its citizens too. The theoretical foundations of this argument again begin with Albert O. Hirschman. As discussed in Chapter 2, Hirschman (1970) argued that government agencies are better oriented to respond to the exercise of voice than to exit. When citizen-consumers choose exit as a response to government failures or distrust, governments are ill suited to react adequately. After all, political institutions are designed to respond to citizen voice, not consumer exit. Representative democracy gives citizen-consumers the opportunity to voice their concerns through formal processes, and functioning democratic institutions respond accordingly. Whether democratic institutions interact with citizens in this way relies on citizen-consumers trusting both the competence and morality of government. Citizens who exercise their voice must believe that the government is both capable of responding to citizen concerns and morally committed to do so. In exchange, governments in functioning democracies reward citizen-consumer trust with quality service provision.

In contrast to the vicious cycle of distrust depicted in previous chapters, this chapter provides evidence for an alternative relationship between citizen-consumers and their government, one in which trust pushes individuals to not only use public services, but also support them, and where an active and engaged citizenry leads to improved service quality. Applied to tap water, this virtuous cycle is depicted in Figure 7.1. Strong government provision and regulation of tap water lead to greater public trust in government and the utilities that provide drinking water. This trust in turn leads citizen-consumers to choose tap water over commercial alternatives. Trust in government and the services provided by government increases the belief that the exercise of voice will have positive impacts on government performance, incentivizing the citizen-consumer to maintain high levels of engagement in political processes. As governments are well situated to respond to the exercise of voice, this increased level of political participation creates stronger incentives for governments to continue investments in water services and rigorous regulation, which results in continued excellent performance, perpetuating a virtuous cycle of trust.

Previous analyses provide strong support for this cycle if the framing of the hypotheses is reversed. For example, the evidence for Hypothesis 1, which posited that tap water failure would lead to decreased trust

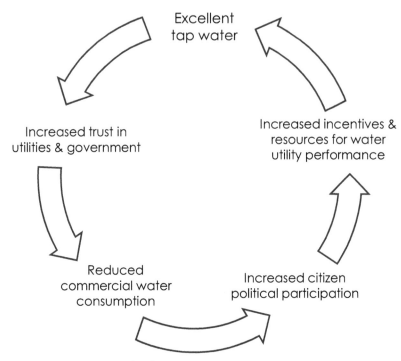

**Figure 7.1** Virtuous cycle of trust in tap water.

*Note*: This chapter reverses the vicious cycle we have examined thus far into a 'virtuous' one, wherein excellent basic service provision increases trust in government, reduces exit to the commercial sector, and increases citizen political participation, thereby increasing the resources available to governments, ensuring excellent basic service provision continues.

(presented in Chapter 3), can also be seen as evidence that good performance will lead to higher levels of trust. Individuals who do not experience tap water failure express higher levels of trust in government. Similarly, the evidence for Hypothesis 5, which suggested that individuals with lower levels of trust in government would be more likely to consume bottled water (Chapter 5), also provides support for the idea that individuals who trust government are more likely to consume tap water. Indeed, nearly all the hypotheses in the book explored thus far could be reframed in this positive way.

In this chapter, we isolate a few of the other expected relationships that come out of this virtuous cycle of trust. Figure 7.2 shows the specific pieces of the virtuous cycle we explore in this chapter, using data on public opinion, voter turnout, and water utility performance.

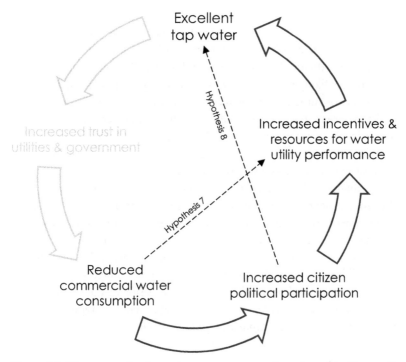

**Figure 7.2** Virtuous cycle of trust in tap water: stages investigated in Chapter 7. *Note*: This chapter examines the relationships between tap water drinkers and political participation, and political participation and tap water quality.

We first explore the possibility that citizen-consumer choice of public services will lead to greater support for investment in public services. This expectation is Hypothesis 7: *Tap water drinkers are more likely than commercial water drinkers to support rate increases aimed at improving service.* To choose government-provided services is to indicate trust in the quality of those services. If an individual chooses to drink tap water instead of bottled water, she sends a strong signal of her belief in both the competence and the morality of the agencies responsible for providing her water. Given this implicit trust, we expect that tap water drinkers will also support investments in public water supplies. A person who trusts the government enough to ensure basic services will also trust government to use public resources effectively to continue to provide high-quality services.

Second, reframing our understanding of the relationship between citizen-consumers and government service provision as a virtuous cycle extends to the relationship between political participation and service quality. We saw how exit from public services and a lack of trust in government reflect a broader exit from political life in Chapter 5. We found that individuals who have been historically politically marginalized are less likely to voice their problems to government, that individuals who consume bottled water are less likely to take political action, and that areas with higher levels of bottled water consumption have lower levels of voter turnout. In Chapter 6, we showed how specific legacies of political marginalization and neglect stoke government distrust and a turn to commercial water.

Fortunately, the reverse is also true. Citizen-consumers who trust the government are willing to voice their concerns to government. Governments that provide public services are well suited to respond to citizens who exercise voice. Governments have reason to expect that good performance will be rewarded with political support and poor performance will lead to public backlash. Therefore, government services where citizens exercise political voice should be superior to governments that serve less politically active citizens. This logic leads to Hypothesis 8: *As voter turnout increases, tap water quality also increases.*

## Tap Water Consumption and Support for Government Services

We begin by analyzing the relationship between choice of public services and support for reinvestment in those services. Specifically, we look at how tap water consumption relates to support for water infrastructure investment. Drinking tap water habitually is a profound act of trust in a water utility and the government that runs and/or regulates it. Amanda Johnson's sentiments about the Columbia water bond in this chapter's epigraph perfectly capture our expectations for the relationship between tap water consumption and support for higher spending on infrastructure: Since she drinks tap water every day, Johnson is happy to vote "yes" to increase infrastructure spending that will improve the quality of her water, even at the cost of higher water rates. In choosing to drink tap water, Johnson has already demonstrated that she trusts the City of Columbia to provide her with a high-quality service. It makes sense that she would trust her local government to use increased spending effectively to improve that service. In voting for the bond referendum, she voiced support for improved government service.

At first blush, Johnson's reasoning might seem obvious: A citizen-consumer who is satisfied with her service is willing to pay more to ensure its continuity. Support for the bond might not be so much an expression of citizen trust as it is of simple consumer satisfaction. But without trust, logic could just as easily lead to the opposite conclusion: A citizen-consumer who is satisfied with his service might see no reason to pay more for it, figuring that "if it ain't broke, don't fix it!" A dissatisfied citizen-consumer might be willing to pay more in order to improve it. *Trust, then, is the linchpin of citizen-consumer logic in the case of support for spending on public services.* Reason compels people who trust government to favor greater spending on collective efforts to improve services because they believe in government's performative and moral capacity to improve. The same logic compels people who do *not* trust government's competence or morality to oppose giving more resources to government in the name of improved services; they do not believe in government's performative or moral capacity to improve. If we are correct, then Amanda Johnson of Columbia, Missouri, is not alone – tap water drinkers' trust in government will make them more likely than commercial water drinkers to support rate increases aimed at improving service.

To test our expectation about the relationship between tap water consumption and support for water rate increases, we analyze data from the Value of Water (VOW) surveys from 2018 and 2020.[5] Similar to the CCES survey discussed in Chapter 5, respondents to the 2018 and 2020 VOW surveys were asked about their drinking water consumption. Respondents received the prompt "Thinking about the water you drink at home, do you most often drink ___," with the following options:

- Unfiltered water straight from the tap;
- Tap water that is filtered in your home, either at the sink, through the refrigerator, or through a pitcher; or
- Bottled water.

In all, 30 percent of respondents said that they drank unfiltered tap water, 41 percent reported drinking filtered tap water, and 29 percent said that their primary source of drinking water was bottled. As in

---

[5] We first introduced the VOW surveys in Chapter 3. More information on this survey is available in Appendix A.

Chapter 5, our analysis is interested primarily in bottled water versus tap water, unfiltered or filtered. In-home filtration is used mainly for aesthetic purposes (as opposed to health or safety), so tap water filtration is a complement to tap water, not a substitute for it (Lanz & Provins 2016).

Respondents to the VOW survey were also asked about their support for rate increases to improve infrastructure that would result in water quality improvements. The survey asked respondents,

Next, suppose your water and wastewater service provider increased rates by a modest amount to pay for infrastructure and water quality improvements, including preventing pollution of local streams and rivers, protecting your area's drinking water supply, and improving wastewater service. Would you be willing or unwilling to pay a modest rate increase in order to improve your water and wastewater service?

A remarkable 76 percent of respondents indicated that they were willing to pay increased rates to support infrastructure improvements, whereas 24 percent were unwilling. This very high proportion is likely due in large part to the wording of the question: The VOW survey emphasizes the benefits of a rate increase, framing its question about support for rate increases in terms of the many positive results that follow such a measure. Meanwhile, the rate increase is described as "modest," thereby minimizing the costs. The survey was sponsored by the US Water Alliance, a water-sector advocacy organization, and the question about support for rate increases was intentionally framed to elicit positive responses. It is hardly surprising that the vast majority of respondents to what amounts to a "push poll" indicated support for rate increases. Indeed, it is astonishing that nearly a quarter of respondents said that they *did not* support a "modest rate increase" that would provide clear benefits.

However, although the skewed wording makes the VOW survey question a dubious source for gauging overall public support for rate increases, it is quite useful for our purposes. Although the framing is clearly positive, a substantial share of respondents does not support rate increases for infrastructure improvements. With the survey deck stacked in favor of support for rate increases, the sizable minority of respondents who nevertheless oppose rate increases are likely expressing something other than a purely instrumental, cost–benefit logic. Opposition to clearly beneficial rate increases suggests that opponents distrust utilities' performative and/or moral capacity to deliver the proffered benefits.

Our expectation is that individuals who primarily use tap water, either filtered or unfiltered, will be more likely to support water rate increases.[6] We investigate the relationship using a logistic regression that predicts positive support for rate increases. The independent variable is also dichotomous: whether the respondent primarily drinks tap water (filtered or unfiltered) or bottled water. To account for general support for government spending, our estimates are adjusted for partisanship.[7] Figure 7.3 shows the results of the analysis.

On average, both bottled water and tap water drinkers are likely to say that they are willing to support water rate increases (probably due to the positive framing of the question). However, as Figure 7.3 shows, tap water drinkers are significantly more likely to express support for higher water rates in exchange for higher water quality. On average, and after adjusting for partisanship, individuals who consume tap water are 6.3 percent more likely than those who drink bottled water to say that they support a rate increase for improved water infrastructure.

These findings cast in stark relief the ways that commercial drinking water competes directly with tap water utilities. Since water utilities are natural monopolies, it can be easy to assume that their revenue is insensitive to competition from commercial water firms. Water for drinking is a small fraction of the volume that utilities sell (most is used for cleaning, bathing, sanitation, and outdoor irrigation), so commercial drinking water sales do not significantly reduce utilities' sales. But as government-owned and/or -regulated organizations, public water utilities rely on citizens' political support for rate increases, just as commercial firms rely on consumer choice. Our evidence suggests that when people exit from tap water to commercial

---

[6] As a test of robustness, we also fitted models that distinguished between plain tap water, filtered tap water, and bottled water drinkers. These models produced ordered effects consistent with our expectations: Plain tap water drinkers were most supportive of rate increases, followed by filtered water drinkers, with bottled water drinkers the least supportive. The difference between plain tap water and filtered tap water drinkers was small, but the difference between plain tap water and bottled water drinkers remained large and statistically significant.

[7] Our models of support for rate increases as a function of drinking water source are intentionally sparse, including only partisanship and drinking water choice. Due to multicollinearity, these models do not control for demographic, geographic, or other variables that strongly predict bottled water consumption.

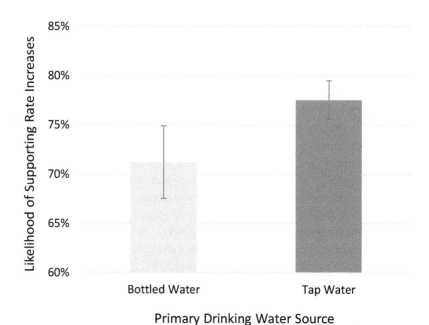

**Figure 7.3** Likelihood of supporting rate increases by primary drinking water.
*Note*: Logistic regression analysis of VOW Survey, assuming Independent partisanship.
Thin bars represent 90% confidence intervals. Produced with logistic regression, control-
ling for partisanship. See Appendix C, Table C39 for full estimation.

water, they take both their consumer dollars and their citizen political
support away from the public water supply. Meanwhile, citizen-
consumers who choose government service are more supportive of
spending on that service. The profits of distrust thus accrue to commercial firms in ways that sap political support – and therefore financial support – from public services.

## Citizen Participation and Government Performance

In Chapter 5, we explored how citizen-consumer exit to private services relates to exercise of political voice. Individuals who consume
bottled water are less likely to participate in the political process,
including taking basic actions such as voting. The democratic implications of this choice are profound. When citizens cease to exercise their
voice in a democratic system, they limit their own ability to exert both
direct and indirect pressure on government to provide better services.

The flip side of this equation, however, is just as important. When citizens exercise voice and engage collectively with government, public officials face strong incentives to provide higher-quality services. Elected officials, regulators, and public managers understand that within an engaged populace is a latent potential for collective action that could result in political backlash if expectations are not met.

Robert Putnam and colleagues (1983, 1988) famously explored this dynamic in their research on successful governance in Italy. They found that the level of citizen engagement was a strong predictor of success across Italian regional governments. Where citizens are active participants who pay attention to political concerns within their community, government performance was high; where citizens are less engaged, government performance suffered. Putnam argued that successful self-governance through political institutions thus depends on the "political culture" of the citizenry.

The relationship between citizen engagement and government performance has long been noted by scholars of environmental justice as well, who have recognized that politically active communities are more likely to mobilize and therefore less likely to face environmental harms (Hird & Reese 1998; Konisky & Reenock 2013). Engaged citizens provide an important check on government and government-provided services, ensuring accountability through engagement. It is the collective action of citizens or, perhaps more accurately, the *potential* for collective action among citizens that mitigates the potential dangers of government failure (Konisky & Reenock 2013). If the government has reason to believe that citizens will punish them for failure, then the government has a greater incentive to get things right in the first place. Indeed, Hirschman (1970), in writing on the operation of voice in democratic systems, recognized that it is not the constant use of voice that allows governments to adequately respond to the citizens, but rather that periods of relative inattention make "it possible for them to react with unexpected vigor ... whenever their vital interests are directly threatened" (32).

We have seen that citizen-consumers who drink tap water are more likely to support water infrastructure improvements with rate increases. Here, we expect that governments providing services in areas with highly engaged citizens will provide better services in general. As in earlier chapters, we measure water utility performance in terms of compliance with the health regulations of the Safe Drinking Water Act

(SDWA). We expect that as citizen political participation increases, compliance with the SDWA will increase as well. We explore the relationship between citizen political participation and basic service quality by looking at voter turnout and SDWA records in the state of California. A large number of water utilities operate in the Golden State, serving a highly diverse population under a single regulatory regime. California also keeps detailed voting and voter registration records, allowing for the development of a measure of voter turnout within water utility service areas. We analyze 408 water utilities in California to investigate the link between citizen participation and the quality of water provision.

Our dependent variable for this analysis is a count of the number of SDWA health violations committed by a utility between 2013 and 2019. SDWA violations in California during this seven-year period are relatively low; utilities averaged .48 violations, with 26 being the most health violations observed. Whether organizations comply with environmental regulations or not is typically theorized as the result of the expected costs of compliance against the expected costs of violation (Konisky & Teodoro 2016; Switzer 2019a; Winter & May 2001). If the expected costs of compliance outweigh the expected costs of violation, then the utility is more likely to violate the SDWA. If a virtuous cycle between citizen-consumers and government is possible, increased citizen participation will raise public officials' expected political costs of poor water service quality generally. Where citizens are more politically active, they are more likely to be aware of and to punish service failures (Dowding & John 2012). The 2018 water bond in Columbia, Missouri, is an instructive example. The presence of citizen groups like the COMO Safe Water Coalition means poor performance is unlikely to go unpunished. This kind of citizen vigilance incentivizes elected officials, utility managers, and environmental regulators to perform well even before the exercise of voice. Importantly, SDWA violations are meant to measure water system quality generally. Our argument is not that citizen-consumers will always observe and react to specific violations, but rather that regulatory compliance is a useful proxy for system performance generally.

If we are correct, then the quality of water services will increase when citizen participation is higher, and therefore the number of SDWA health violations will be lower as voter turnout increases. To measure citizen participation, we developed a measure of voter turnout using data from the California Statewide Database (University of California 2020), which contains detailed voter and election information for California elections. We matched the election precincts with the geographic boundaries of California water systems, obtained from the California Environmental Health Tracking Program, which allowed us to create aggregate measures of participation within each water utility. We examine voter turnout in the 2016 general election, measured as the percentage of registered voters who cast a ballot in the election. The 2016 election falls exactly in middle of our period of analysis. For the utilities in the analysis, voter turnout averaged 74 percent, ranging from 53 to 88 percent.

We once again employ a statistical model to examine the relationship between citizen participation and the quality of water services. We fitted a negative binomial regression to investigate the relationship between turnout and health violations. We also account for a number of relevant variables, including major party registration, race, ethnicity, water source, socioeconomic status, and the logged size of the population being served by the utility.

Results of the analysis are consistent with our expectations: Levels of political participation are significantly associated with the number of health violations committed by a utility. We find that as voter turnout increases, the number of SDWA health violations decreases. This relationship can be seen in Figure 7.4, which displays the estimated number of SDWA health violations by voter turnout in the 2016 election. These numbers are statistically significant and substantively strong. A utility with a turnout of 66 percent of registered voters (one standard deviation below average) is expected to commit approximately .87 health violations of the SDWA over the seven-year period, whereas a utility with an 82 percent turnout (one standard deviation above average) is expected to commit just .20 violations over the same period – a startling 77 percent decline in violations. This difference is quite striking, as SDWA health violations are relatively rare events.

As expected, higher levels of citizen participation are associated with stronger compliance with drinking water regulations. This finding is important for the possibility and potential of a more virtuous relationship between citizen-consumers and their governments. If political participation is a signal of trust in government, it is crucial that governments reciprocate with excellent performance and ethical conduct. Our finding that higher levels of voter turnout are associated with

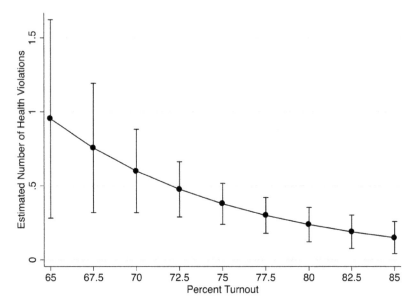

**Figure 7.4** California utility SDWA health violations, 2013–2019, by 2016 presidential election turnout.

*Note*: Negative binomial regression analysis of SDWA violations. Thin bars represent 90% confidence intervals. Produced with negative binomial regression, controlling for partisanship, race, ethnicity, groundwater, purchased water, logged population, and socioeconomic status. See Appendix C, Table C41 for full estimation.

higher-quality services demonstrates that the relationship between citizen-consumers and their governments can function in the way that democratic theory demands.

## Voice, Basic Services, and Democracy

The picture that emerges from this chapter and the last is at once gloomy and hopeful; the reciprocal relationship between citizen and state can go well or poorly. Where political institutions alienate or disregard citizens, those citizens learn to distrust government and turn to commercial firms for sustenance. Where political institutions respect, respond to, and provide for their citizens' needs, citizens trust governments and reward them with support. Taken together, some important lessons about citizen voice and basic services emerge that point the way to a restoration of citizen trust and democratic legitimacy.

It is possible to interpret the analyses of this chapter in a negative way, as we have in much of this book. Rather than thinking about consumers who choose government services over commercial options, or citizens who support increased public investment, we could easily emphasize the opposite: Citizen-consumers who choose commercial options over public services are less likely to support paying for public services. Rather than showing that increased public participation leads to better performance, we could suggest that lower participation worsens government performance. Taken together with Chapter 6, the results here also present concerns about the nature of equity in the exercise of voice. Political science research has long recognized that political participation is uneven along racial, ethnic, and socioeconomic lines (Brady, Verba, & Schlozman 1995; Verba et al. 1993). These disparities are especially pronounced in local government, where turnout is often low and participation generally favors privileged groups (Hajnal & Lewis 2003). These differential levels of participation can potentially lead to inequities in service delivery and perpetuate inequitable policy decisions (Einstein, Palmer, & Glick 2019). When the inequities in the exercise of voice lead to inequitable outcomes, this may further exacerbate distrust among marginalized communities. It is not enough for the exercise of voice to ensure good outcomes for some while others persist in experiencing poor services. This concern is central to our concluding arguments that follow in Chapter 8.

There is good reason, however, to emphasize the positive nature of these relationships – it allows us to imagine a better way forward.

After the passage of Columbia's water bond in 2018, the COMO Safe Water Coalition did not close up shop. The coalition continued to push the government of Columbia to improve water quality after the bond passed. In August 2020, the group continued to use its voice, posting on Facebook a critique of how long the utility was taking in approving a contract to start design and pilot testing for the treatment plant. Importantly, embedded in this critique was a tacit approval of the process and a belief that exercising voice would lead to change (COMO Safe Water Coalition 2020):

We appreciate Mayor Brian Treece and Fifth Ward Council Member Matt Pitzer asking the hard questions of staff and the consultant and truly listening to what we have been saying for years.... We believe that our repeated attempts to hold city leaders accountable for past errors [have] heightened the sense of urgency and appreciation for what must get done.

The post concluded with a call for citizens to contact their council members to push for water infrastructure improvements (COMO Safe Water Coalition 2020). Discontent with their water utility did not drive the members of the COMO Safe Water Coalition to exit for commercial alternatives; rather, they raised their voices. Implicit in their use of voice are performative and moral trust. If the COMO Safe Water Coalition did not believe that local officials were capable of responding in good faith and with good performance, then there would be no point in citizens calling on them to do so. Whether the City of Columbia will meet all of its citizens' concerns is an open question. What is not in question is that the city benefits from citizens who push their government to improve, and that the people of Columbia benefit from a government that listens.

# 8 | Basic Services and Rebuilding Legitimacy
The Water–Trust Cycle, from Virtuous to Vicious and Back Again

If the people cannot trust their government to do the job for which it exists – to protect them and to promote their common welfare – all else is lost.

Barack Obama,[1] *An Honest Government – A Hopeful Future*

The easiest thing is fixing pipes, the hardest will be getting people's trust back.

Jimmy Kerr,[2] Martin County (KY) Water Board member

A central tenet – arguably *the* central tenet – of liberal political theory is that the legitimacy of any government rests on its ability to secure its people's basic needs. The cycle of distrust between basic service provision and people's faith in government that we have explored in this book has profound and troubling implications for democracy itself. The centuries-long project of building the American state is a tale of a government developing political institutions, regulatory regimes, and administrative systems to "provide for the common defense, promote the general welfare, and secure the blessings of liberty." In the nineteenth and early twentieth centuries, American government evolved from fragmented fledgling to consolidated democracy through the hard, unglamorous work of service provision: postal delivery, canal construction, road maintenance, pension administration, forest management, financial regulation, and agricultural inspection. Water and sewer systems were among the most important of these developments, as we observed in Chapter 1. Modern American political parties emerged as enterprising politicians forged coalitions that built the infrastructures that sustain life and undergird an advanced economy. The visible, tangible improvements in health and prosperity that

---

[1] Obama (2006).    [2] Lakhani (2020).

followed public investments and state regulation established American governments as competent and benevolent.

In the early twenty-first century, faith in this protective state edifice is shaky. Democratic governments in the United States and around the world face increasing challenges to their legitimacy. Beyond the inefficiency and distributional inequity wrought by distrust, political scientist Donald Kettl (2017) warns that generalized distrust of government increases ideological polarization, encourages corruption, and weakens political institutions in ways that invite violence and, ultimately, risks systemic collapse. The burgeoning crisis of legitimacy besetting democratic governments across the globe has emerged in large part because many citizens no longer trust authorities to secure their basic needs. We have argued that faltering trust in governance institutions relates directly to Americans' experiences with basic services, which in turn affect their behaviors as citizens and consumers.

## The Vicious and Virtuous Cycles

Drinking water is perhaps the most basic of basic human needs, and so the examination of Americans' drinking water choices, trust in government, and political behavior in the preceding chapters offers deeper insights into American democracy. High-profile water contamination crises in Pittsburgh, Corpus Christi, Newark, Washington, DC, and especially Flint have weakened public confidence in America's water systems and the governments that operate them; parallels to the broader crises of trust in American governance institutions are not difficult to see. Tap water quality in the United States is meant to be ensured by a comprehensive government regulatory regime. But when government services are disappointing or damaging, or when regulatory agencies do not protect the public, those failures shake trust in government itself.

In this book, we have shown that problems with tap water are associated with reduced trust in government and that commercial water demand increases where tap water failures occur. We have also shown that behavioral effects of poor water quality transcend service areas and political borders: Distrust of tap water is contagious, and the contagion is most potent among the politically alienated. Political inequality thus amplifies service inequality, which manifests as defensive spending on commercial drinking water. We have seen this citizen-consumer logic play out in response to discontent with tap water. Chapter 3 showed that problems with tap water predict lower trust in government and that tap water quality failures predict commercial drinking water demand. In Chapter 4, we saw that the effects of tap water failure on public trust transcend political and service area boundaries. Chapter 5 demonstrated that low-income members of ethnic minority groups are less likely to complain to government about tap water problems and more likely to drink commercial water. In turn, commercial water drinkers trust government less and are less engaged in politics and civic life compared with tap water drinkers. Chapter 6 traced some of these pathological patterns of citizen-consumer behavior to their institutional origins. In short, the vicious cycle of distrust is on full display in the American drinking water sector.

But we have also seen that the cycle can be virtuous. In Chapter 7, we examined how safe, reliable tap water engenders performative trust in government, observable in lower demand for commercial drinking water. When government ensures basic service quality, trusting citizen-consumers reciprocate by engaging in civic life. With their greater trust in government, tap water drinkers are more willing than commercial water drinkers to pay higher water rates that support improvements in water quality. This support gives governments the resources they need to maintain high-quality basic services. As Chapter 7 showed, the vicious cycle of distrust at the tap can turn virtuous.

In this concluding chapter, we pull back from our focus on drinking water to consider the wider implications of our theory for democracy. Returning to the general theory of citizen-consumers that we introduced in Chapter 2, we retrace the vicious cycle of distrust and introduce its happy inverse: a virtuous cycle of basic services that fosters trust in government. With this virtuous cycle in full view, we argue that restoring government legitimacy ought to begin with sound public administration. In the balance of the chapter, we argue that government leaders must initiate efforts to break and reverse the cycle of distrust, and so begin a new, virtuous, trust-building cycle. To that end, we set out three conditions that governments must meet to maintain and continue to build trust through their provision of basic services: *excellence*, *openness*, and *equity*.

The ideas set forth here apply to basic services and government generally, not only to drinking water. We lay out reform proposals for the water sector specifically in a coda called "The Plan: Better Water for a More Perfect Union."

## The Importance of Basic Services

People are simultaneously citizens and consumers. The presence of commercial exit as a viable alternative to democratic voice creates a tension between person-as-consumer and person-as-citizen. We have argued that when governments fail to provide for basic services, performative trust in institutions declines. Where commercial firms offer private alternatives to collective goods and services, distrustful citizen-consumers will increasingly opt for these commercial competitors. Dissatisfied citizen-consumers who nonetheless retain trust in government's morality may voice their discontent to officials, believing that better outcomes will follow. But for politically marginalized segments of the population and for people who identify with victims of government failure, poor basic services also damage moral trust in government. Decline in moral trust will drive citizen-consumers to commercial alternatives even when their own basic services are objectively good. As moral trust in institutions declines, so does political participation and civic engagement. With less scrutiny, support, and accountability, service quality deteriorates further, government's moral trustworthiness declines, more citizen-consumers become alienated, and the cycle deepens. Distrustful citizen-consumers opt for the market, and commercial firms reap the profits of distrust from the most politically marginalized segments of society. As we have seen, this vicious cycle threatens government's capacity to perform, civic life, and democracy generally.

Yet the mechanisms that drive this dismal dynamic hold the key to building and maintaining government legitimacy. Excellent basic services, provided openly and honestly, can set into motion a positive feedback cycle. In Chapter 7, we introduced this virtuous cycle of trust in tap water (Figure 7.1); Figure 8.1 is a generalized version of this cycle that can apply to any basic service. Beginning at the top of Figure 8.1 and moving counterclockwise, excellent basic services cause trust in government to grow. As trust increases, citizen-consumers will increasingly prefer government services rather than their commercial alternatives. Increased reliance on collective basic services and trust in governance institutions leads to increased political participation. In turn, greater demand for and expectation of high-quality services increases the resources available to government agencies and creates stronger incentives for politicians to deliver excellent service. These

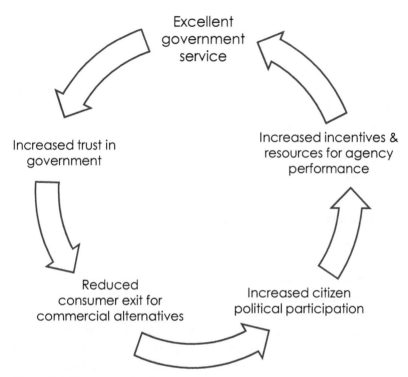

**Figure 8.1** Virtuous cycle of trust.

*Note*: This chapter reverses the vicious cycle of basic services and distrust depicted in Figure 2.5 into a virtuous cycle, wherein excellent basic service provision increases trust in government, reduces exit to the commercial sector, and increases citizen political participation, thereby increasing the resources available to governments, ensuring that excellent basic service provision continues.

increased resources and incentives feed back into stronger performance, and the cycle continues.

The most important lesson distilled from our political theory of citizen-consumer behavior and exploration of drinking water, then, is that basic services – the mundane but essential necessities of daily life – hold the promise of redeeming and strengthening American democracy. Grandiose visions and lofty achievements will not suffice to win legitimacy if citizens cannot rely on the state to secure their basic needs.

Sound administration of basic services is thus a keystone in the edifice of government. Arresting and reversing the tide of skepticism requires earning citizens' trust at what Kettl (2017) calls "the retail level": the basic services and protections that governments are supposed to provide. Kettl argues that citizens' "retail trust," formed through direct experiences and observations, contributes to trust at the "wholesale level": faith in the institutions of government itself. "The path to a new social contract starts with good solutions to day-to-day problems," argues Kettl, with fellow political scientist Anne Khademian (2020). The patterns of trust in government, consumer behavior, and citizen political participation in this book testify to the significance of public administration for government legitimacy writ large.

## Earning Trust

Trust is relational, involving a truster and a trustee. As we laid out in Chapter 2 and demonstrated empirically in Chapters 3–5, trust operates on two dimensions: performative trust and moral trust. The cycle of distrust that afflicts American government reflects the relationship between citizens (trusters) and the state (trustee) on both of these dimensions, but this downward spiral is neither inevitable nor irreversible. Halting and turning that cycle from vicious to virtuous requires that citizens, or government, or both citizens *and* government act countercyclically. The headwinds driving against such a turn are strong and many, but we believe that establishing and/or restoring trust in government is possible. The pages that follow outline a strategy toward that goal, rooted in the theory and evidence that emerge from the chapters of this book.

### *Why Governments Must Lead*

For both practical and normative reasons, we believe that government leaders must make the first move toward rebuilding trust by demonstrating government's competence and morality. The cycle depicted in Figure 8.1 implies that, in theory, dissatisfied citizens may reverse the cycle of distrust by opting for what Dowding and John (2012) call *collective voice*: organizing to demand better services from government. Where exit costs are high, Dowding and John argue that citizens can mobilize politically to "throw politicians and parties out of power if they do not deliver" (141). This potential for accountability is at the core of democratic theory, of course, and we agree entirely that facilitating voice and accountability is critical to a healthy state.

We are skeptical, however, that collective voice can catalyze wide-spread, wholesale trust building. Collective political action is always difficult, and political mobilization costs for basic services are especially high since their benefits are highly diffuse and their costs are, on average, concentrated (Wilson 1974). The political organizer's appeals to identity, ideology, or other purposive benefits that typically arouse mass participation (Olson 1965) are unlikely to motivate citizens to agitate for universal basic services. Where commercial firms can benefit from providing alternatives, exit is likely to be less costly and more certain for dissatisfied citizen-consumers. As we explained in Chapter 2, exit to commercial firms is always the rational response to failing basic services for politically alienated citizens whose moral distrust of government runs deep. Eager to reap the profits of distrust, commercial firms proliferate wherever faith in government falters, and these firms will sap strength from any mass movement that would threaten those profits. It is possible for dissatisfied and distrustful citizens to defy the logic of exit and mobilize to voice demands for basic services.[3] But such efforts are likely to be spasmodic, isolated, or quixotic.

Ethically, we also question whether people whom government has failed should be responsible for restoring government's legitimacy. If the social contract between citizen and state is weak or broken, the weakness and breakdown emerge from government's failures, not citizens' defections. Governments may get an unduly bad rap in many cases, and Americans' distrust of the public sector may be more wide-spread than public agency performance really warrants (Kettl 2017; Lerman 2019; Mettler 2011). But the patterns of basic service failure, institutional exclusion, and consumer behavior uncovered in our analyses show that distrust does not arise *ex nihilo*. Many Americans have good reason to distrust their government, either because they have

---

[3] A striking example of a citizen-driven movement for basic services is the work of We the People of Detroit (WPD), a grassroots community organization formed in 2008 to advocate for quality of life in the Motor City generally, and for water quality and affordability specifically. The organization has achieved impressive local and state legislative victories. Much of WPD's work in majority-Black Detroit invokes the rhetoric of justice and anti-racism typical of successful environmental justice appeals (Čapek 1993).

directly experienced basic service failures (as we showed in Chapter 3), or because they identify with others who have experienced such failures (Chapter 4), or because they have been systematically excluded from political life (Chapter 6).

Calling on the public to rebuild government legitimacy by exercising voice instead of exit is profoundly regressive against this backdrop. Asking alienated citizens to organize for improved services places the burden of rebuilding trust in governance institutions upon those already burdened by those very institutions. Citizens who repeatedly witness or experience performative and/or procedural failure of government can develop what Sally A. Nuamah (2021) calls a "collective participatory debt." In an ethnographic study of political participation in US cities, Nuamah found that many poor, minority citizens formed a deep disillusionment and mistrust of policy processes that invite engagement but fail to deliver tangible improvements to their lives. "Over time, it becomes more difficult for citizens to justify their participation due not only to a distrust of the system but also to mobilization fatigue, which leaves them disillusioned about the prospect of future participation," observed Nuamah (2021, 1125–1126). Appeals for greater political engagement with poor and/or minority communities only place greater costs on those who already suffer from government failure.

Expecting mass mobilization of dissatisfied and alienated citizens to emerge demanding high-quality, universal basic services is therefore neither realistic nor ethically defensible. Breaking the cycle of distrust requires leadership from within government: Visionary politicians or enterprising administrators must make the first moves in demonstrating to a wary public that the government is worthy of their trust. Rather than sidestepping basic service challenges because they are difficult, costly, or unglamorous, public-sector leaders must embrace those challenges and champion solutions to them. Government enterprises' general sensitivity to voice and insensitivity to exit means that government leaders have little incentive to break the cycle of distrust in the absence of pressure to improve. Building trust through sound management is not flashy or thrilling; it is costly and painstaking. But with their democracies in a crisis of legitimacy, leaders who really want to govern, and not merely indulge in the trappings of power, will see the investment in administration of basic services as worthwhile.

## What Governments Must Do

Earning trust requires that governments provide basic services with excellence, openness, and equity. By *excellence*, we mean that services providing citizens' basic needs – physical security, shelter, food, water, sanitation, and so on – are decent, reliable, and affordable. By *openness*, we mean that government's performance must be easily observable, administrative procedures must be visible, its decision processes must engage ordinary citizens proactively, and its officials must be responsible for success and failure alike. By *equity*, we mean that government must ensure excellence and openness everywhere and for everyone. The hyperopic effect of government performance and morality is a central and novel insight that emerges in our research: Government failure anywhere erodes trust everywhere. It is not enough that basic services are good for most people, or that government is transparent most of the time; basic services must be good for everyone, everywhere, with public officials accountable all of the time. Here, we take up each of these facets of basic service.

### Excellence

Competence is the first dimension of trust, so earning and maintaining citizens' trust begins with quality performance in the provision of basic goods and services. Crime must be low, food and housing safe, emergency services swift and effective, and energy and sanitation reliable. And of course, as we showed in Chapters 3 and 4, tap water must be healthy and affordable. Strong performance in the provision of basic services creates observable outcomes that give the public reasons to trust government (Van Ryzin 2007, 2011) and help build government agencies' performative and technical reputations (Carpenter & Krause 2012). Management consultancy McKinsey & Company (D'Emidio et al. 2019) issued similar advice in studies that found strong correlations between satisfaction with agency services and citizen trust.

Importantly, we argue that government must *provide* for excellent basic goods and services, not necessarily that government must *produce* those goods and services. That is, governments must create and sustain conditions in which all citizens receive what they need to be safe, healthy, and productive, but the government itself need not produce all of citizens' basic needs. Governments need not grow vegetables or cook meals to provide for adequate food, for example, nor must governments build and maintain apartment buildings to provide for adequate housing. For purposes of establishing and maintaining trust in government, we are agnostic with respect to who produces basic services. Where government agencies produce basic services, production must be reliable and of high quality. Where governments provide for basic services by regulating private producers, regulation must be rigorous and thorough.[4] What is important for building trust and institutional legitimacy is that all people receive excellent, open, and equitable basic goods and services, and that citizen-consumers recognize that government is responsible for ensuring basic service quality.

Many of the local, state, and federal agencies that produce or regulate these services in the United States already perform very well; others are less successful. Thanks to this variation and more than a century of scientific research, public administration scholars know a good deal about what makes government agencies more or less effective. This research is vast and varied, offering important lessons for effective management. For example, larger, more professionalized agencies tend to perform better than smaller, less professionalized agencies (Brewer & Selden 2000; Lee & Whitford 2013; Scutchfield et al. 2004). Human capital (i.e., employees' collective knowledge, skills, education, and experience) positively predicts agency performance (Ballou & Podgursky 1999; Crook et al. 2011; Meier, Favero, & Compton 2016; O'Toole & Meier 2009). Research on staffing turnover suggests that public agencies perform best with moderate levels of personnel change (An 2019; Lee 2018; Meier & Hicklin 2008). Executive recruitment and retention shape organizational innovation and performance (LeRoux & Pandey 2011; O'Toole & Meier 2009; Teodoro 2011). This litany is the thinnest sliver of a voluminous body of research on effective public management that governments may put to use.

Since securing citizen trust starts with performance, governments keen on building trust would do well to draw on existing public administration research and invest in more of it. Rigorous research on public management can help identify best (and worst) practices and

---

[4] With regard to drinking water specifically, Mathias Risse (2014) argues that even the human right to water does not mean that government agencies must supply water. Governments may secure consistent, affordable access to safe water through regulation of private firms.

facilitate their widespread adoption (or abandonment). Analysis and evaluation should accompany the implementation of every government policy. For their part, academic institutions can and should do much more to promote the dissemination and application of public administration research. The National Academy of Public Administration (NAPA) offers one useful model for putting research into practice. Chartered by Congress in 1967, NAPA is a network of leading scholars and veteran public administrators who provide management advice and assistance to Congress and federal agencies. Some similar organizations exist at the state level. Expanded use of administrative science across all levels of government can help agencies perform better and thus help strengthen citizen trust in government's competence.

## Openness

Morality is the second dimension of trust; it is not enough for government agencies to perform excellently – processes matter too (Van Ryzin 2011, 2015). Citizen trust in government requires that public administration be fair and consistent, but also flexible and compassionate.[5] Government officials must be honest with the citizens whom they serve. Politicians and agency leaders who are scrupulously fair and honest will develop the kind of procedural and moral reputations that engender citizen trust (Carpenter & Krause 2012). In practical terms, building trust in government's morality requires openness. Openness includes both *transparency* in government's performance and processes and active *engagement* with the public. As such, our call for openness aligns with Kettl's (2017) call for transparency, as well as Dowding and John's (2012) and Lerman's (2019) calls for government to facilitate public participation.

### *Transparency*

To win citizens' trust, governments must lavishly share information about their agencies' performance and processes. Traditionally, "transparency" in government has been interpreted to mean that citizens, journalists, and researchers should have access to government records, that official meetings are open to the public, that government decisions

---

[5] Management consultancy Deloitte issued similar advice to governments (Eggers et al. 2021). The Deloitte study argued that, along with demonstrating competence through excellent performance, governments must demonstrate "humanity" and "transparency" in order to secure trust.

are subject to citizen scrutiny, and so on. A watchdog mentality under-lies such transparency practices – the idea that information will allow citizens to hold governments accountable for failures. We wholeheart-edly endorse such measures, but they reflect a narrow understanding of transparency, with government agencies as passive responders to public queries. Passive transparency implies merely that governments make information available, with no active obligation to make that information digestible or actionable for citizens. By using the word *openness*, we mean to imbue transparency with an active overtone: Governments should proactively provide citizens with accurate, mean-ingful, easy-to-understand information about their agencies' work in providing basic services.[6]

One useful way for government to provide transparency actively and meaningfully is to issue organizational report cards (Gormley & Weimer 1999). Organizational report cards distill complex agency performance on multiple dimensions into simple, intuitive ordinal scales. Perhaps the most noteworthy examples are US hospital ratings created through a joint effort by the Health Quality Alliance (HQA), a public–private joint organization that works with Medicare adminis-trators to publish ratings of American hospitals. Since 2005, these ratings have summarized data on timeliness and effectiveness of care, complications and deaths, unplanned hospital visits, psychiatric ser-vices, value of care, and patient satisfaction into overall ratings on a 1–5-star scale. These ratings provide patients and consumers with valuable information in selecting health care facilities for needs. More importantly for purposes of building trust in government, hos-pital ratings provide a way for citizens to assign credit (or blame) to politicians and administrators for good (or bad) performance. Similar report cards could be developed for all basic services so that citizens may hold officials accountable for failures. Less obviously but no less importantly, report cards give elected officials and agency administra-tors positive motivation to achieve and maintain excellent basic ser-vices for which they can claim credit.

Another part of transparency involves actively demonstrating the work that government agencies do to provide basic services. In *The Submerged State*, political scientist Suzanne Mettler traces Americans' declining trust in government to the structure of public policies (2011).

[6] Kettl (2017) uses "transparency" with this kind of active meaning.

Mettler argues that Americans distrust government in part because they do not recognize all that government does for them. Public policies that provide indirect subsidies, tax expenditures, or behavioral "nudges" to achieve their goals may be effective and efficient, but such policies obscure the role of the state in citizens' lives. Mettler argues that the invisibility of such indirect policies weakens democracy because citizens tend to associate their benefits with the market, rather than government. Making agencies' work more visible would strengthen their accountability and government's legitimacy.

A recent series of studies from Boston yields some exciting findings for governments looking to build trust through better administration. From 2013 to 2015, Ryan Buell, Ethan Porter, and Michael Norton used data from Citizens Connect, the City of Boston's proprietary smartphone application, to test whether information about city agencies' work shapes people's trust in government (2020). Citizens Connect allows Bostonians who spot problems to submit service requests to city agencies (e.g., broken playground equipment, potholes in city streets, graffiti or other vandalism). Originally, residents who submitted requests through their smartphones would receive a text message or notification on their smartphone application when the service issue was resolved. In late 2014, the city began including photographs of completed work and/or the city workers who responded to the service requests. These photographs showed more explicitly that city agencies had responded to service requests, demonstrating the city's administrative competence through positive service outcomes. Unsurprisingly, residents who received the images of work in progress or completed work were much more likely to submit requests in the future. Buell, Porter, and Norton interpret Bostonians' willingness to submit more requests after receiving more explicit information about government's work as an indication of greater citizen trust. A series of laboratory experiments seems to affirm this interpretation, as the researchers found that providing participants more and more explicit information about government work yielded greater trust in government.

In his subsequent book on the subject, Porter builds on the findings of the Boston study to argue that citizens' trust in government increases when they know more about government's work because they evaluate government goods and services through the same psychological processes with which they evaluate consumer products. "The efforts that government undertakes on citizens' behalf should be highlighted," argues Porter. "What matters is the *operations* of government, including and *especially those that pertain to citizens*" (2020, 11; italics added). Greater operational transparency makes familiar and tangible the unfamiliar and obscure work of government, demonstrating the value that governments provide. In the language of our own theory of the citizen-consumer, operational transparency is the link between performative and moral trust: Effective administration establishes government's competence, and clear communication demonstrates government's procedural fairness.[7]

### Engagement

Beyond transparency, openness involves facilitating citizen voice in shaping the quality and delivery of basic services. Hirschman (1970) observed the pathologies that arise when citizen-consumers respond with exit to governments that are attuned to voice but insensitive to exit. Conceptually, remedies include raising the cost of exit and/or reducing the cost of exercising voice. To raise the cost of exit, governments could tax or prohibit outright commercial alternatives to their products and services. We see that approach as untenable, regressive, and potentially harmful to people who suffer from government failure and so rely upon commercial alternatives. Instead, the more promising and progressive course is for agencies to make it easier for citizens to voice their preferences and discontent, individually and collectively (Dowding & John 2012). Governments seeking to build trust must open wide and dredge deep the channels of communication between citizens and the state.

Public agencies have at their disposal several means of easing the exercise of citizen voice. One common example is the ombudsman's office, which many agencies at all levels of American government have established. Drawing from a popular Scandinavian administrative model, an ombudsman is meant to hear grievances from and advocate on behalf of ordinary citizens in their dealings with bureaucratic agencies (Rowat 1964). With new information technologies have come new, more direct channels for citizens to voice discontent. For governments that are willing and able to invest in them, telephone hotlines (311 in many American cities), internet portals, and smartphone

---

[7] Fittingly, Porter's book (2020) is entitled *The Consumer Citizen*.

applications like Citizens Connect allow people to report service problems to government. Encouragingly, increasing numbers of American state governments publish physical and online documents in multiple languages, further reducing the barriers to public participation (Benavides et al. 2020). Maintaining and/or expanding such channels can help establish government's moral trustworthiness (West 2004).

A critical limitation of these passive engagement channels, however, is that they rely on citizens to initiate contact and may inadvertently deepen existing inequities in public services, thus exacerbating political alienation. As with other forms of civic participation, research on ombudsmen and 311 participation finds that reporting correlates positively with socioeconomic status and negatively with racial and/or ethnic minority demographics (Cavallo, Lynch, & Scull 2014; Minkoff 2016; Van Roosbroek & Van de Walle 2008). Although passive engagement programs reduce the citizen's cost of voice, they nonetheless rely upon the citizen to initiate engagement and so place the burden of breaking the cycle of distrust upon the alienated citizen. That citizen-initiated engagement programs might risk such democratic hazards does not negate their value but suggests that passive approaches alone are not enough to rebuild widespread moral trust in government.

In addition to traditional passive engagement channels, then, government agencies may build moral trust by actively soliciting voice from citizens who might otherwise not offer it. Carefully designed and executed surveys of public attitudes and satisfaction can give agency leaders and policy makers valuable information about how their citizens perceive basic service quality (Van Ryzin, Immerwahr, & Altman 2008). Similarly, public agency leaders may connect proactively with residents and minority-affiliated organizations outside of government in ways that both improve service and engender trust. Governments also can institutionalize broad representation and advocacy within their agencies by diversifying their administrators (Meier & Steward 1992; Mosher 1982; Riccucci & Saidel 1997). We address active engagement further in our discussion of equity, below.

### Beyond "Public Relations"
By calling for government leaders to share information lavishly, we do not mean that public agencies should merely engage in advertising, branding, or public relations activities that serve mainly to laud

agencies. Transparency and engagement can involve advertising and branding insofar as they familiarize citizen-consumers with an agency's work, but the openness that we envision involves more than trumpeting government's virtues or building political support for its leaders. Openness means that agencies are as transparent about their failures as they are about their successes, and that channels of engagement are equally accessible to praise and discontent. Openness requires government leaders to take responsibility for and respond to failure proactively, rather than to obfuscate or react to failure defensively.[8]

The line between openness and advertising is often blurry; what looks like public information to an administrator can look like propaganda to a critic (Lee 2011). But a meaningful, operational distinction is possible. Openness means that agencies are transparent about success and failure alike, and that their channels of engagement are equally accessible to praise and discontent. Openness requires government leaders to take responsibility for and respond to failure proactively, rather than to conceal, deflect, or lash back. As one example, an organizational report card that is scored on objective standards provides transparency, whereas a press release or social media post emblazoned with an agency's logo announcing the same report card is advertising. This sort of advertising can enhance transparency. By contrast, a press release about a report card that proclaims the high marks and omits the poor ones is mere propaganda. In a similar vein, a public opinion survey that seeks to understand citizens' perceptions of or satisfaction with agency performance can be a useful means of citizen engagement. But a "push poll" that seeks to sway public opinion in favor of an agency through biased sampling or manipulative language is a particularly cynical sort of propaganda.

## Equity

Our calls for excellence and openness in public administration of basic services to this point echo other observers' prescriptions for the ails of distrust in government (e.g., Kettl 2017; Lerman 2019; Porter 2020). To these we add a third condition necessary for building trust: *equity*.

---

[8] Experimental evidence suggests that the public responds more positively to governments that are responsive rather than defensive in the face of crisis (Lerman 2019).

A novel finding that emerges in this book is that basic service failure anywhere damages trust in government everywhere, and that the effects of failure on distrust are strongest for people who identify with the victims of government failure. Equity informs both performative and moral dimensions of trust. To earn citizens' performative trust, it is not enough for basic services to be excellent on average or for the majority of people; government must be competent for everyone. To earn citizens' moral trust, government cannot be merely transparent most of the time or engaged with most people; government must be open with and to everyone.

A concern for equity makes the distributional implications of public management as important a consideration as efficiency or effectiveness. Decades ago, political scientist Theodore Lowi (1972) observed that public policies themselves shape political processes in ways that can support or damage democracy, and he argued that the implications of public policies for the democratic process ought to guide political scientists' evaluation of government actions. Alongside its effects on outcomes, we may judge a public policy as good or bad depending on whether it strengthens or weakens democratic governance.[9] If inequality in basic services undermines trust in government, then rebuilding trust requires building equity into every public policy and every public agency – especially those responsible for basic services.

In practical terms, governments should evaluate distributional impacts of their decisions as carefully and as rigorously as they evaluate policy efficiency or net benefits. When designing policies or evaluating their impacts, analysts should pay attention not only to median or average effects, but also to the effects of policies across the population. In statistical terms, justice is in the tails of the distribution. Policies that are efficient on average but create or exacerbate inequalities in ways that burden politically marginalized populations risk damaging government legitimacy, particularly if basic services and quality of life are involved.

Governments can build equity into public management systems by establishing administrative offices that are charged with active engagement and advocating for citizens whose political voices are otherwise muted. Perhaps most notably, in 1957 Congress established the Civil

---

[9] Lowi (1972) argued that evaluating the effects of public policy on the quality of democracy was the main end of political science as a discipline.

Rights Division within the US Justice Department and tasked the agency with enforcement of federal laws prohibiting racial, ethnic, sex, religious, disability, and other forms of discrimination. State public utilities regulators operate consumer protection or ratepayer advocacy offices that monitor pricing and/or quality regulation on behalf of ordinary citizen-consumers. These advocacy agencies serve as important checks on the dangers of regulatory capture by industry (Stigler 1971). For example, the City of Seattle operates an office for Environmental Justice and Service Equity (EJSE) that actively solicits citizen preferences and analyzes the distributional impacts of city policy and management. The EJSE's work mainly involves evaluating basic services such as trash collection and stormwater infrastructure. Building equity directly into administrative systems creates internal advocates for equity and watchdogs against discrimination. Embedding equity advocacy within agencies makes active engagement a part of the organization's work, drastically reducing the cost of voice for politically marginalized citizens.

## Why Trust Requires All Three

Each of these three basic service conditions – excellence, openness, and equity – is necessary to build and maintain citizens' trust in government; none of the three is sufficient on its own. Excellence is the most intuitive of the three, and our finding that tap water quality positively predicts trust in government aligns with ample public administration and political development research linking service quality to trust. But strong performance alone does not engender trust if citizens do not recognize that government is responsible for good outcomes. In other words, it is not enough for public agencies to perform well – citizens must recognize that government is responsible for good performance.

Trust in government thus also requires governments to communicate and engage openly with the citizens they serve. However, the salutary effects of openness depend on strong, or at least improving, government agency performance. Governments cannot simply solicit citizen views or claim that they perform well; actions must match rhetoric, and objective, observable conditions in lived experiences must affirm government claims of excellence. Attempts to win trust through communication alone will ring hollow if basic services are not sound;

citizen engagement efforts will only breed cynicism if public administration is lax or inept.

Finally, the contagiousness of distrust makes equity a necessary condition of trust in government. Government agencies everywhere must treat people with respect, fairness, and honesty in order to secure trust in government everywhere. Excellence and openness without equity will only deepen political alienation. But if governments provide for basic services with all three virtues – excellence, openness, and equity – performative and moral trust in government will increase. This renewed trust will give governments the resources and incentives to continue to provide excellent, open, and equitable service in a virtuous cycle.

## Basic Services and Trust: Local, State, and Federal Roles

The marble cake of American federalism presents both opportunities and challenges for the project of rebuilding trust in governance institutions. As Morton Grodzins (1964) observed decades ago, American government is characterized by "chaos and cooperation" with federal agencies, state and tribal institutions, and tens of thousands of local governments operating simultaneously in virtually every area of public policy. In policy areas as varied as healthcare, housing, transportation, and law enforcement, an array of local, state, and federal entities governs the provision of public services. Building trust in government through basic services thus necessarily involves every level of American federalism. But local, state, and federal authorities bring different qualities to the effort that make them more or less suited to different aspects of basic service provision.

### Local Governments

State and especially national politics dominate headlines, but the governments that matter most in the day-to-day lives of most Americans are local. Nearly 90,000 counties, cities, towns, villages, school districts, special districts, and authorities provide services directly to their residents. Although US local governance authority is highly fragmented – a subject that we take up in "The Plan" for water sector reform at the end of the book – local governments remain the most effective implementers of basic services. Local authorities are in most instances well situated to administer basic services, owing to their immediate understanding of local demands and conditions. At their best, local governments' proximity to the citizenry can reduce the cost and raise the potential payoff of political participation. Indeed, the ability of American local governments to encourage engagement in civic life through the provision of basic services was recognizable to Alexis de Tocqueville ([1835] 2004) during his travels in the United States during the nineteenth century. Tocqueville suggested that while local governments were indeed well suited to provide basic services, it was in their ability to engender the civic engagement of citizens that they derived the greatest value. With help and oversight from state and federal authorities, local governments are well situated to provide for excellent and open public services.

## State Governments

State agencies occupy a peculiar role in US basic service provision. In most instances, states do not directly administer basic services. Rather, state agencies provide resources and/or regulatory oversight to the local agencies that provide those services. State agencies wield carrots and sticks, at once enabling and coercing local governments. When it comes to basic service provision, we view state governments as effective facilitators and capacity builders. State governments are well situated to address resource inequities across communities. This balancing can involve statewide revenue-sharing arrangements. Less obviously but perhaps more importantly, state governments can augment local implementation capacity in ways that markedly improve basic services through training, data management, reporting, and coordinating efforts among local agencies. Such efforts can bolster basic service quality (which builds performative trust) and equity (which builds moral trust).

## Federal Government

The federal government can and does provide significant funding for basic services and regulates service quality in ways that can improve performance and transparency. But we believe that the principal way in which the federal government can strengthen basic services is not as a funder, but as a guardian of equity. Federal authorities can help ensure procedural equity in basic services through monitoring and enforcement of civil rights. The Justice Department's enforcement of the Voting Rights Act (discussed in Chapter 6) is an excellent example. Federal agencies charged with oversight of basic services should champion equity by building distributional analyses – that is, examining who gets what, when, and how (Lasswell 1936) – into rulemaking and by demanding transparency from state and local agencies. The federal government also ought to stand sentinel against egregious cases of procedural or substantive discrimination that would erode moral trust in government, pursuing civil or criminal prosecutions as necessary.

## Faith in Democracy through Trust at the Tap

With government legitimacy as the end and basic services as the means, we conclude this book where it began: the water that Americans drink. Perhaps the most intimate relationship between citizen and government takes form in the liquid that flows through taps. Water is a life-sustaining product that governments regulate and send into people's homes, a product in which people immerse themselves and their children, a product that people take into their bodies. It is difficult to imagine any government maintaining its legitimacy without providing for this most basic of basic needs.

The rise of commercial drinking water in the United States is a symptom of the broader erosion of trust in governance institutions that afflicts the country. Water bottles on a conference table in a city with excellent tap water say to those in attendance that the private, commercial product is superior to the collective, government-regulated product. Water kiosks on the streets of a city with a sound water utility are visible, physical manifestations of the same distrust. An aqueduct emphasizes shared identity and achievement; the water kiosk is an expression of political alienation. The water tower is collective, the water kiosk isolated and isolating. The profits of distrust that flow to bottled water and kiosk companies drag down the economy and pollute the environment; even more troubling, they erode our civic life.

But tap water also holds the potential to (re)establish trust in American government. Governments must attack head-on the water sector's crumbling infrastructure, its uneven public communication, and its service failures that disproportionately fall upon low-income racial and ethnic minority communities. We outline specific proposals for reforming the US drinking water sector in "The Plan" at the end of this book. Providing tap water is not the nation's most dire or intractable challenge. Indeed, its very tractability is part of what makes drinking water so important for government's legitimacy. Other grand challenges such as fighting climate change, curing cancer, protecting against international terrorism, or preventing the proliferation of nuclear weapons are complex and fraught with uncertainty. Drinking water problems are easy by comparison; the fundamental scientific knowledge needed to provide safe tap water already exists, by and large. The main barriers to progress in the US water sector are social, economic, and organizational; overcoming those barriers is principally a political challenge. A small but growing vanguard of forward-thinking water sector leaders is already working to drive the investments, craft the policies, and develop the management systems needed to redeem America's tap water and, with it, public trust. With excellence, openness, and equity at the tap, governments can earn the legitimacy necessary to tackle the world's most dire problems. Without trust, these problems are hopeless; with trust, they are surmountable.

Rebuilding democratic governance thus begins with literal rebuilding. The nation's tap water problems are soluble; solving them will demonstrate to citizens that democracy can fulfill the promise of a better life. Sound public services – run by competent, compassionate, and responsible people – can establish performative and moral trust between citizen and state. The ubiquitous, life-sustaining infrastructure buried beneath our streets holds not only water, but also the chance for visionary leaders to restore faith in America.

Healthier water systems make a healthier republic.

# The Plan
## Better Water for a More Perfect Union

Nothing is more essential to the life of every single American than clean air, pure food, and safe drinking water.

Gerald R. Ford,[1] on signing the Safe Drinking Water Act, 1974

If we are thoughtful, however, we will see bottled water for what it is – the result of a failure to provide satisfactory public water systems and services for everyone – and realize that our obsession with bottled water can be overcome if we address the reasons that people seek it out.

Peter Gleick,[2] *Bottled & Sold*

Here we offer twelve proposals to make tap water service in the United States more excellent, open, and equitable, following the framework we prescribed in Chapter 8. Each proposal is consistent with the main theory and evidence advanced in this book, and each enjoys support from research on the water sector or other areas of public administration. What follows is not a detailed, all-encompassing blueprint for water sector reform; each idea merits much lengthier articulation and investigation. But the proposals are more than aphorisms or vague calls to "think differently," "perform better," or "engage more."

Each of our proposals is practicable, and none requires a technological leap forward. Some are structural transformations that must be driven by state and national authorities. Others are specific programs or management measures that are best championed by local leaders and water sector professional organizations. Some of these proposals are bold and ambitious, whereas others are narrower in scope and could be deployed immediately. Some of our proposals are cheap; others involve significant financial investments. Some of our ideas could be implemented immediately, others within five to ten

---

[1] www.fordlibrarymuseum.gov/library/speeches/740305.htm.
[2] Gleick (2010, 180).

years. Some of the proposals are fairly innocuous while others may be provocative. However, all of these ideas are pragmatic, without any specific ideological valence. We believe that these proposals are politically viable in a moment when distrust of government abounds and our national politics are fractured and polarized. We hope that readers with interests outside of the water sector may find inspiration in these tangible recommendations to address problems within their own areas of interest.

## Tap Water Excellence

Basic service excellence requires that every American have access to safe, affordable drinking water from the tap. Although tap water is safe and reliable in most of the United States, significant parts of the country suffer from poor or unreliable tap water, driving distrust in government and boosting commercial drinking water profits – even in places where tap water is safe and reliable. Our first set of proposals aims to improve water utility performance through institutional restructuring, regulatory reform, and capital investment.

### Reform #1: Consolidation

There are too many drinking water utilities in the United States. The energy sector provides a useful comparison. In the United States today there are about 3,200 electrical utilities and perhaps 1,400 gas utilities; by comparison, *there are about 50,000 active community water systems.*[3] As Figure 9.1 shows, these systems are highly skewed in size. More than 40,000 of America's 50,000 community water systems are very small, serving populations of fewer than 3,300. Roughly half of these small systems are owned and operated by governments, with the remaining half controlled by investor-owned firms. Meanwhile, the largest 1,000 water utilities serve nearly 60 percent of the total US population.

---

[3] This count comes from the Safe Drinking Water Information System, which counts "community water systems" as physically distinct drinking water supply systems. Most of these are independent systems operated by a single utility organization. However, in some cases, this coding scheme means that multiple water systems are counted separately even when they are operated by a single organization. For example, in Ohio, Greene County operates eight community water systems serving a total population of 45,000. Aqua America, an investor-owned utility company, operates 36 small community water systems serving a total of 365,000 people across Ohio.

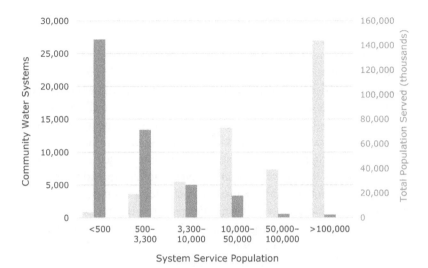

**Figure 9.1** US community water systems by size.

*Source*: EPA Safe Drinking Water Information System (SDWIS), January 2019. Dark bars depict the count of community water systems by EPA's size categories; light bars depict the total population served by utility size categories (in thousands).

Organizational consolidation of community water systems is perhaps the single most important, badly needed water sector reform. Many of the other reforms proposed here will work best after significant consolidation. We urge a sweeping national program of water system consolidation that would reduce the number of water utilities in the United States to about 5,000.

It is difficult to overstate the problems that follow from the water sector's extreme fragmentation. Many of the tiny systems that form the majority of the nation's water utilities lack the capability to operate effectively and efficiently (Levin et al. 2002). Multiple studies over the past decade have found that SDWA compliance correlates very strongly and positively with utility size (Allaire, Wu, & Lall 2018; Marcillo & Krometis 2019; Scott, Moldogaziev, & Greer 2018; Schaider et al. 2019; Switzer & Teodoro 2017). Careful perusal of the Environmental Protection Agency's (EPA) Safe Drinking Water Information System (SDWIS) records shows that some utilities perennially commit multiple water quality violations each year. Small systems are among the most egregious violators. Managing modern drinking water supply, treatment, storage, and distribution systems is technically demanding, requiring a level of organizational capacity beyond what many small utilities can muster (Teodoro & Switzer 2016). Like many small organizations, smaller utilities struggle to attract and retain talented employees (Switzer, Teodoro, & Karasik 2016).

Water service is also more expensive on average in small systems, and consolidation can translate directly into lower water bills (Jensen et al. 2020; Teodoro 2019). Compared with larger utilities, smaller utilities pay higher prices for chemicals and equipment, as well as higher interest rates for capital finance, because of their limited buying power. These higher costs translate into higher service rates because smaller utilities have fewer customers over whom to spread fixed costs. Similarly, smaller systems are more vulnerable to annual and seasonal revenue fluctuations, so smaller utilities tend to price tap water service more regressively than larger utilities. In terms of both quality and price, water utilities show enormous economies of scale.

The problems of small water systems are widely known among utility professionals. The Safe Drinking Water Act's (SDWA) congressional authors understood the problems of limited organizational capacity for small systems when they drafted the law decades ago, but they believed that small systems would naturally consolidate in order to comply with the law (National Research Council 1997). Unfortunately, the widespread consolidation that Congress anticipated did not happen in the decades since the SDWA's passage, and the landscape of America's drinking water utilities remains extremely fragmented. Additionally, monitoring and enforcement of drinking water rules for tens of thousands of small systems is difficult and costly for federal, state, and tribal regulatory agencies responsible for SDWA implementation. Smaller utilities often lack the capabilities to comply with complicated regulations, and the sheer number of utilities means regulatory agencies may lack the capacity to enforce them effectively.

The clear solution to these problems is to reduce the number of water utilities through consolidation. Without significant consolidation, implementation of regulatory reforms and major investment initiatives will be stymied. Consolidation can happen when multiple utilities merge, a bigger utility takes over a smaller one, or a nonprofit organization or an investor-owned firm acquires small systems and operates them as a single utility. The best consolidation approach will vary from one place to another. Importantly, *physical* integration of multiple community water systems is often best, but not necessary:

Small water systems can be folded into larger organizations even when they are physically separate. Telemetry and automation allow multiple small water systems to be operated by a single organization. Several local government, nonprofit, and investor-owned utilities currently operate under this organizationally consolidated, physically dispersed model.

The chief barriers to water utility consolidation are political. Consolidation often faces fierce resistance from staff who fear losing jobs or from local interest groups who fear losing control of their (often inefficient, poorly performing) systems. The legal and financial complexities of consolidation are significant, and in some cases, it can be difficult to find larger utilities that are willing to take on the responsibility for smaller, failing systems. Histories of racial or ethnic conflict between communities also often create barriers to consolidation. Some state governments have taken steps to encourage or compel small system consolidation with various financial carrots and, on rare occasions, regulatory sticks.

Moral appeal and empirical evidence have been insufficient to overcome the political barriers to consolidation; consequently, a joint effort by federal and state governments is the best avenue for progress. Federal and state funding programs for local water and sewer systems must be contingent on system sustainability. For small systems that lack the technical, hydrological, financial, and/or organizational resources to be sustainable and self-sufficient, federal and state grants must be awarded only with consolidation. For larger systems, federal and state grants should be awarded only to utilities that agree to merge with nearby or adjacent unsustainable systems. Financial regulation of investor-owned utilities should be structured in ways that encourage consolidation.[4] State governments should streamline the legal processes for merging utility organizations and provide technical assistance to support consolidation.

---

[4] Under consolidated or "single-tariff" water pricing, utility assets for multiple community water systems may be combined into a single rate base for purposes of setting prices, so that customers of physically separate systems operated by a single utility pay the same price for service (Beecher 1999). Consolidated rate bases provide important economies of scale in regulatory compliance and provide greater financial stability. Single-tariff pricing necessarily involves some degree of inter-customer subsidy since short-term average costs naturally vary across utilities.

*Reform #2: Regulatory Implementation*

Substantial improvements to America's drinking water regulatory regime are also needed, beginning with more rigorous enforcement of existing rules. The agencies charged with SDWA enforcement have few effective levers with which to compel compliance for utilities that violate water quality regulations. Criminal prosecutions under the SDWA are rare. Since most Americans receive tap water service from their local governments, any civil fines levied against utilities for SDWA violations ultimately punish the same people whom the law is supposed to protect. In most cases, regulatory agencies cannot credibly threaten to put a local government water system out of business and cannot provide the financial resources or human capital necessary to bring systems into compliance.

Aware of these constraints, regulatory officials are understandably reluctant to crack down on failing systems with limited capacity – especially when these systems are operated by local governments.[5] EPA and many state-level regulators set less stringent operational rules and water quality standards for small systems and also enforce those looser standards less rigorously. Smaller communities thus effectively receive weaker regulatory protection. When moving the goalposts fails, regulatory officials try, with varying degrees of success, to cooperate with local managers to bring systems into compliance. The result is that many water utilities, especially smaller systems, violate the SDWA frequently and chronically.

Rigorous, consistent enforcement of the SDWA, the Clean Water Act (CWA), and other water regulations is paramount to achieving excellent drinking water service. Testing procedures should capture water quality frequently across a representative sample of in-home taps. Regulators must eliminate loopholes and exemptions for small systems. State regulators should move swiftly to condemn and/or force consolidation of chronically failing systems. Criminal prosecution should be routine for utility personnel who evade or flout drinking water rules, and for regulators who turn a blind eye to egregious violations.

---

[5] Regulators are, on average, more willing to impose sanctions on investor-owned utilities to force compliance (Konisky & Teodoro 2016).

More rigorous regulatory compliance will mean higher costs for water service in some circumstances. Consolidation can offset these costs to a great extent, but the higher quality that rigorous enforcement compels will likely translate into more expensive service on average. However, we have seen that tap water quality problems lead citizen-consumers to exit for commercial drinking water. Regulators' well-intentioned tolerance of chronically failing water systems in the name of affordability makes drinking water orders of magnitude more expensive when distrust drives people away from the tap and toward bottles and kiosks. As we have demonstrated, these costs weigh most heavily upon those who have the least resources at their disposal. Regulatory neglect disproportionately affects communities with low socioeconomic status or high ethnic minority populations (Konisky 2009; Konisky & Schario 2010; Teodoro, Haider, & Switzer 2018).

Our evidence indicates that improvements to tap water quality would reduce commercial drinking water consumption in ways that could offset moderate rate increases. Chapter 7 demonstrates that citizen-consumers who trust their tap water are more supportive of rate increases to ensure tap water quality. In the long run, higher tap water quality will mean lower drinking water costs as citizen-consumers come to trust the tap and decrease their spending on commercial water.

Although enforcement of existing regulations is paramount, expansion of contaminants regulated under the SDWA can also help build confidence in tap water. EPA and state regulators should move aggressively to address emerging contaminants like PFAS through source water protection and treatment.[6] Beyond the public health benefits of water regulation, vigorous action on water quality demonstrates to the public that utility managers and regulatory officials are working hard to protect them. Utility leaders and water sector professional organizations should be leaders, not laggards, in advancing new regulations.

---

[6] Per- and polyfluoroalkyl substances (PFAS) are man-made chemicals that have been in a variety of industries since the 1940s. These chemicals are persistent in the environment and in the human body, accumulating over time, with potentially serious health effects. At the time of this writing, EPA, state, and tribal regulatory agencies were working on regulatory strategies to address PFAS through the SDWA and CWA.

*Reform #3: Tap Water Aesthetics*

Our evidence suggests that water utilities and regulators would do well to prioritize the aesthetic aspects of drinking water. The SDWA has two sets of water quality standards: *primary* and *secondary*. Primary standards set limits for contaminants that are associated with risks to human health. Exceedances of these standards are among the most serious health violations that we analyze throughout this book. Utilities are supposed to meet these primary standards, and regulators are empowered to enforce them. Secondary standards are contaminant limits related to the aesthetic properties of drinking water, including taste, odor, and color. As currently interpreted, the SDWA does not obligate utilities to meet these secondary standards, and the EPA is not authorized to enforce compliance with them.

We urge the water sector to embrace secondary standards and to take the aesthetic aspects of water seriously so that tap water is not merely safe, but truly excellent. Compliance with primary standards is crucial, of course, but primary standards should be seen as water quality guardrails, not targets. Tap water that meets SDWA health requirements but is odd-tasting, foul-smelling, or cloudy erodes trust, even if that water poses no demonstrable threat to health (Pierce et al. 2019). Past research demonstrates that the *taste* of tap water drives preferences for commercial drinking water, and in Chapter 3 we found that dissatisfaction with tap water taste significantly correlates with trust in government. In Chapter 7, we showed that citizen-consumers recognize the value of high-quality tap water, as tap water drinkers are more supportive of rate increases than are bottled water drinkers. Citizen-consumers use taste and odor as indicators of water quality, whether or not these perceptions are scientifically associated with health risks. At a minimum, achievement of secondary standards should be considered a professional goal for water utility managers. Regulators should make attainment of secondary standards a legitimate goal when awarding grants and assistance or evaluating rate increases. In the long run, legislators should expand regulatory authority to include tap water aesthetics. Americans now spend more than $36 billion annually on commercial drinking water; the increased utility costs associated with improved taste, odor, and color will be offset to a great extent by reduced bottled water consumption if more citizen-consumers like the taste of their tap water and come to trust its providers.

## *Reform #4: Infrastructure Investment*

America's drinking water utilities face perhaps a trillion dollars in replacement and upgrade costs over the next twenty-five years (American Water Works Association 2017). Removal and replacement of lead service lines and other immediate hazards will be expensive but necessary to ensure healthy tap water. Improvements in aesthetics and investments in human capital (discussed further, below) will drive that price tag up further. Still, it is difficult to imagine many domestic issues more important than the provision of safe, reliable, affordable drinking water.

There are many ways to channel financial capital into physical water infrastructure. With so much of the nation's water infrastructure owned by local governments, the most obvious avenue for investment is for the counties, cities, towns, and special districts that operate water systems to borrow from the bond market. Too many local officials have been unwilling to raise the taxes and rates necessary to maintain and upgrade infrastructure, even with municipal bond rates at historic lows.[7] More rigorous enforcement of water regulations can check this tendency to some degree. Alternatively, federal and/or state governments might provide significant new funding for water infrastructure, much as they did in the 1970s and 1980s. In 2021, Congress passed an infrastructure bill that will pour tens of billions of dollars into water and sewer systems. However, in the long run, major state and federal funding for local utilities risks disincentivizing local investment in routine maintenance, replacements, and upgrades. In fact, the prospect of state or federal grants can create a perverse incentive for local politicians to run their water systems to failure, with the idea that a failing system will qualify for more grant money.

Finally, governments might facilitate private financing of water infrastructure, either through new investment instruments or by encouraging privatization of undercapitalized water systems under government regulation. Identifying corporate ownership as a possible solution to America's water infrastructure problems will surely ruffle some ideological feathers. We do not advocate privatization categorically, but we believe that it would be foolish to leave aside private

---

[7] Long-term interest rates are at historic lows at the time of this writing; by some reckoning, interest rates are negative in real terms.

investment in public water systems as a potential solution. Although local government ownership of a water system allows for more direct democratic engagement in utility governance, excellent, open, and equitable tap water is paramount to trust in government. State legitimacy depends on basic service quality. In this regard, high-quality, privately produced water service is preferable to poor-quality water from a government. Critically, the benefits of privatization are contingent on strong regulatory regimes, not privatization per se. Whether it is local government producing high-quality drinking water or state/federal government regulation ensuring strong private production through stringent regulation, the path to safe drinking water, and the trust it engenders, begins and ends with government excellence. The best ownership and management models for channeling investment into water systems will vary across this diverse country.

Serious investment in water systems will involve increasing service prices significantly in many instances. A perennial fear, approaching conventional wisdom in the American water sector, is that citizens prefer low service rates above all, and that significant rate increases, no matter how well justified, will invite the wrath of angry voters (Hughes, Pincetl, & Boone 2013; Postel 1999; Teodoro, Zhang, & Switzer 2020; Timmins 2002). Elected officials and local government utility managers are thus reluctant to make needed investments for fear of sparking a backlash. Famously, three city council members in Tucson, Arizona, were recalled in 1977 after raising water rates (Logan 2006). More recently, there have been repeated attempts to recall city council members in Westminster, Colorado, after large increases in water rates (Aguilar 2021).

Despite these notable cases, there is strong emerging evidence that increasing water rates does not lead voters to punish political leaders. Hansen, Eskaf, and Mullin (2022) analyze the relationship between water rate increases and incumbent vote shares for 165 municipalities in North Carolina between 2007 and 2017. They find no evidence that increasing water rates led to lower vote shares for incumbents. In fact, water rate increases were associated with an *increase* (albeit statistically insignificant) in vote share for incumbents. Even when the rate increases were quite large, incumbents did not appear to suffer electorally (Hansen, Eskaf, and Mullin 2022). This result is consistent with our findings in Chapter 7 about support for rate increases associated with improved water and sewer service quality. In short, available evidence indicates that rate increases are unlikely to lead to a widespread political backlash, and they may in fact generate political benefits, so long as citizen-consumers recognize a link between the rate increases and service improvements.

## Reform #5: Human Capital

Along with physical infrastructure, the water sector needs significant reinvestment in human capital. When passing the CWA and SDWA, Congress not only mandated national water quality standards, but also created state-level water and sewer operator certification programs and invested $275 million (about $1.5 billion in 2020 inflation-adjusted terms) for three years of training and technical assistance to help build the skilled workforce needed to operate advanced water and sewer systems. By 2020, federal investment in water sector human capital was just $75 million annually, even as water systems have become increasingly complex. Each state has different training and licensing regimes for water and sewer operators, with separate licensing programs for treatment, distribution, and collection systems, resulting in a confusing and frustrating patchwork. Significant increases in research and training are needed to build America's water workforce; state and federal governments are best situated to support these programs. The EPA also should work with national water sector organizations to harmonize and streamline licensing regimes for water sector personnel with national standards and a national accreditation system for workers and training institutions.

## Tap Water Openness

Openness in America's drinking water sector requires utilities' performance to be readily observable by citizen-consumers. Utility managers and regulators must engage proactively with the public in developing and implementing policy. In choosing openness rather than merely transparency or accountability, we aim to put water systems on a positive footing. Water and sewer facilities are civic jewels that sustain healthy and vibrant communities, and they should be celebrated as such. The people who operate water systems are hardworking, fiercely dedicated professionals. Transparency in water system performance and active engagement between utilities, regulators, and the public should not be feared, but rather embraced as a chance to recognize and inspire excellence. To these ends, our second set of proposals seeks to make water system operations and performance transparent and to foster engagement between water utilities and their citizen-consumers.

## *Reform #6: Water System Report Cards*

Although tap water flows into millions of homes, water systems are little known or understood by utility consumers. Much of the critical water infrastructure that sustains everyday life is literally buried, so most people can only evaluate their water utilities' performance in terms of monthly bills, taste, and service failures such as main breaks. In economic terms, tap water quality is a case of *asymmetrical information*: Utility managers understand the chemical and biological properties of tap water that determine its safety, but the general public does not.[8] To reduce the gap between public and professional knowledge, Congress amended the SDWA in 1996 with new rules that require water systems to notify the public of water quality violations and to publish annual Consumer Confidence Reports (CCRs). These CCRs relate levels of various regulated contaminants in tap water. Unfortunately, many utility managers treat the CCR requirement as an exercise in minimal compliance. The resulting CCRs are often poorly designed, are difficult to comprehend, and do not improve customers' trust in tap water (Johnson 2000; Roy et al. 2015). Moreover, CCRs as mandated under the SDWA do not provide customers with information about other aspects of utility performance, such as capital investments, system integrity, utility financial stability, reliability, security, and equity.

Instead of (or in addition to) traditional CCRs, every American water utility should receive an annual report card from an independent organization that communicates clearly and simply how well it is performing. In schools, the report card is a "powerful instrument because of its capacity to draw distinctions across subjects, across time, and across persons; because of its capacity to enlighten and embarrass; and because of its capacity to propel students forward," observe

---

[8] Information asymmetry about product quality is one of the main rationales for regulation in a market economy (Breyer 1984).

political scientists William Gormley and David Weimer. Applied to organizations, report cards "encourage accountability to external audiences and provide valuable feedback to service providers" (Gormley & Weimer 1999, 1). A simple, comprehensive report card, published in multiple languages, would give a utility's leaders a powerful, intuitive way to communicate performance and progress to their citizen-consumers. Report cards should highlight the quality of a utility's service on key dimensions including water quality, reliability, resilience, affordability, equity, and security.

Utility report cards would provide opportunities to raise and praise excellent performance and to name and shame poor performance. With report cards in hand, utility managers could set clear improvement targets and show how their efforts improved the system's grade point average. Mayors, council members, regulators, and utility shareholders could trumpet improvements and strong performance, helping to demonstrate the value of unpleasant rate increases. By the same token, politicians and activists could demand accountability from utilities that persistently perform poorly or backslide. To avoid grade inflation, grading standards should be established and report cards should be issued by an independent organization, rather than by government agencies that operate or regulate utilities.[9] Government regulators' involvement in the grading process ought to be limited to collecting and validating data.

Organizational report cards are used in several other fields, so lessons learned elsewhere can be applied to water utilities. Perhaps the most promising model is Hospital Compare, a ratings system for US hospitals that grades each hospital on a one- to five-star scale. Launched in 2002, Hospital Compare is a joint creation of Medicare and the Hospital Quality Alliance, a public–private collaborative enterprise that collects and publishes data on hospital quality along five dimensions: timely and effective care, complications and deaths, unplanned hospital visits, psychiatric services, and payment/value of care. Hospital Compare added patient survey data to its rating system in 2008. Patients, insurers, and hospital managers all have easy access to these ratings through a searchable, easy-to-navigate website.

---

[9] Regulatory agencies such as the EPA and professional organizations such as the American Water Works Association that rely on utilities for membership dues would have clear conflicts of interest in establishing grading standards and issuing report cards.

We envision a similar rating system for water and sewer utilities. Ideally, a water utility report card regime would be funded and administered by a new, independently funded organization. Creating, curating, and maintaining such a system will require significant investment of time and expertise over many years, but the Hospital Compare ratings system provides an encouraging model to follow.

## *Reform #7: Water Infrastructure as Civic Architecture*

From ancient Rome to nineteenth-century New York City, enterprising politicians have looked for ways to celebrate public water supplies with monumental architecture. As we observed in Chapter 1, in the early twentieth century, US cities designed aqueducts, reservoirs, treatment plants, and fountains not only to deliver water, but also to make visible the achievement of these public works. By the mid-twentieth century, tap water service had become ubiquitous and governments had largely abandoned the idea of water facilities as civic architecture as frivolous and wasteful. Instead, thrift and economy dominated water infrastructure design. Post-9/11 security concerns over terrorist attacks drove water facilities further from public view. Reservoirs and treatment plants were hidden, and ornamental public fountains were no longer parts of water systems.

Architect Christopher Pohlar's description of the tension between ethos and economy at the heart of water infrastructure design in Cincinnati, Ohio, merits quoting at length:

Infrastructural networks embody a social ideology dependent upon the cultural framework. Their aesthetics speak consciously or unconsciously for the society or parts of society that create it. The government is usually the medium that communicates social concerns into public infrastructure. The elements of government administration that directly control the installation and upkeep of a community's infrastructure usually follow financial instead of aesthetic imperatives. These two qualities are often divorced from each other, the monetary as conscious necessity and the aesthetic being the unconscious result of that necessity. Aesthetic and financial concerns often combat each other within the framework of our society. To many, the financial is allied with the practical and pragmatic. As Kathy Allen, a Cincinnati Water Works Administrator said in an interview with the author, "infrastructure is a utility, not a luxury, and the investment should be no more than the absolute minimum to meet the functional requirements." (2010, x)

Greater Cincinnati Water Works (GCWW) constructed the world's largest steam engine to run its massive new water treatment in 1907, and by 1908 typhoid fever cases in the city plummeted by 90 percent. GCWW housed its state-of-the-art lift station and treatment plant in beautiful Romanesque stone structures on the banks of the Ohio River and built a golf course around its reservoirs. When the "Old River Plant" went out of service in 1963, it was replaced by a low-slung spartan structure, and the ultraviolet treatment facility GCWW added in 2013 was housed next door in a nondescript rectangular building.

Public infrastructure communicates public values. A consequence of literally burying public water infrastructure is that government provision of this vital service is invisible. We urge a widespread return to a design ethic that makes water facilities visible and engaging civic monuments to increase transparency and public engagement with these facilities. Water towers should regain iconic status in urban as well as rural communities: creatively designed, illuminated, and proclaiming public values. Just as kiosks stand as visible mausoleums depicting where public faith in government has withered, public water infrastructure should stand as monuments proclaiming civic pride.

Water infrastructure should be visible, and as open and inviting to the public as practically possible. This ethos can apply to "smaller" infrastructure as well. For example, water dispensers commonly found in airports should be placed prominently in public buildings and branded with utility logos. QR codes posted on public fountains and dispensers should communicate water quality and utility performance information through smartphones.

Improved visibility may include engaging space within public infrastructure. Several American water and wastewater treatment facilities built over the past twenty years include parklike gardens, community meeting spaces, and educational facilities. Such measures engage the public and demystify water organizations. In Washington, DC, the DC Water headquarters building overlooks the Anacostia River and includes nearly 20,000 square feet of event space. Louisville Water in Kentucky hosts weddings, corporate meetings, and community events in a historic water tower and built the WaterWorks Museum in a retired 1860 pump station. This movement toward more open facilities is particularly strong in California. The City of Petaluma's Ellis Creek plant includes four miles of walking trails around its constructed wetland. The San Francisco Public Utilities Commission's new

45,000-square-foot Southeast Community Facility includes a large special events space, multipurpose spaces for meetings, classes, social gatherings, and childcare services, and space to host social services and workforce development offices. The Sweetwater Authority, a water district serving a southern California population of 190,000, built a classroom into its groundwater desalination plant and hosts grade school programs on conservation, ecology, and water treatment technology.

In increasing the visibility of water infrastructure, it is important that people like what they see. Along with large facilities like water towers, treatment plants, and reservoirs, utilities should build and maintain public drinking fountains such as the iconic "Nasoni" in Rome or "Benson Bubblers" in Portland, Oregon. These fountains are functional and beautiful, providing relief on hot city days and character to neighborhoods. Far from frivolous, they are familiar and beloved street-level symbols of community.

## *Reform #8: Active Outreach*

Communication with customers must be a core aspect of water system service. As discussed in Chapter 8, we do not mean that utilities should only trumpet their successes or try to convince citizen-customers that their water is great through advertising campaigns alone. Rather, water organizations must open channels for *and actively encourage* citizen-consumer voice. The public meetings, advisory boards, telephone lines, and internet portals that government agencies typically employ are useful, but insufficient to build trust. These traditional means of public engagement only engage citizen-consumers who already have sufficient moral trust in government to believe that their voices will shape decisions and outcomes (Nuamah 2021). The politically marginalized populations who are most likely to drink commercial water instead of tap water are unlikely to communicate with utilities that they distrust (Nuamah 2021).

To reach these populations, the utilities that operate water systems and the agencies that regulate water must actively establish relationships with and gather information from all of the communities that they serve. Promising models for this style of engagement are already in use. The Northeast Ohio Regional Sewer District (NEORSD), a large wastewater utility that serves the greater Cleveland area, runs a "Good

Neighbor Ambassador" program to connect the utility with the communities that it serves. Recruited from the neighborhoods where they work, ambassadors are employed by the NEORSD to act as liaisons between the utility, the community, and business organizations. Ambassadors actively distribute information about the utility's work, serve as points of contact with the NEORSD, and lead street-level maintenance and cleanup efforts.

Some utilities employ scientific survey methods to evaluate performance and policies from representative samples of their service populations. When evaluating a possible change to its trash collection schedule in 2013, Seattle Public Utilities ran pilot demonstrations in a diverse handful of neighborhoods and used scientific surveys to evaluate residents' attitudes toward the change. The pilot proved cost-effective in terms of efficient trash collection, but surveys revealed stark differences in support for the change across neighborhoods: although a majority of respondents supported the change, residents of Seattle's lower-income and predominantly nonwhite areas were strongly opposed to the change. The city abandoned the idea due to its disparate and inequitable impacts. Importantly, scientific surveys and active engagement open channels of communication *at the utility's expense*. These measures give voice to citizen-consumers who would be otherwise unheard in water system management and policymaking.

## Tap Water Equity

Tap water quality and access are now widely understood to be matters of environmental justice (Davis et al. 2016; Pauli 2019; Schaider et al. 2019; Switzer & Teodoro 2017, 2018). As we demonstrated in Chapter 4, egregious failures in tap water anywhere undermine trust at the tap everywhere, especially among people who identify with the victims of that failure. Similarly, historically alienated populations are more likely to purchase commercial water products (Chapter 6). Equity in tap water means that tap water service is excellent everywhere, and utility and regulatory organizations are open to everyone. Our third set of proposals includes measures to achieve equity through universal service, decision frameworks that emphasize distributional impacts, regulatory institutions, and administrative reforms.

## Reform #9: Universal Service

Recent estimates indicate that more than 1.1 million people do not have water service; startlingly, nearly half of this population are in major metropolitan areas (Meehan et al. 2020). Although the share of population without water service is miniscule (about 0.3 percent), the sheer number of homes without water service is an ongoing indictment of government's capacity to provide for basic needs. Universal in-home piped water service should be a national priority.[10]

The cost to extend service to residences without water access is difficult to estimate, as there currently are no reliable national data on exactly which homes have full water access. However, the cost of universal water service is likely to be substantial. In many places, extending existing community water systems to serve new customers is a reasonable approach. New "distributed infrastructure" technology for potable water deployed at the neighborhood or household level, such as communal gray water/rainwater treatment or point-of-use treatment systems, provides potentially economical means of attaining universal service (Makropoulos & Butler 2010). EPA and state regulators should encourage development and deployment of distributed infrastructure to this end.

Given the scope of the challenge, funding for universal service should come from the state or federal levels. One possible model is the structure of federal funding for telecommunications services. Federal funding for universal telecommunications service through the Federal Communications Commission (FCC) has been in place for nearly ninety years (initially to support telephone service, later extended to broadband Internet). The FCC's Universal Service Fund supports a variety of programs that subsidize system construction and maintenance in rural areas or underwrite "lifeline" rates for low-income customers. The Universal Service Fund is paid for by mandatory contributions by telecommunications firms, which are typically passed on to end users as fees. Similar programs at the state and/or federal level could be used to underwrite universal water service.

---

[10] Truly universal piped water access in the strict sense is practically impossible, as some extremely remote homes are "off the grid." Much as the 1972 Clean Water Act called for "elimination" of pollution from the nation's waters, our call for "universal" tap water service is aspirational.

## Reform #10: Distributional Analysis

Under the CWA and SDWA (and several other environmental laws), water quality regulations are subject to cost–benefit analyses that weigh compliance costs against their environmental and/or health benefits. The use of cost–benefit analysis in environmental rulemaking became widespread following President Ronald Reagan's Executive Order 12291. The CWA and SDWA allow exemptions and/or compliance delays for utilities that demonstrate limited financial capability. Implicit in the use of cost–benefit and financial capability analysis is a concern for *total* or *average* costs and benefits of environmental rules. No formal consideration is given to the *distributional* effects of environmental rules.

When evaluating rules or management procedures, regulators and utilities should analyze the distributional effects of rules across the population in addition to examining the average or total effects. Regulations that are cost-beneficial on average but distribute costs or benefits disproportionately to different people or places should be rejected or amended to address distributional inequities. Conversely, measures that are not cost-beneficial on average but redress or ameliorate existing demographic or socioeconomic inequities may merit implementation (Solis 2020). Extreme water quality problems that affect relatively small portions of the population deserve consideration in rulemaking – especially if those experiencing harms are poor or members of racial and ethnic minorities. Along with cost–benefit analysis, then, we urge regulators to analyze the distribution of water quality rules and enforcement rigorously and systematically. As with many other environmental conditions, water quality is distributed spatially, and a variety of spatial and distributional methods are available for such analysis. An executive order requiring distributional analysis in water quality rulemaking and enforcement could lead to major improvements in drinking water equity.

## Reform #11: Expanded Mandates for Public Utilities Commissions

Regulators should embrace equity by building advocacy for underrepresented citizen-consumers into their organizations. State public utilities commissions (PUCs) across the country already safeguard consumer interests with offices of consumer advocacy that serve as watchdogs for utility quality and prices. The missions and mandates of these offices should be expanded to include monitoring the distributional effects of water utility investments and prices, as well as low-income access and affordability. PUCs should consider such distributional impacts in their oversight of public utilities.

We also recommend significant expansion of state PUC jurisdiction to include all water utilities. In most of the country PUCs regulate only investor-owned utilities. Since the energy sector is operated mostly by investor-owned firms, energy utilities receive much closer regulatory scrutiny than water utilities receive because the latter are predominantly owned by local governments. Local governments in most states are formally "self-regulated" with respect to pricing and service quality, so they are not subject to PUC consumer protections. PUCs in Indiana, Maine, and Rhode Island regulate some or most municipal water systems. Wisconsin is the only state in which *all* water utilities, government and investor-owned alike, are subject to state regulation. Expanding PUC authority to all water utilities would greatly increase transparency and accountability for utility finance for local government water systems, especially in smaller communities. PUC regulation of local government utilities would also extend consumer protections that private utility customers enjoy to municipal utility customers. Although the local "self-regulation" of water rates allows for the voice of citizens to be heard through local political processes and therefore theoretically provides such protections, traditionally marginalized groups may have a more difficult time being heard in these settings. State regulation would provide an additional safeguard against policies that could negatively impact marginalized populations.

## Reform #12: Equity Embedded in Administration

Utilities, too, should embed voices for equity into their organizations by hiring and empowering champions for equity within their operational ranks. Building equity directly into administrative systems creates internal advocates for equity and watchdogs against discrimination. Embedding equity advocacy within agencies drastically reduces or eliminates the cost of voice for politically marginalized citizens and may shift an organization's culture toward prioritizing these issues. A notable model is the Environmental Justice and Service Equity (EJSE) division within Seattle Public Utilities. Much more than symbolic, the EJSE team actively solicits citizen preferences and analyzes the distributional impacts of city policy and management (e.g., the trash pickup proposal analysis discussed earlier was developed by EJSE).

## The Way Forward

These twelve proposals to make tap water service in the United States more excellent, open, and equitable follow the framework we prescribed in Chapter 8. Each proposal is practicable and consistent with the theory and evidence advanced in this book. Though specific to water in our case, we hope that readers with interests in other basic services will find inspiration in these tangible recommendations to address problems within their own areas of interest.

# Appendix A: Survey Methodology

The analyses of public opinion, experiences, and consumer behavior reported in this book are based on three national surveys: the Texas A&M University Energy-Food-Water NEXUS (NEXUS) survey, the Cooperative Congressional Election Study (CCES) survey, and the Value of Water (VOW) survey.

## The NEXUS Survey

The 2015 NEXUS survey was sponsored and deployed by the Institute for Science, Technology, and Public Policy (ISTPP) at the Bush School of Government and Public Service at Texas A&M University. The questionnaire was designed by an interdisciplinary team of Texas A&M researchers to gather a variety of behavioral and attitudinal data related to energy, agriculture, and water policy. ISTPP contracted with a private polling firm, the GfK Group, to administer the survey.[1]

### Sampling

GfK's KnowledgePanel served as the survey's sampling frame. KnowledgePanel is a probability-based panel of approximately 60,000 survey participants, recruited and selected to allow representative samples for the overall US population, as well as various geographically and demographically defined subsamples. The NEXUS survey sample was designed to be representative of the US adult population, stratified to include oversamples from the State of Texas and the City of Houston. GfK provided inverse-probability sampling weights to adjust for nonrandomness introduced by stratification. We applied

---

[1] In 2018, the GfK Group's KnowledgePanel was acquired by Ipsos, which continues to operate it.

US national sampling weights in all of the analyses of NEXUS data reported in this book.

## Administration

The NEXUS survey was administered via the Internet on a secured website. To help guard against nonresponse bias due to technology, GfK provided computers and internet access to KnowledgePanel participants who do not have a computer or internet access. Data were collected from July 17 through August 29, 2015. The median respondent completed the survey in twenty-four minutes. GfK sent invitations to 3,362 KnowledgePanel participants. A total of 1,979 completed the questionnaire, for a response rate of 58.9 percent.

## The Cooperative Congressional Election Study Survey

The Cooperative Congressional Election Study (CCES) is an annual survey administered by YouGov. In congressional election years, it involves asking more than 50,000 adults in the United States a series of questions related to politics. The survey involves two waves during election years. The pre-election wave occurs between late September and late October, and the post-election wave is administered in November. Half of the CCES questionnaire is common content that is asked of all respondents. The other half of the questionnaire is created by individual teams who design surveys for a subset of 1,000 respondents. The data used in the analysis here come from a combination of the 2018 CCES common content and a team module created by a team at the University of Missouri.

## Sampling

The CCES sample consists of 60,000 adults interviewed before and after the 2018 election. The CCES uses YouGov's matched random sample methodology. This involves the creation of a random target sample that is meant to be representative of the target population – in this case, the adult population of the United States. Based on the characteristics of the target sample, YouGov selects matching members from a pool of opt-in respondents. This involves finding respondents who are as close as possible to each member of the target sample. The sample is then weighted to adjust for any remaining imbalance between the target sample and the respondents.

## Administration

The CCES is administered on the Internet. The pre-election interviews took place in October 2018, and the post-election interviews took place in November 2018. A large number of the respondents to the CCES survey are YouGov panelists. Others are recruited to participate using online advertisements or recruited through other survey providers. The survey is designed to take about twenty minutes for the pre-election wave and about ten minutes for the post-election wave.

## The Value of Water Survey

The Value of Water (VOW) survey was conducted annually from 2015 to 2021 by the US Water Alliance, a nonpartisan, nonprofit advocacy organization. The US Water Alliance provided us with data from the 2018, 2019, 2020, and 2021 waves of the survey; each survey wave employed a different questionnaire. The VOW questionnaires were developed by US Water Alliance staff. The main goal of the survey was to demonstrate popular support for public infrastructure investment. The US Water Alliance contracted with a bipartisan pair of polling firms, FM3 Research (Democratic) and New Bridge Strategies (Republican), to administer the survey.

## Sampling

The VOW survey target population was registered voters in the United States. For the VOW sampling frame, FM3 Research and New Bridge Strategies used national voter registration databases maintained by the private analytics firm TargetSmart. FM3/New Bridge drew a random sample of 100,000 registered voters for survey administration. Voters from this sample were contacted up to four times for participation until complete responses reached the target of at least 1,000 each year. The resulting margin of sampling error is 3.1 percent for each year of the survey.

**Table A.1.** *Value of Water survey administration, 2018–2021*

| Year | Dates of administration | Total responses | Margin of error |
|------|------------------------|-----------------|-----------------|
| 2021 | March 15–21 | 1,007 | ±3.1% |
| 2020 | March 7–18 | 1,056 | ±3.1% |
| 2019 | February 14–24 | 1,000 | ±3.1% |
| 2018 | March 11–15 | 1,001 | ±3.1% |

## Administration

The VOW survey was administered via telephone from a call center to landlines and mobile phones. Data were collected over a period of five to ten days in February or March each year. Table A.1 summarizes key aspects of VOW survey administration shared with us.

# Appendix B: Kiosk Data Collection and Validation

Reliable location data for public policy research can be difficult to acquire. Typically, local spatial data are expensive to collect or purchase: Either they are owned by a private company and a researcher must purchase the data, or researchers must invest significant time and energy in data collection. No national data set on commercial drinking water kiosks existed at the outset of this study. We could easily print a list of locations from company websites, but there was no way to ensure the accuracy of the addresses. When spatial data are collected remotely (i.e., not in person), best practice recommends that researchers should validate the accuracy of the data via a process called *ground truthing*. In effect, researchers should physically travel to specific locations to confirm that the observations exist at those locations. With thousands of water kiosks scattered across the United States, physical ground truthing was practically impossible. Instead, we developed a way to ground-truth the locations of kiosks without leaving our offices: "traveling" via Google Maps and Google Street View.

Google mapping products are useful data collection and validation platforms because they give users the sensation of physically being in a place and produce reliable and valid data. Many peer-reviewed studies use Google mapping products to collect data for analysis (e.g., Contreras & Brodie 2010; Madin, Madin, & Booth 2011; Myers 2010; Vega, Craig, & Lindo 2011; Yee et al. 2011).

The novel data collection insight in our book is that Google Street View can be used to validate data on local public policy environments via ground truthing. Because Google Street View captures 360-degree imagery and is designed to give "the viewer the feeling of virtually being on the street" (Clarke et al. 2010, 1225), we can use the platform to replicate "traveling" to a specific location to validate data. Studies in sociology demonstrate that data collection via Google Street View is as reliable as in-person data collection (Clarke et al. 2010;

Rundle et al. 2011). Clarke et al. (2010) demonstrate that data collection on the conditions of Chicago neighborhoods via Google Street View is just as accurate as in-person data collection. Rundle et al. (2011) demonstrate the same findings comparing Google Street View data collection and in-person data collection in New York City. With these models in mind, we collected and validated data on US kiosks using the Google Maps platform.

In spring 2017, we recruited a team of six undergraduate students at Texas A&M University through the Aggie Research Scholars program to help collect data on water kiosk locations in the United States. The Aggie Research Scholars program pairs undergraduate students seeking research experience with graduate students seeking research assistance. We were fortunate to work with six talented and hardworking students. We collected data on the locations of kiosks operated by two major kiosk companies: Watermill Express and Ice House America. We selected these two companies for our national kiosk data set for three main reasons. First, both of these companies have a physically independent presence; these kiosks typically exist as stand-alone structures in parking lots or as roadside stops. Other kiosk companies, such as Primo (which bought Glacier in 2017), also have a national presence but typically exist as vending machines within other stores, such as grocery chains, big-box stores, or gas stations. Purchasing water from Glacier or Primo kiosks as part of a grocery trip may reflect a different theoretical process than driving to a specific location to solely purchase water. Second, Watermill Express and Ice House America are franchises, allowing them to respond organically to local demand. Watermill Express was listed on a top growing franchise list in the United States (Watermill Express 2017); Glacier and Primo have different business models, possibly including corporate partnerships, which drive their locations. Finally, we excluded smaller, localized kiosks companies that do not have a national presence. Some companies operate just a single kiosk; others operate a handful in a single community. Though we initially inventoried some of these companies in the West and Northeast, we ultimately did not collect data on them or include them in our final data set to ensure national comparability.

We followed a two-step process to collect the kiosk data. First, we collected the addresses of kiosks from kiosk company websites. In 2017, both Watermill Express and Ice House America had a kiosk location feature on their websites. We collected the location of water kiosks in the continental United States from these company websites. Our undergraduate team recorded these locations using the addresses provided on the company websites using Google My Maps, a Google product that allows users to create their own maps. Similarly, we were able to search for additional, unlisted kiosk locations using the search feature of Google My Maps. We searched for kiosks by company name. Google Maps contains the locations of businesses because owners and individuals can add the locations of businesses to Google Maps. Searching for additional kiosks ensured we collected kiosk locations not listed on company websites. For example, in Texas we started with a list of 550 kiosks from the Watermill Express website and then identified an additional 78 Watermill Express kiosks using the search feature of Google Maps.

Second, we validated the presence of a kiosk at each kiosk location we recorded. Given the franchising model of kiosk companies, the central companies' location information may be incomplete or out of date. To validate the location of kiosks, we took advantage of Google Maps' Satellite View and Street View features. Kiosks are easily identifiable in Google Maps' Satellite View given their distinct appearances. For example, Watermill Express kiosks are shaped like windmills and have a bright blue roof, and Ice House America kiosks are large rectangles with deep blue roofs. Using Google Street View, our team "traveled" to each location in our kiosk data set and "walked" down the street. This strategy is valid, given Google Street View is designed to give users the feeling of walking down the street (Anguelov et al. 2010), and reliable, given Google Street View's accuracy compared to in-person data collection (Clarke et al. 2010; Rundle et al. 2011). If a kiosk was visible at the location where it was listed, it remained in our data set. If no kiosk could be found at the location where it was listed, we removed the location from our data set. Frequently, kiosks were not located at the exact address provided by companies. These kiosks were often found within a block or two of the original address or at the opposite side of a large parking lot. For example, in Texas we identified twenty-two kiosks that were not located where they were listed on the companies' websites. Changes in exact kiosk location were easily identified and updated using Google Street View by dragging pins to the exact location of the kiosk in question. This validation process resulted in a precise and accurate recording of kiosk locations in the continental United States.

Once we were confident in the kiosk locations marked in Google My Maps, we exported these data as a spatial data file and converted it into a shapefile for analysis in ArcMap GIS. The resulting data set included more than 2,100 water kiosks.

# Appendix C: Statistics

This appendix reports descriptive statistics, full estimation results, and relevant analytical notes for the statistical models reported throughout the book. Tables and the figure are organized in parallel with the chapter organization (Tables C.1–C.41).

## Chapter 3 Statistics

Table C.1. *NEXUS survey descriptive summary*

| Variable | Mean | Standard deviation | Minimum | Maximum |
|---|---|---|---|---|
| **Trust in government (0–10)** | | | | |
| Local government | 2.68 | 2.44 | 0 | 10 |
| State government | 4.36 | 2.42 | 0 | 10 |
| Federal government | 3.93 | 2.66 | 0 | 10 |
| **Drinking water problems (0/1)** | | | | |
| Tastes bad | 0.32 | 0.47 | 0 | 1 |
| Dirty or cloudy | 0.20 | 0.40 | 0 | 1 |
| Low pressure | 0.29 | 0.46 | 0 | 1 |
| Causes illness | 0.04 | 0.19 | 0 | 1 |
| **Party identification (1–7)** | 4.14 | 2.09 | 1 | 7 |
| **Demographics** | | | | |
| Female (0/1) | 0.51 | 0.50 | 0 | 1 |
| Black (0/1) | 0.11 | 0.31 | 0 | 1 |
| Hispanic (0/1) | 0.14 | 0.35 | 0 | 1 |
| Age | 50.19 | 17.31 | 18 | 93 |
| Homeowner (0/1) | 0.73 | 0.44 | 0 | 1 |
| Education | 10.23 | 2.10 | 1 | 14 |
| Household income ($000) | 72.33 | 51.04 | 2.5 | 200 |

$N = 1,979$

*Note*: Unweighted values. Inverse probability weights applied in estimation.

Table C.2. *Models of trust in local government (NEXUS survey)*

| OLS regression | Water tastes bad | Water dirty or cloudy | Low water pressure | Water causes illness |
|---|---|---|---|---|
| Tap water problem | −0.630 | −0.411 | −0.415 | −1.208 |
| | (0.000) | (0.036) | (0.015) | (0.002) |
| Party identification | 0.105 | 0.098 | 0.102 | 0.100 |
| (1–7, Republican– | (0.005) | (0.009) | (0.007) | (0.008) |
| Democrat) | | | | |
| Female | 0.100 | 0.113 | 0.115 | 0.120 |
| | (0.494) | (0.443) | (0.437) | (0.411) |
| Black | 0.343 | 0.294 | 0.270 | 0.315 |
| | (0.168) | (0.249) | (0.293) | (0.217) |
| Hispanic | 0.247 | 0.300 | 0.273 | 0.313 |
| | (0.336) | (0.244) | (0.289) | (0.218) |
| Homeowner | −0.034 | −0.015 | −0.055 | −0.049 |
| | (0.852) | (0.936) | (0.763) | (0.787) |
| Age | 0.008 | 0.008 | 0.008 | 0.008 |
| | (0.058) | (0.042) | (0.053) | (0.065) |
| Income ($000) | 0.001 | 0.001 | 0.001 | 0.001 |
| | (0.724) | (0.454) | (0.474) | (0.479) |
| Constant | 3.858 | 3.665 | 3.742 | 3.688 |
| | (0.000) | (0.000) | (0.000) | (0.000) |
| Observations | 1,204 | 1,204 | 1,203 | 1,199 |
| $R^2$ | 0.031 | 0.021 | 0.022 | 0.026 |

*Note*: Cells contain coefficients generated by ordinary least squares regression (OLS; *p*-values in parentheses). Inverse probability weights applied in estimation.

Table C.3. *Models of trust in state government (NEXUS survey)*

| OLS regression | Water tastes bad | Water dirty or cloudy | Low water pressure | Water causes illness |
|---|---|---|---|---|
| Tap water problem | −0.367 | −0.349 | −0.166 | −1.108 |
| | (0.024) | (0.069) | (0.322) | (0.005) |
| Party identification | 0.166 | 0.163 | 0.163 | 0.161 |
| (1–7, Republican– | (0.000) | (0.000) | (0.000) | (0.000) |
| Democrat) | | | | |
| Female | 0.296 | 0.302 | 0.307 | 0.325 |
| | (0.041) | (0.037) | (0.034) | (0.023) |
| Black | 0.424 | 0.386 | 0.374 | 0.415 |
| | (0.085) | (0.122) | (0.134) | (0.097) |
| Hispanic | 0.269 | 0.309 | 0.288 | 0.299 |
| | (0.290) | (0.219) | (0.257) | (0.229) |
| Homeowner | −0.174 | −0.167 | −0.182 | −0.180 |
| | (0.339) | (0.361) | (0.319) | (0.319) |
| Age | 0.010 | 0.010 | 0.010 | 0.009 |
| | (0.018) | (0.015) | (0.016) | (0.025) |
| Income ($000) | 0.001 | 0.001 | 0.001 | 0.001 |
| | (0.551) | (0.426) | (0.396) | (0.458) |
| Constant | 3.104 | 3.018 | 3.007 | 3.040 |
| | (0.000) | (0.000) | (0.000) | (0.000) |
| Observations | 1,206 | 1,207 | 1,205 | 1,202 |
| $R^2$ | 0.045 | 0.043 | 0.041 | 0.048 |

*Note*: Cells contain coefficients generated by OLS regression ($p$-values in parentheses).
Inverse probability weights applied in estimation.

Table C.4. *Models of trust in federal government (NEXUS survey)*

| OLS regression | Water tastes bad | Water dirty or cloudy | Low water pressure | Water causes illness |
|---|---|---|---|---|
| Tap water problem | −0.481 | −0.231 | −0.112 | −0.905 |
| | (0.004) | (0.238) | (0.520) | (0.047) |
| Party identification | 0.388 | 0.385 | 0.384 | 0.383 |
| (1–7, Republican– | (0.000) | (0.000) | (0.000) | (0.000) |
| Democrat) | | | | |
| Female | 0.228 | 0.232 | 0.235 | 0.251 |
| | (0.125) | (0.122) | (0.117) | (0.093) |
| Black | 0.431 | 0.387 | 0.382 | 0.417 |
| | (0.079) | (0.120) | (0.125) | (0.096) |
| Hispanic | 0.346 | 0.381 | 0.377 | 0.392 |
| | (0.177) | (0.135) | (0.145) | (0.123) |
| Homeowner | −0.192 | −0.185 | −0.195 | −0.195 |
| | (0.303) | (0.321) | (0.297) | (0.292) |
| Age | 0.001 | 0.001 | 0.001 | 0.001 |
| | (0.833) | (0.752) | (0.739) | (0.852) |
| Income ($000) | 0.004 | 0.005 | 0.005 | 0.005 |
| | (0.013) | (0.004) | (0.004) | (0.005) |
| Constant | 2.069 | 1.911 | 1.895 | 1.933 |
| | (0.000) | (0.000) | (0.000) | (0.000) |
| Observations | 1,207 | 1,208 | 1,206 | 1,202 |
| $R^2$ | 0.128 | 0.122 | 0.120 | 0.124 |

*Note*: Cells contain coefficients generated by OLS regression (*p*-values in parentheses). Inverse probability weights applied in estimation.

Table C.5. *Model of trust in local government with taste–party ID interaction (NEXUS survey)*

| OLS regression | Trust in local government |
| --- | --- |
| Water tastes bad | −0.267 |
|  | (0.495) |
| Party identification | 0.127 |
| (1–7, Republican– | (0.002) |
| Democrat) |  |
| Water tastes bad | −0.083 |
| × Party identification |  |
|  | (0.308) |
| Female | 0.100 |
|  | (0.493) |
| Black | 0.355 |
|  | (0.152) |
| Hispanic | 0.236 |
|  | (0.356) |
| Homeowner | −0.041 |
|  | (0.824) |
| Age | 0.008 |
|  | (0.060) |
| Income ($000) | 0.001 |
|  | (0.745) |
| Constant | 3.774 |
|  | (0.000) |
| Observations | 1,204 |
| $R^2$ | 0.032 |

*Note*: Cells contain coefficients generated by OLS regression (*p*-values in parentheses). Inverse probability weights applied in estimation.

**Table C.6.** *Cooperative Congressional Election Study (CCES) survey, descriptive summary*

| Variable | Mean | Standard deviation | Minimum | Maximum |
|---|---|---|---|---|
| **Trust in government (0/1)** | | | | |
| Local government | 0.384 | 0.487 | 0 | 1 |
| State government | 0.316 | 0.465 | 0 | 1 |
| Federal government | 0.221 | 0.415 | 0 | 1 |
| **Unsatisfied with tap water (0/1)** | | | | |
| Any reason | 0.220 | 0.414 | 0 | 1 |
| Health or safety | 0.090 | 0.287 | 0 | 1 |
| Taste | 0.115 | 0.319 | 0 | 1 |
| Political ideology (1–5) | 2.999 | 1.239 | 1 | 5 |
| **Demographics** | | | | |
| Female (0/1) | 0.584 | 0.493 | 0 | 1 |
| Black (0/1) | 0.089 | 0.285 | 0 | 1 |
| Hispanic (0/1) | 0.113 | 0.317 | 0 | 1 |
| Education | 3.654 | 1.531 | 1 | 6 |
| Immigrant (0/1) | 0.061 | 0.239 | 0 | 1 |

$N = 1,000$

**Table C.7.** *Models of trust in government (2018 CCES survey)*

| Logistic regression | Trust in local government | Trust in state government | Trust in federal government |
|---|---|---|---|
| Unsatisfied with tap water | −0.713 | −0.727 | −0.413 |
| | (0.002) | (0.004) | (0.148) |
| Female | −0.215 | −0.039 | −0.235 |
| | (0.202) | (0.832) | (0.265) |
| Conservative | −0.085 | 0.011 | 0.127 |
| | (0.201) | (0.877) | (0.110) |
| Black | 0.224 | 0.246 | 0.737 |
| | (0.442) | (0.397) | (0.017) |
| Hispanic | −0.292 | 0.311 | 0.367 |
| | (0.355) | (0.343) | (0.318) |
| Education | −0.076 | −0.264 | −0.344 |
| | (0.197) | (0.000) | (0.000) |
| Immigrant | 0.622 | 0.974 | 1.054 |
| | (0.122) | (0.024) | (0.016) |
| Constant | 0.300 | 0.236 | −0.448 |
| | (0.429) | (0.553) | (0.317) |
| Observations | 916 | 916 | 916 |
| $X^2$ | 17.00 | 33.36 | 41.74 |

*Note*: Cells contain coefficients generated by logistic regression ($p$-values in parentheses). Inverse probability weights applied in estimation.

Table C.8. *Models of reasons for dissatisfaction with water and trust in government (2018 CCES survey)*

| Logistic regression | Trust in local government | Trust in state government | Trust in federal government |
|---|---|---|---|
| Unsatisfied taste | −0.405 | −0.428 | −0.476 |
| | (0.179) | (0.231) | (0.254) |
| Unsatisfied safety | −1.096 | −1.148 | −0.529 |
| | (0.003) | (0.005) | (0.202) |
| Female | −0.224 | −0.050 | −0.254 |
| | (0.185) | (0.783) | (0.229) |
| Conservative | −0.085 | 0.011 | 0.146 |
| | (0.192) | (0.873) | (0.062) |
| Black | 0.267 | 0.293 | 0.785 |
| | (0.349) | (0.301) | (0.011) |
| Hispanic | −0.299 | 0.301 | 0.429 |
| | (0.350) | (0.366) | (0.239) |
| Education | −0.076 | −0.264 | −0.335 |
| | (0.203) | (0.000) | (0.000) |
| Immigrant | 0.489 | 0.845 | 0.870 |
| | (0.247) | (0.065) | (0.052) |
| Constant | 0.301 | 0.244 | −0.529 |
| | (0.425) | (0.541) | (0.235) |
| Observations | 915 | 915 | 915 |
| $X^2$ | 17.01 | 34.36 | 41.37 |

*Note*: Cells contain coefficients generated by logistic regression ($p$-values in parentheses). Inverse probability weights applied in estimation.

**Table C.9. 2021 Value of Water (VOW) survey, descriptive summary**

| Variable | Mean | Standard deviation | Minimum | Maximum |
|---|---|---|---|---|
| **Trust in government (1–4)** | | | | |
| Local | 2.39 | 0.41 | 1 | 4 |
| State | 2.17 | 0.50 | 1 | 4 |
| Federal | 1.93 | 0.49 | 1 | 4 |
| **Water problem frequency (1–4)** | | | | |
| Water main breaks | 1.91 | 0.89 | 1 | 4 |
| Sewer backups or overflows | 1.58 | 0.83 | 1 | 4 |
| Contamination | 1.84 | 0.95 | 1 | 4 |
| **Trust in tap water (1–4)** | 3.39 | 0.92 | 1 | 4 |
| **Party identification (1–7)** | 4.05 | 2.32 | 1 | 7 |
| **Demographics** | | | | |
| Female (0/1) | 0.48 | 0.51 | 0 | 1 |
| Black (0/1) | 0.07 | 0.25 | 0 | 1 |
| Hispanic (0/1) | 0.04 | 0.20 | 0 | 1 |
| Age | 54.81 | 18.01 | 19 | 98 |

$N = 1,007$

**Table C.10.** *Models of trust in local government by water infrastructure problem type (2021 VOW)*

| OLS regression | Water main breaks | Sewer backups or overflows | Waterfront closure due to pollution or algae bloom |
|---|---|---|---|
| **Problem frequency** | | | |
| Rarely | 0.037 | –0.010 | –0.078 |
| | (0.335) | (0.772) | (0.042) |
| Occasionally | –0.057 | –0.104 | –0.047 |
| | (0.133) | (0.003) | (0.229) |
| Frequently | –0.091 | –0.120 | –0.085 |
| | (0.011) | (0.001) | (0.021) |
| **Party identification** | –0.199 | –0.207 | –0.206 |
| **(1–7, Democrat–** | (<.001) | (<.001) | (<.001) |
| **Republican)** | | | |
| **Demographics** | | | |
| Female | 0.046 | 0.052 | 0.041 |
| | (0.176) | (0.129) | (0.252) |
| Black | –0.090 | –0.072 | –0.108 |
| | (0.011) | (0.041) | (0.003) |
| Hispanic | –0.058 | –0.058 | –0.047 |
| | (0.098) | (0.098) | (0.194) |
| Age | 0.015 | 0.023 | 0.001 |
| | (0.665) | (0.507) | (0.990) |
| Constant | 2.656 | 2.679 | 2.753 |
| | (<.001) | (<.001) | (<.001) |
| Observations | 830 | 829 | 759 |
| $R^2$ | 0.054 | 0.061 | 0.053 |

*Note*: Cells contain standardized coefficients generated by OLS regression (*p*-values in parentheses). Dependent variable is trust in government on 4-point scale: 1 (*never trust*) to 4 (*just about always trust*).

**Table C.11.** *Models of trust in state government by water infrastructure problem type (2021 VOW)*

| OLS regression | Water main breaks | Sewer backups or overflows | Waterfront closure due to pollution or algae bloom |
|---|---|---|---|
| **Problem frequency** | | | |
| Rarely | 0.002 | –0.038 | –0.061 |
| | (0.954) | (0.279) | (0.108) |
| Occasionally | –0.090 | –0.132 | –0.040 |
| | (0.017) | (<.001) | (0.299) |
| Frequently | –0.061 | –0.101 | –0.045 |
| | (0.082) | (0.003) | (0.219) |
| **Party Identification** | –0.236 | –0.239 | –0.236 |
| **(1–7, Democrat–** | (<.001) | (<.001) | (<.001) |
| **Republican)** | | | |
| **Demographics** | | | |
| Female | 0.097 | 0.116 | 0.104 |
| | (0.004) | (0.722) | (0.004) |
| Black | –0.004 | 0.012 | –0.012 |
| | (0.913) | (0.722) | (0.733) |
| Hispanic | –0.031 | –0.030 | –0.008 |
| | (0.372) | (0.374) | (0.829) |
| Age | 0.058 | 0.068 | 0.031 |
| | (0.087) | (0.046) | (0.386) |
| Constant | 2.349 | 2.534 | 2.409 |
| | (<.001) | (<.001) | (<.001) |
| Observations | 830 | 829 | 760 |
| $R^2$ | 0.065 | 0.086 | 0.071 |

*Note*: Cells contain standardized coefficients generated by OLS regression (*p*-values in parentheses). Dependent variable is trust in government on 4-point scale: 1 (*never trust*) to 4 (*just about always trust*).

Table C.12. *Models of trust in federal government by water infrastructure problem type (2021 VOW)*

| OLS regression | Water main breaks | Sewer backups or overflows | Waterfront closure due to pollution or algae bloom |
|---|---|---|---|
| **Problem frequency** | | | |
| Rarely | −0.005 | −0.000 | −0.017 |
| | (0.897) | (0.998) | (0.617) |
| Occasionally | −0.063 | −0.102 | −0.038 |
| | (0.073) | (0.001) | (0.286) |
| Frequently | −0.024 | −0.089 | 0.021 |
| | (0.057) | (0.005) | (0.534) |
| **Party Identification** | −0.456 | −0.461 | −0.447 |
| **(1–7, Democrat–** | (<.001) | (<.001) | (<.001) |
| **Republican)** | | | |
| **Demographics** | | | |
| Female | 0.035 | 0.042 | 0.037 |
| | (0.260) | (0.175) | (0.265) |
| Black | −0.005 | 0.014 | 0.003 |
| | (0.877) | (0.657) | (0.929) |
| Hispanic | 0.019 | 0.022 | 0.028 |
| | (0.544) | (0.481) | (0.396) |
| Age | 0.043 | 0.045 | 0.017 |
| | (0.171) | (0.156) | (0.603) |
| Constant | 2.473 | 2.479 | 2.489 |
| | (<.001) | (<.001) | (<.001) |
| Observations | 827 | 827 | 758 |
| $R^2$ | 0.211 | 0.220 | 0.207 |

*Note*: Cells contain standardized coefficients generated by OLS regression ($p$-values in parentheses). Dependent variable is trust in government on 4-point scale: 1 (*never trust*) to 4 (*just about always trust*).

**Table C.13.** *Models of trust in local, state, and federal government by trust in tap water (2021 VOW)*

| OLS regression | Local | State | Federal |
|---|---|---|---|
| Trust in tap water | 0.213 | 0.163 | 0.118 |
| (1 = strongly distrust, 4 = strongly trust) | (<.001) | (<.001) | (<.001) |
| Party identification | −0.183 | −0.215 | −0.449 |
| (1–7, Democrat–Republican) | (<.001) | (<.001) | (<.001) |
| Female | 0.073 | 0.123 | 0.047 |
| | (0.036) | (<.001) | (0.138) |
| Black | −0.059 | 0.009 | 0.023 |
| | (0.086) | (0.817) | (0.491) |
| Hispanic | 0.044 | −0.001 | 0.036 |
| | (0.217) | (0.828) | (0.340) |
| Age | 0.002 | 0.055 | 0.042 |
| | (0.953) | (0.117) | (0.202) |
| Constant | 2.029 | 1.781 | 2.083 |
| | (<.001) | (<.001) | (<.001) |
| Observations | 803 | 804 | 801 |
| $R^2$ | 0.084 | 0.092 | 0.226 |

*Note*: Cells contain standardized coefficients generated by OLS regression (*p*-values in parentheses). Dependent variable is trust in government on 4-point scale: 1 (*never trust*) to 4 (*just about always trust*).

**Table C.14.** *Utilities and kiosk data summary*

| Variable | Mean | Standard deviation | Minimum | Maximum |
|---|---|---|---|---|
| Total kiosks, 2017 | 1.15 | 6.06 | 0 | 144 |
| Health violation count, 2010–2016 | 1.84 | 6.43 | 0 | 164 |
| Health violations, binary, 2010–2016 | 0.45 | 0.50 | 0 | 1 |
| % Hispanic | 19.62 | 19.59 | 0.80 | 97.33 |
| % Black | 14.09 | 14.72 | 0.34 | 96.71 |
| % Renters | 39.42 | 12.88 | 4.46 | 81.29 |
| Socioeconomic status | 0.00 | 1.00 | −3.02 | 3.22 |
| Population (logged) | 11.45 | 0.79 | 10.60 | 15.93 |
| Groundwater source | 0.25 | 0.43 | 0 | 1 |
| Private owner | 0.11 | 0.32 | 0 | 1 |

$N = 1,185$

## Socioeconomic Status (SES) Factor Score

Following Switzer and Teodoro (2018), we use factor analysis to create a single variable that captures multiple dimensions of socioeconomic status (SES). This variable combines measures of the percent of the utility's population living below the poverty level, the percent of the population with a bachelor's degree, the percent of the population with a high school diploma, and the median income using factor analysis. Factor analysis mathematically identifies latent underlying factors among related variables using eigenvalues (Zwick & Velicer 1982). Applied to our data, factor analysis mathematically identifies the underlying dimensions that connect education, poverty, and income. Analysis revealed a single factor with an eigenvalue of 2.64, accounting for 88 percent of the variance within the variables of interest, indicating that there is a single underlying factor among the variables. Loadings from this factor analysis were used in a regression to generate standardized factor scores with a mean of 0 and standard deviation of 1.0. An SES score of 0 represents a socioeconomically average community within the data set, a value of +1 represents a community that is one standard deviation higher than average, and a value of −1 is one standard deviation below average. Figure C.1 shows the distribution of the resulting SES factor score. This SES factor score more fully represents socioeconomic status than any single measure of income, education, or poverty.

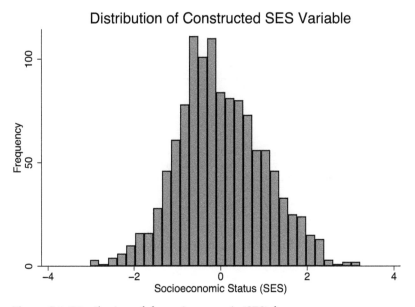

**Figure C.1** Distribution of the socioeconomic (SES) factor score.

Table C.15. *Model of total water kiosks located within a utility service area*

| Zero-inflated negative binomial regression | Kiosks |
|---|---|
| **Stage 2: Kiosk count** | |
| SDWA health violations (total) | 0.022 |
| | (0.040) |
| % Hispanic | −0.002 |
| | (0.616) |
| % Black | −0.008 |
| | (0.159) |
| % Renters | −0.021 |
| | (0.003) |
| SES | −0.947 |
| | (0.000) |
| Population (logged) | 1.133 |
| | (0.000) |
| Constant | −11.931 |
| | (0.000) |
| **Stage 1: Kiosk presence** | |
| SDWA health violations (binary) | −0.563 |
| | (0.070) |
| Population (logged) | −0.271 |
| | (0.131) |
| Groundwater | −0.149 |
| | (0.691) |
| Private utility | −0.380 |
| | (0.407) |
| Constant | 2.189 |
| | (0.367) |
| State fixed effects? | Yes |
| Observations | 1,185 |
| AIC | 1,961.450 |
| BIC | 2,271.177 |

*Note*: Cells contain coefficients from a zero-inflated negative binomial model ($p$-values in parentheses).

**Table C.16.** *Models of at least one water kiosk in a utility service area*

| Logistic regression | At least one kiosk | At least one kiosk |
|---|---|---|
| SDWA health violations (binary) | 0.400 | |
| | (0.026) | |
| SDWA health violations (total) | | 0.078 |
| | | (0.002) |
| Population (logged) | 0.766 | 0.785 |
| | (0.000) | (0.000) |
| Groundwater | 0.224 | 0.153 |
| | (0.362) | (0.535) |
| Private utility | 0.250 | 0.330 |
| | (0.435) | (0.306) |
| State fixed effects? | Yes | Yes |
| Constant | −8.988 | −9.153 |
| | (0.000) | (0.000) |
| Observations | 884 | 884 |
| AIC | 885.833 | 880.168 |
| BIC | 1,034.151 | 1,028.486 |

*Note*: Cells contain coefficients from logistic regression models (*p*-values in parentheses). These estimates inform the likelihood of at least one kiosk being present in a utility service area.

## Chapter 4 Statistics

### Spatial Model Specification

In Chapter 4, we employ a spatial lag of X (SLX) spatial econometric model (Vega & Elhorst 2015) to assess the effects of government distrust across demographically similar communities. We believe that the use of an SLX model is appropriate, given the theory we are testing. However, alternative spatial lags (e.g., a spatially lagged dependent variable, a spatially lagged error term, or some combination of spatial lags) have power against each other (Anselin 1988; Cook, Hays, & Franzese 2015). A traditional spatial econometric model specification should follow a general-to-specific specification search (Hendry 1995) following statistical tests of spatial autocorrelation such as Moran's I (Cook, Hays, & Franzese 2020). We present the results of Moran's I tests for spatial autocorrelation below.

In a recent appeal for SLX models, Wimpy, Williams, and Whitten (2021) demonstrate that general-to-specific testing is rarely undertaken in political science and most researchers default to using the spatial autoregressive (SAR) model. However, they argue an SLX model allows for better flexibility and more accurate theoretical testing of particular concepts. Ultimately, we employ an SLX model because this model best reflects our theoretical expectations that a neighbor's SDWA health violations (i.e., a spatially lagged predictor) increases the presence of kiosks within another unit.

## W *Specification*

We discuss the specification of our weights or neighbor matrix, **W**, at length in Chapter 4. The chapter refers to this important component of spatial econometric modeling as "neighbors" for ease of interpretation. In addition to the **W** specifications we describe in the main text, all of our **W** matrices are spectrally normalized. To calculate our various measures of social distance, first we calculated the difference between the demographic variable of interest for each pairing of observations in our data set. Smaller values indicated observations were more alike, while larger values indicated observations were less alike. To give greater weight to these smaller values, we next calculated the inverse social distance using double-power distance weights prior to normalization.

## *Moran's I*

While there are different types of tests for spatial autocorrelation, we rely on the Moran's I test to determine whether spatial autocorrelation is present in our data. The null hypothesis of the Moran's I test is that the error term is independent and identically distributed (i.i.d.); in other words, no spatial autocorrelation is present within the residuals. To reject the null hypothesis means that spatial autocorrelation is present conditional on the specification of **W**, the weights (or neighbor) matrix. Following best practices, we conduct Moran's I tests on our key variables of interest for each of our **W** specifications.

Table C.17. *Moran's I test results for key variables under various W specifications*

| Dependent variable | W specification | Result |
|---|---|---|
| SDWA Health violations (2010–2016) | Inverse distance | $\chi^2 = 0.01$ (0.924) |
| | SES inverse distance | $\chi^2 = 0.18$ (0.668) |
| | % Black inverse distance | $\chi^2 = 0.58$ (0.447) |
| | % Hispanic inverse distance | $\chi^2 = 0.50$ (0.481) |
| Total kiosks | Inverse distance | $\chi^2 = 0.00$ (0.963) |
| | SES inverse distance | $\chi^2 = 0.18$ (0.670) |
| | % Black inverse distance | $\chi^2 = 0.47$ (0.493) |
| | % Hispanic inverse distance | $\chi^2 = 6.39$ (0.012) |

*Note*: Cells contain $\chi^2$ values for Moran's I test (*p*-values in parentheses).

The Moran's I test results indicate that health violations are not spatially clustered within the data across any of our definitions of space. There is spatial clustering in total kiosks only when **W** is defined based on communities' Hispanic population. A strict interpretation of these results would suggest employing a spatial model only using this network specification. However, the Moran's I test was developed for use against interval data; its application to count data is possibly limited and should be cautiously interpreted. Further, given our theoretical interests and that we are using the SLX model to test and adjudicate between different theoretical mechanisms, we employ all of our specifications of **W** in spite of the Moran's I test results.

Table C.18. *Model of number of kiosks in utility service areas, with neighbors defined by inverse geographic distance*

| SLX zero-inflated negative binomial regression | Kiosks | Kiosks |
|---|---|---|
| **Stage 2: Kiosk count** | | |
| SDWA health violations | 0.022 | 0.022 |
| | (0.040) | (0.039) |
| Spatial lag: SDWA health violations | | −0.126 |
| | | (0.349) |
| % Hispanic | −0.002 | −0.003 |
| | (0.616) | (0.560) |
| % Black | −0.008 | −0.008 |
| | (0.159) | (0.151) |
| % Renters | −0.214 | −0.021 |
| | (0.003) | (0.003) |
| SES | −0.947 | −0.950 |
| | (0.000) | (0.000) |
| Population (logged) | 1.133 | 1.129 |
| | (0.000) | (0.000) |
| Constant | −11.931 | −11.859 |
| | (0.000) | (0.000) |
| **Stage 1: Kiosk presence** | | |
| SDWA health violations (binary) | −0.563 | −0.550 |
| | (0.070) | (0.076) |
| Population (logged) | −0.271 | −0.274 |
| | (0.131) | (0.126) |
| Groundwater | −0.149 | −0.147 |
| | (0.691) | (0.693) |
| Private utility | −0.380 | −0.380 |
| | (0.456) | (0.405) |
| Constant | 2.189 | 2.236 |
| | (0.367) | (0.352) |
| State fixed effects? | Yes | Yes |
| Observations | 1,185 | 1,185 |
| AIC | 1,961.450 | 1,962.597 |
| BIC | 2,271.177 | 2,277.402 |

*Note*: Cells contain coefficients from an SLX zero-inflated negative binomial regression ($p$-values in parentheses).

Table C.19. *Model of number of kiosks in utility service areas, with neighbors defined by similarity in socioeconomic status*

| SLX zero-inflated negative binomial regression | Kiosks | Kiosks |
|---|---|---|
| **Stage 2: Kiosk count** | | |
| % Hispanic | –0.002 | 0.004 |
| | (0.616) | (0.422) |
| % Black | –0.008 | –0.007 |
| | (0.159) | (0.212) |
| % Renters | –0.021 | –0.026 |
| | (0.003) | (0.000) |
| Population (logged) | 1.113 | 1.057 |
| | (0.000) | (0.000) |
| SES | –0.947 | –0.998 |
| | (0.000) | (0.000) |
| SDWA health violations | 0.022 | 0.023 |
| | (0.040) | (0.026) |
| Spatial lag: SDWA health violations | | 3.737 |
| | | (0.000) |
| Constant | –11.931 | –18.056 |
| | (0.000) | (0.000) |
| **Stage 1: Kiosk presence** | | |
| SDWA health violations (binary) | –0.563 | –0.606 |
| | (0.070) | (0.049) |
| Population (logged) | –0.271 | –0.332 |
| | (0.131) | (0.069) |
| Groundwater | –0.149 | –0.041 |
| | (0.691) | (0.913) |
| Private utility | –0.380 | –0.396 |
| | (0.407) | (0.392) |
| Constant | 2.189 | 2.895 |
| | (0.367) | (0.238) |
| State fixed effects? | Yes | Yes |
| Observations | 1,185 | 1,185 |
| AIC | 1,961.450 | 1,942.860 |
| BIC | 2,271.177 | 2,257.665 |

*Note*: Cells contain coefficients from an SLX zero-inflated negative binomial regression ($p$-values in parentheses).

Table C.20. *Model of number of kiosks in utility service areas, with neighbors defined by similarity in percent Black population*

| SLX zero-inflated negative binomial regression | Kiosks | Kiosks |
|---|---|---|
| **Stage 2: Kiosk count** | | |
| % Hispanic | −0.002 | 0.001 |
| | (0.616) | (0.811) |
| % Black | −0.008 | 0.014 |
| | (0.159) | (0.186) |
| % Renters | −0.021 | −0.023 |
| | (0.003) | (0.001) |
| Population (logged) | 1.113 | 1.101 |
| | (0.000) | (0.000) |
| SES | −0.947 | −0.939 |
| | (0.000) | (0.000) |
| SDWA health violations | 0.022 | 0.024 |
| | (0.040) | (0.023) |
| Spatial lag: SDWA health violations | | 1.672 |
| | | (0.011) |
| Constant | −11.931 | −14.972 |
| | (0.000) | (0.000) |
| **Stage 1: Kiosk presence** | | |
| SDWA health violations (binary) | −0.563 | −0.585 |
| | (0.070) | (0.063) |
| Population (logged) | −0.271 | −0.247 |
| | (0.131) | (0.178) |
| Groundwater | −0.149 | −0.120 |
| | (0.691) | (0.752) |
| Private utility | −0.380 | −0.401 |
| | (0.407) | (0.392) |
| Constant | 2.189 | 1.844 |
| | (0.367) | (0.464) |
| State fixed effects? | Yes | Yes |
| Observations | 1,185 | 1,185 |
| AIC | 1,961.450 | 1,956.983 |
| BIC | 2,271.177 | 2,271.788 |

*Note*: Cells contain coefficients from an SLX zero-inflated negative binomial regression ($p$-values in parentheses).

**Table C.21.** *Model of number of kiosks in utility service areas, with neighbors defined by similarity in percent Hispanic population*

| SLX zero-inflated negative binomial regression | Kiosks | Kiosks |
|---|---|---|
| **Stage 2: Kiosk count** | | |
| % Hispanic | −0.002 | 0.004 |
| | (0.616) | (0.599) |
| % Black | −0.008 | −0.007 |
| | (0.159) | (0.213) |
| % Renters | −0.021 | −0.023 |
| | (0.003) | (0.001) |
| Population (logged) | 1.113 | 1.114 |
| | (0.000) | (0.000) |
| SES | −0.947 | −0.982 |
| | (0.000) | (0.000) |
| SDWA health violations | 0.022 | 0.021 |
| | (0.040) | (0.042) |
| Spatial lag: SDWA health violations | | 0.533 |
| | | (0.236) |
| Constant | −11.931 | −12.735 |
| | (0.000) | (0.000) |
| **Stage 1: Kiosk presence** | | |
| SDWA health violations (binary) | −0.563 | −0.561 |
| | (0.070) | (0.069) |
| Population (logged) | −0.271 | −0.285 |
| | (0.131) | (0.114) |
| Groundwater | −0.149 | −0.139 |
| | (0.691) | (0.710) |
| Private utility | −0.380 | −0.387 |
| | (0.407) | (0.397) |
| Constant | 2.189 | 2.366 |
| | (0.367) | (0.328) |
| State fixed effects? | Yes | Yes |
| Observations | 1,185 | 1,185 |
| AIC | 1,961.450 | 1,962.076 |
| BIC | 2,271.177 | 2,276.881 |

*Note*: Cells contain coefficients from an SLX zero-inflated negative binomial regression ($p$-values in parentheses).

## Counterfactual Effects on Providence, Rhode Island

To calculate the indirect effect of health violations in Flint, Michigan, on water kiosks in Providence, Rhode Island, we isolated the connection between Flint and Providence within each of our **W** matrices ($\mathbf{w}_{ij}$). Using this value, we calculated the indirect marginal effect of SDWA health violations in Flint on kiosks in Providence. Specifically, we calculated the predicted number of kiosks within Providence using $\mathbf{w}_{ij}$ and Providence's observed utility service area data and then calculated the marginal effect of a single health violation in Flint.

Table C.22. *Predicted probabilities of kiosks in Providence given SDWA health violations in Flint*

| **W** | $\mathbf{w}_{ij}$ | Predicted kiosks, given zero health violations in Flint | Predicted kiosks, given one health violation in Flint | Indirect effect of Flint on Providence |
|---|---|---|---|---|
| Socioeconomic status | 0.00088714 | 0.0020911 | 0.002098 | 0.0000069 |
| % Black population | 0.00063604 | 0.1102971 | 0.1104145 | 0.0001174 |
| % Hispanic population | 0.00067998 | 0.9532465 | 0.9535921 | 0.0003456 |

*Note*: Cells contain predicted probabilities and marginal effects calculated from an SLX zero-inflated negative binomial regression.

To calculate the indirect effect of health violations in all of Providence's neighbors on water kiosks in Providence, Rhode Island, we calculated the indirect marginal effect of SDWA violations in all of Providence's neighbors on kiosks in Providence. For each definition of neighbors (i.e., each **W** specification), we first calculated the predicted number of kiosks within Providence using all of its neighbors' SDWA health violations. Next, we calculated the predicted outcome of kiosks within Providence as if it were an "island" and had no neighbors. Using these paired values, we calculated the marginal effect of all of Providence's neighbors' SDWA violations on kiosks in Providence.

Table C.23. *Predicted number of kiosks in Providence given SDWA health violations in data set*

| W | Predicted kiosks in Providence, given neighbors' health violations | Predicted kiosks, given no neighbors | Indirect effect of all neighbors on Providence |
|---|---|---|---|
| Socioeconomic status | 2.199027 | 0.0020911 | 2.1969359 |
| % Black population | 2.604712 | 0.1102971 | 2.4944149 |
| % Hispanic population | 2.404085 | 0.9532465 | 1.4508385 |

*Note*: Cells contain predicted probabilities and marginal effects calculated from an SLX zero-inflated negative binomial regression.

## Chapter 5 Statistics

Table C.24. *Model of complaints to utility about tap water problems (NEXUS survey)*

| Outcome model: Probit regression | Probability of reporting tap water problems |
|---|---|
| Black | −2.935 |
| | (0.046) |
| Hispanic | −2.068 |
| | (0.178) |
| Log income | −0.283 |
| | (0.000) |
| Black × Log income | 0.285 |
| | (0.037) |
| Hispanic × Log income | 0.162 |
| | (0.255) |
| Homeowner | 0.339 |
| | (0.003) |
| Respondent pays water bill directly | 0.506 |
| | (0.000) |
| Party identification (1–7, Republican–Democrat) | 0.018 |
| | (0.417) |
| Constant | 1.328 |
| | (0.044) |

| Selection model: Probit regression | Likelihood of having a tap water problem |
|---|---|
| Log income | −0.201 |
| | (0.000) |
| Black | 0.149 |
| | (0.215) |
| Hispanic | −0.040 |
| | (0.735) |
| Constant | 2.058 |
| | (0.000) |
| Rho | 0.996 |
| Independence $X^2$ | 13.70 |
| Observations | 1,208 |
| $X^2$ | 53.86 |
| AIC | 2,323.318 |

*Note*: Cells contain coefficients generated by probit regression with Heckman selection (*p*-values in parentheses). Inverse probability weights applied in estimation.

Table C.25. *Models of bottled water consumption (CCES survey)*

| Logistic regression | Bottled water use (local distrust) | Bottled water use (state distrust) | Bottled water use (federal distrust) |
|---|---|---|---|
| Never trust local | 0.472 (0.087) | | |
| Never trust state | | 0.448 (0.068) | |
| Never trust federal | | | 0.424 (0.057) |
| Conservative | −0.037 (0.634) | −0.041 (0.605) | −0.013 (0.869) |
| Black | 0.771 (0.013) | 0.832 (0.009) | 0.790 (0.010) |
| Hispanic | 0.961 (0.005) | 0.984 (0.005) | 0.952 (0.009) |
| Income | −0.083 (0.006) | −0.080 (0.010) | −0.088 (0.004) |
| Female | −0.160 (0.425) | −0.172 (0.394) | −0.212 (0.299) |
| Age | 0.001 (0.933) | 0.001 (0.904) | −0.000 (0.960) |
| Constant | −0.380 (0.437) | −0.421 (0.391) | −0.425 (0.400) |
| Observations | 794 | 785 | 790 |
| $X^2$ | 26.77 | 26.69 | 26.17 |

*Note*: Cells contain coefficients generated by logistic regression ($p$-values in parentheses). Inverse probability weights applied in estimation.

**Table C.26.** *Models of political participation (CCES survey)*

| OLS/logit regression | Index of political participation (OLS) | Any political participation (logit) |
|---|---|---|
| Bottled water use | −0.337 | −0.626 |
| | (0.000) | (0.002) |
| Conservative | −0.238 | −0.284 |
| | (0.000) | (0.000) |
| Black | −0.393 | −0.377 |
| | (0.000) | (0.236) |
| Hispanic | −0.291 | −0.418 |
| | (0.042) | (0.213) |
| Income | 0.062 | 0.103 |
| | (0.000) | (0.000) |
| Female | −0.080 | 0.037 |
| | (0.399) | (0.831) |
| Age | 0.008 | 0.021 |
| | (0.004) | (0.000) |
| Constant | 0.971 | −1.124 |
| | (0.000) | (0.005) |
| Observations | 834 | 834 |
| $R^2$ | 0.117 | |
| $X^2$ | | 57.14 |

*Note*: Cells in left column contain coefficients generated by OLS regression; columns at right contain coefficients generated by logistic regression (*p*-values in parentheses). Inverse probability weights applied in estimation.

**Table C.27.** *Voter turnout and bottled water consumption (2011–2017), descriptive summary*

| Variable | Mean | Standard deviation | Minimum | Maximum |
|---|---|---|---|---|
| Turnou, gubernatorial elections (2011–2017) | 44.652 | 13.599 | 8.314 | 95.580 |
| Bottled water consumption | 58.885 | 5.141 | 43.589 | 129.493 |
| % Black | 10.295 | 15.270 | 0.000 | 85.900 |
| % Hispanic | 7.587 | 12.145 | 0.000 | 95.700 |
| SES | 0.000 | 1.000 | −4.517 | 3.299 |
| Unemployment | 8.277 | 3.634 | 0.000 | 29.600 |
| % Renter | 28.095 | 8.011 | 6.912 | 80.888 |
| Democratic % of major party | 39.286 | 14.882 | 1.100 | 90.100 |

N = 4,155

**Table C.28.** *Model of voter turnout in gubernatorial elections, 2011–2017*

| OLS regression | Turnout |
|---|---|
| Avg. bottled water expenditure per household | −0.259 |
| | (0.000) |
| % Black | 0.159 |
| | (0.000) |
| % Hispanic | −0.047 |
| | (0.000) |
| SES | 5.059 |
| | (0.000) |
| % Unemployed | −0.199 |
| | (0.000) |
| % Renter | −0.260 |
| | (0.000) |
| % Democratic vote | 0.032 |
| | (0.001) |
| Year 2011 | −0.613 |
| | (0.492) |
| Year 2012 | 19.065 |
| | (0.000) |
| Year 2013 | −3.951 |
| | (0.000) |
| Year 2014 | 3.339 |
| | (0.000) |
| Year 2015 | −0.522 |
| | (0.555) |
| Year 2016 | 23.967 |
| | (0.000) |
| Constant | 58.749 |
| | (0.000) |
| Observations | 4,155 |
| $R^2$ | 0.626 |

*Note*: Cells contain coefficients generated by OLS regression (*p*-values in parentheses).

## Chapter 6 Statistics

Table C.29. *North Carolina bottled water analysis, descriptive summary*

| Variable | Mean | Standard deviation | Minimum | Maximum |
|---|---|---|---|---|
| Bottled water sales per capita, 2017 | 24.321 | 1.338 | 20.462 | 27.529 |
| Not covered by Section 5, 1965 | 0.610 | 0.490 | 0 | 1 |
| SES, 2016 | 0.000 | 1.000 | 1.831 | 2.807 |
| % Renters, 2016 | 30.603 | 6.904 | 16.698 | 48.125 |
| % Black, 2016 | 21.537 | 16.639 | 0.400 | 62.300 |
| Population (logged), 2016 | 10.899 | 1.071 | 8.326 | 13.827 |

$N = 100$

*Note*: Unit of analysis is counties in North Carolina.

Table C.30. *Model of North Carolina bottled water sales by county, 2017*

| OLS regression | Bottled water per capita | Bottled water per capita |
|---|---|---|
| County not covered by Section 5 | 0.800 | 0.607 |
| | (0.014) | (0.024) |
| SES | 0.697 | 0.650 |
| | (0.000) | (0.000) |
| % Renters | −0.012 | −0.001 |
| | (0.632) | (0.966) |
| % Black | 0.012 | |
| | (0.274) | |
| Population (logged) | −0.128 | −0.150 |
| | (0.427) | (0.347) |
| Constant | 25.332 | 25.616 |
| | (0.000) | (0.000) |
| Observations | 100 | 100 |
| $R^2$ | 0.307 | 0.298 |

*Note*: Cells contain coefficients generated by OLS regression (*p*-values in parentheses).

**Table C.31.** *Appalachian bottled water sales analysis,*
*descriptive summary*

| Variable | Mean | Standard deviation | Minimum | Maximum |
|---|---|---|---|---|
| Bottled water revenue per capita | 23.726 | 1.662 | 12.879 | 32.058 |
| Appalachian county | 0.383 | 0.486 | 0 | 1 |
| SES | 0.328 | 1.077 | −3.412 | 4.565 |
| % Black | 18.083 | 18.951 | 0.000 | 86.200 |
| % Renters | 365.031 | 97.806 | 123.559 | 873.871 |
| Population (logged) | 10.590 | 1.193 | 7.209 | 14.774 |

N = 1,098

*Note*: Unit of analysis is counties in Appalachian region.

**Table C.32.** *Model of bottled water sales in Appalachian*
*states by county, 2017*

| OLS regression | Bottled water sales per capita |
|---|---|
| Appalachian county | 0.383 |
| | (0.001) |
| SES | 0.639 |
| | (0.000) |
| % Black | 0.003 |
| | (0.331) |
| % Renters | 0.001 |
| | (0.191) |
| Population (logged) | 0.009 |
| | (0.873) |
| Constant | 23.375 |
| | (0.000) |
| Observations | 1,098 |
| $R^2$ | 0.166 |

*Note*: Cells contain coefficients generated by OLS regression (*p*-values in parentheses).

**Table C.33.** *Houston, Texas, kiosk analysis, descriptive summary*

| Variable | Mean | Standard deviation | Minimum | Maximum |
|---|---|---|---|---|
| Total kiosks, 2017 | 0.213 | 0.564 | 0 | 4 |
| % Hispanic | 40.149 | 25.454 | 0.000 | 98.900 |
| % Black | 21.195 | 21.924 | 0.000 | 93.200 |
| SES | −0.001 | 1.00 | 2.404 | 2.702 |
| % Renters | 45.031 | 25.185 | 0.952 | 100.000 |
| Population (logged) | 8.539 | 0.595 | 2.197 | 11.021 |

N = 757

*Note*: Unit of analysis is Houston census tracts.

**Table C.34.** *Model of kiosks in Houston, Texas, census tracts, 2017*

| Negative binomial regression | Total kiosks |
|---|---|
| % Hispanic | 0.033 |
| | (0.000) |
| % Black | 0.004 |
| | (0.580) |
| SES | −0.020 |
| | (0.941) |
| % Renters | 0.004 |
| | (0.397) |
| Population (logged) | 0.075 |
| | (0.688) |
| Constant | −4.164 |
| | (0.016) |
| lnalpha | −0.123 |
| | (0.751) |
| Observations | 757 |
| $X^2$ | 88.22 |

*Note*: Cells contain coefficients generated by negative binomial regression (*p*-values in parentheses).

**Table C.35.** *Phoenix, Arizona, kiosk analysis, descriptive summary*

| Variable | Mean | Standard deviation | Minimum | Maximum |
|---|---|---|---|---|
| Total kiosks | 0.242 | 0.553 | 0 | 3 |
| % Hispanic | 38.319 | 27.121 | 1.400 | 94.000 |
| % Black | 7.605 | 7.002 | 0.000 | 44.700 |
| SES | 0.007 | 0.997 | 2.476 | 2.684 |
| % Renters | 45.803 | 22.891 | 1.892 | 99.528 |
| Population (logged) | 8.304 | 0.497 | 3.850 | 9.260 |

N = 393

*Note*: Unit of analysis is Phoenix census tracts.

**Table C.36.** *Model of kiosks in Phoenix, Arizona, census tracts, 2017*

| Negative binomial regression | Total kiosks |
|---|---|
| % Hispanic | 0.022 |
| | (0.014) |
| % Black | −0.002 |
| | (0.906) |
| SES | −0.430 |
| | (0.151) |
| % Renters | 0.005 |
| | (0.520) |
| Population (logged) | 0.519 |
| | (0.027) |
| Constant | −7.335 |
| | (0.000) |
| Observations | 393 |
| $X^2$ | 82.97 |

*Note*: Cells contain coefficients generated by negative binomial regression (*p*-values in parentheses).

Table C.37. *Southwestern state kiosk analysis, descriptive summary*

| Variable | Mean | Standard deviation | Minimum | Maximum |
|---|---|---|---|---|
| Total kiosks | 2.230 | 11.549 | 0 | 187 |
| % Hispanic | 27.166 | 21.544 | 0.500 | 99.000 |
| SES | −0.087 | 1.028 | 3.754 | 3.731 |
| % Black | 4.932 | 5.635 | 0.000 | 34.600 |
| % Renters | 30.056 | 8.377 | 6.912 | 73.684 |
| Population (logged) | 10.192 | 1.783 | 4.331 | 16.124 |
| Population density (pop. per square kilometer) | 64.141 | 336.463 | 0.044 | 6999.064 |

$N = 547$

*Note*: Unit of analysis is counties in southwestern states (i.e., California, Colorado, Nevada, New Mexico, Oklahoma, Texas, and Utah).

**Table C.38.** *Model of kiosks per county in eight southwestern states, 2017*

| Negative binomial regression | Total kiosks |
| --- | --- |
| % Hispanic | 0.020 |
| | (0.001) |
| SES | −0.425 |
| | (0.001) |
| % Black | −0.008 |
| | (0.669) |
| % Renters | 0.010 |
| | (0.522) |
| Population (logged) | 1.376 |
| | (0.000) |
| Population density | −1673.017 |
| | (0.001) |
| California | −0.922 |
| | (0.026) |
| Colorado | −0.812 |
| | (0.141) |
| Nevada | −0.051 |
| | (0.939) |
| New Mexico | 0.302 |
| | (0.537) |
| Oklahoma | 2.069 |
| | (0.000) |
| Texas | 0.786 |
| | (0.059) |
| Utah | −17.169 |
| | (0.992) |
| Constant | −16.972 |
| | (0.000) |
| Observations | 547 |
| $X^2$ | 429.03 |

*Note*: Cells contain coefficients generated by negative binomial regression (*p*-values in parentheses). Analysis of counties in Arizona, California, Colorado, Nevada, New Mexico, Oklahoma, Texas, and Utah. Arizona is the reference category. Population density entered as population per square meter.

## Chapter 7 Statistics

**Table C.39.** *Model of support for rate increases (2018, 2020 VOW survey)*

| Logistic regression | Tap vs. bottled | Plain tap vs. filtered tap vs. bottled |
|---|---|---|
| **Primary drinking water** | | |
| Tap water (plain or filtered) | 1.390 | |
| | (0.033) | |
| Plain tap | | 1.533 |
| | | (0.018) |
| Filtered tap | | 1.298 |
| | | (0.121) |
| Party identification | 0.833 | 0.833 |
| (1–7, Democrat– | (0.000) | (0.000) |
| Republican) | | |
| 2020 | 0.803 | 0.808 |
| | (0.123) | (0.132) |
| Constant | 5.800 | 5.793 |
| | (0.000) | (0.000) |
| Observations | 1737 | 1737 |
| $X^2$ | 41.79 | 42.44 |

*Note*: Analysis of 2018 and 2020 Value of Water survey data. Cells contain odds ratios generated by logistic regression (*p*-values in parentheses). Inverse probability weights applied in estimation.

**Table C.40.** *Turnout and SDWA compliance analysis, descriptive summary*

| Variable | Mean | Standard deviation | Minimum | Maximum |
|---|---|---|---|---|
| SDWA health violations, 2013–2019 | 0.480 | 2.168 | 0 | 26 |
| % Turnout | 74.318 | 7.734 | 52.898 | 88.325 |
| %Registered Democratic voters | 58.489 | 15.705 | 24.592 | 93.449 |
| % Black | 4.340 | 5.134 | 0.000 | 42.402 |
| % Hispanic | 36.425 | 22.875 | 4.061 | 97.488 |
| Groundwater (0/1) | 0.350 | 0.478 | 0.000 | 1.000 |
| Purchased water (0/1) | 0.434 | 0.496 | 0.000 | 1.000 |
| Logged population | 10.566 | 1.130 | 7.395 | 15.185 |
| SES | 0.000 | 1.000 | –2.187 | 3.713 |

*N* = 408

*Note*: Unit of analysis is water utilities in California.

**Table C.41.** *Model of SDWA violations in California, 2013–2019*

| Negative binomial regression | Health violations |
|---|---|
| % Turnout | −0.092 |
| | (0.014) |
| % Registered Democratic voters | 0.002 |
| | (0.864) |
| % Black | −0.074 |
| | (0.125) |
| % Hispanic | 0.020 |
| | (0.218) |
| Groundwater | −1.258 |
| | (0.020) |
| Purchased water | −1.330 |
| | (0.006) |
| Logged population | −0.447 |
| | (0.004) |
| SES | 0.274 |
| | (0.456) |
| Constant | 10.817 |
| | (0.003) |
| Observations | 408 |
| $X^2$ | 30.51 |

*Note*: Cells contain coefficients generated by negative binomial regression (*p*-values in parentheses).

# References

Aaker, David A. 2009. *Managing Brand Equity.* New York: Simon & Schuster.

Aberbach, Joel D., & Jack L. Walker. 1973. *Race in the City: Political Trust and Public Policy in the New Urban System.* Boston: Little, Brown.

Abrahams, Nii Adote, Bryan J. Hubbell, & Jeffrey L. Jordan. 2000. "Joint production and averting expenditure measures of willingness to pay: Do water expenditures really measure avoidance costs?" *American Journal of Agricultural Economics* 82(2): 427–437.

Aguilar, John. 2021. "Campaign to recall city leaders over Westminster's water price hikes heads to court." *Denver Post,* January 20. www .denverpost.com/2021/01/08/westminster-water-bills-recall-election/.

Allaire, Maura, Haowei Wu, & Upmanu Lall. 2018. "National trends in drinking water quality violations." *PNAS* 118(9): 2078–2083.

Alsan, Marcella, & Marianne Wanamaker. 2018. "Tuskegee and the health of black men." *Quarterly Journal of Economics* 133(1): 407–455.

American Water Works Association (AWWA). 2017. *Buried No Longer: Confronting America's Water Infrastructure Challenge.* Denver, CO: AWWA.

An, Seung-Ho. 2019. "Employee voluntary and involuntary turnover and organizational performance: Revisiting the hypothesis from classical public administration." *International Public Management Journal* 22 (3): 444–469.

Anguelov, Dragomir, Carole Dulong, Daniel Filip, Christian Frueh, Stéphane Lafon, Richard Lyon, Abhijit Ogale, Luc Vincent, and Josh Weaver. 2010. "Google Street View: Capturing the world at street level." *Computer* 43(6): 32–38.

Anoll, Allison P. 2018. "What makes a good neighbor? Race, place, and norms of political participation." *American Political Science Review* 112(3): 494–508.

Anselin, Luc. 1988. "Lagrange multiplier test diagnostics for spatial dependence and spatial heterogeneity." *Geographical Analysis* 20(1): 1–17.

Appalachian Regional Commission. 2015. "Appalachia then and now: Examining changes to the Appalachian region since 1965." Center for

Regional   Economic   Competitiveness.   www.arc.gov/wp-content/
uploads/2020/06/AppalachiaThenAndNowCompiledReports.pdf

Arcipowski, Erin, John Schwartz, Lisa Davenport, Meghan Hayes, and
Tracy Nolan. 2017. "Clean water, clean life: Promoting healthier,
accessible water in rural Appalachia." *Journal of Contemporary
Water Research & Education* 161(1): 1–18.

Arumugam, Nadia. 2011. "Why minorities reach for bottled water over tap
& how marketers persuade them." *Forbes*, August 11. www.forbes
.com/sites/nadiaarumugam/2011/08/11/why-minorities-reach-for-
bottled-water-over-tap-how-marketers-drive-habit/?sh=39ef77475d70.

Balazs, Carolina, Rachel Morello-Frosch, Alan Hubbard, and Isha Ray.
2011. "Social disparities in nitrate-contaminated drinking water in
California's San Joaquin Valley." *Environmental Health Perspectives*
119(9): 1272–1278.

Balazs, Carolina L., and Isha Ray. 2014. "The drinking water disparities
framework: On the origins and persistence of inequities in exposure."
*American Journal of Public Health* 104(4): 603–611.

Ballou, Dale, & Michael Podgursky. 1999. "Teacher recruitment and retention in public and private schools." *Journal of Policy Analysis and
Management* 17(3): 393– 417.

Bartlett, Steve, Henry Cisneros, Patrick Decker, George Heartwell, & Aldie
Warnock. 2017. *Safeguarding Water Affordability*. Washington, DC:
Bipartisan Policy Center.

Beck, Nathaniel, Kristian Skrede Gleditsch, & Kyle Beardsley. 2006. "Space
is more than geography: Using spatial econometrics in the study of
political economy." *International Studies Quarterly* 50(1): 27–44.

Beecher, Janice A. 1999. "Consolidated water rates: Issues and practices in
single-tariff pricing." Report to the US Environmental Protection
Agency and the National Association of Regulatory Utility
Commissioners. Washington, DC: US EPA.

Benavides, Abraham David, Julius Nukpezah, Laura Marie Keyes, & Ismail
Soujaa. 2020. "Adoption of multilingual state emergency management
websites: Responsiveness to the risk communication needs of a multilingual society." *International Journal of Public Administration* 44(5):
409–419.

Bevir, Mark. 2013. "Legitimacy and the administrative state: Ontology,
history, and democracy." *Public Administration Quarterly* 37(4):
535–549.

Bliss, Laura. 2016. "How democracy died in Flint." Bloomberg CityLab,
January 20. www.bloomberg.com/news/articles/2016-02-04/first-con
gressional-hearing-on-flint-water-crisis-shows-how-democracy-failed.

Bowler, Betty Miller. 1985. "That ribbon of social neglect: Appalachia and the media in 1964." *Appalachian Journal* 12(3): 239–247.

Brady, Henry, Sidney Verba, & Kay Lehman Schlozman. 1995. "Beyond SES: A resource model of political participation." *American Political Science Review* 89(2): 271–294.

Braumeister, Roy F., Ellen Bratslavsky, Catrin Finkenauer, & Kathleen D. Vohs. 2001. "Bad is stronger than good." *Review of General Psychology* 5(4): 323–370.

Brentwood Associates. 2021. "Brentwood Associates invests in Watermill Express." Press release, May 3.

Brewer, Gene A., & Sally Coleman Selden. 2000. "Why elephants gallop: Assessing and predicting organizational performance in federal agencies." *Journal of Public Administration Research and Theory* 10(4): 685–712.

Breyer, Stephen. 1984. *Regulation and Its Reform*. Cambridge, MA: Harvard University Press.

Bridges, Amy. 1999. *Morning Glories: Municipal Reform in the Southwest*. Princeton, NJ: Princeton University Press.

Brown, Mary Jean, & Stephen Margolis. 2012. "Lead in drinking water and human blood levels in the United States." *Morbidity and Mortality Weekly Report*, Vol. 61 Supplement: 1–9. Centers for Disease Control and Prevention.

Buell, Ryan W., Ethan Porter, & Michael I. Norton. 2020. "Surfacing the submerged state: Operational transparency increases trust in and engagement with government." *Manufacturing & Service Operations Management* 23(4). https://doi.org/10.1287/msom.2020.0877.

Čapek, Stella M. 1993. "The 'environmental justice' frame: A conceptual discussion and an application." *Social Problems* 40(1): 5–24.

Carlson, Darren K. 2002. "Racial divide: Crime and police protection." *Gallup Poll Tuesday Briefing*, October 29.

Carpenter, Daniel. 2000. "State building through reputation building: Coalitions of esteem and program innovation in the national postal system, 1883–1913." *Studies in American Political Development* 14 (2): 121–155.

   2001. *The Forging of Bureaucratic Autonomy*. Princeton, NJ: Princeton University Press.

   2010. "Reputation, information and confidence: The political economy of pharmaceutical regulation." In Daniel A. Farber and Anne Joseph O'Connell, *Research Handbook on Public Choice and Public Law*. Cheltenham, UK: Edward Elgar.

Carpenter, Daniel, & George A. Krause. 2012. "Reputation and public administration." *Public Administration Review* 72(1): 26–32.

Cascio, Elizabeth U., and Ebonya Washington. 2014. "Valuing the vote: The redistribution of voting rights and state funds following the Voting Rights Act of 1965." *Quarterly Journal of Economics* 129(1): 379–433.

Cavallo, Sara, Joann Lynch, & Peter Scull. 2014. "The digital divide in citizen-initiated government contacts: A GIS approach." *Journal of Urban Technology* 21(4): 77–93.

Clark, William Roberts, Matt Golder, & Sona N. Golder. 2017. "An exit, voice and loyalty model of politics." *British Journal of Political Science* 47(4): 719–748.

Clarke, Philippa, Jennifer Ailshire, Robert Melendez, Michael Bader, & Jeffrey Morenoff. 2010. "Using Google Earth to conduct a neighborhood audit: Reliability of a virtual audit instrument." *Health & Place* 16(6): 1224–1229.

Cobb-Walgren, Cathy J., Cynthia A. Ruble, & Naveen Donthu. 1995. "Brand equity, brand preference, and purchase intent." *Journal of Advertising* 24(3): 25–40.

COMO Safe Water Coalition. 2020. Facebook post, August 4. www.facebook.com/COMOSafeWater/.

Contreras, Daniel A., & Neil Brodie. 2010. "The utility of publicly-available satellite imagery for investigating looting of archaeological sites in Jordan." *Journal of Field Archaeology* 35(1): 101–114.

Cook, Scott J., Seung-Ho An, and Nathan Favero. 2019. "Beyond policy diffusion: Spatial econometric models of public administration." *Journal of Public Administration Research and Theory* 29(4): 591–608.

Cook, Scott J., Jude C. Hays, and Robert J. Franzese. 2015. "Model specification and spatial interdependence." American Political Science Association conference paper. http://www.sas.rochester.edu/psc/polmeth/papers/Cook_Hays_Franzese.pdf.

  2020. "Model specification and spatial interdependence." In Luigi Curini and Robert Franzese, eds., *The SAGE Handbook of Research Methods in Political Science and International Relation*. London: Sage, 730–747.

Crook, T. Russell, Samuel Y. Todd, James G. Combs, David J. Woehr, & David J. Ketchen Jr. 2011. "Does human capital matter? A meta-analysis of the relationship between human capital and firm performance." *Journal of Applied Psychology* 96(3): 443–456.

Dahl, Robert A. 1961. *Who Governs?* New Haven, CT: Yale University Press.

Davis, Matthew M., Chris Kolb, Lawrence Reynolds, Eric Rothstein, & Ken Sikkema. 2016. *Flint Advisory Task Force Final Report*. Office of the Governor of Michigan.

Debbler, Luka Johanna, Martina Gamp, Michael Blumenschein, Daniel Keim, & Britta Renner. 2018. "Polarized but illusory beliefs about tap and bottled water: A product- and consumer-oriented survey and blind tasting experiment," *Science of the Total Environment* 643: 1400–1410.

DeHoog, Ruth Hoogland, David Lowery, & William E. Lyons. 1990. "Citizen satisfaction with local governance: A test of individual, juris-dictional, and city-specific explanations." *Journal of Politics* 52(3): 807–837.

D'Emidio, Tony, Jonah Wagner, Sarah Greenberg, Kevin Heidenrich, Julia Klier, & Thomas Weber. 2019. "The global case for customer experi-ence in government." McKinsey & Company. www.mckinsey.com/industries/public-and-social-sector/our-insights/the-global-case-for-cus tomer-experience-in-government.

Dolifka, Lani. 2017a. "My passion for clean water advocacy catapulted my business." *Business Daily News*, November 5. www.businessnewsdaily .com/9857-lani-dolifka-watermill-express.html.

2017b. "Why we need clean water here." *Water Online*, March 17. www .wateronline.com/doc/why-we-need-clean-water-here-0001.

Doria, Miguel de França, Nick Pidgeon, & Paul R. Hunter. 2009. "Perceptions of drinking water quality and risk and its effect on behav-ior: A cross-national study." *Science of the Total Environment* 407(21): 5455–5464.

Douglas, Thomas J. 1976. "Safe Drinking Water Act of 1974: History and critique." *Environmental Affairs* 5: 501–543.

Dowding, Keith, & Peter John. 1996. "Exiting behavior under Tiebout conditions: Towards a predictive model." *Public Choice* 88(3–4): 393–406.

2012. *Exits, Voices and Social Investment: Citizens' Reaction to Public Services*. Cambridge: Cambridge University Press.

Drewnowski, Adam, Colin D. Rehm, & Florence Constant. 2013. "Water and beverage consumption among adults in the United States: Cross-sectional study using data from NHANES 2005–2010." *BMC Public Health* 13: 1068.

Dupont, Diane P., & Nowshin Jahan. 2012. "Defensive spending on tap water substitutes: The value of reducing perceived health risks." *Journal of Water and Health* 10(1): 56–68.

Eggers, William D., Bruce Chew, Joshua Knight, Robert Krawiec, & Mahesh Kelkar. 2021. "Rebuilding trust in government." Deloitte Insights. www2.deloitte.com/content/dam/insights/articles/6971_DI-Building-greater-trust-in-government/DI_Building-greater-trust-in-governmen t_2.pdf.

Einstein, Katherine Levine, Maxwell Palmer, and David M. Glick. 2019. "Who participates in local government? Evidence from meeting minutes." *Perspectives on Politics* 17(1): 28–46.

Elhorst, J. Paul. 2014. *Spatial Econometrics: From Cross-Sectional Data to Spatial Panels* (Vol. 479). Berlin: Springer.

Erdem, Tülin, & Joffre Swait. 1998. "Brand equity as a signaling phenomenon." *Journal of Consumer Psychology* 7(2): 131–157.

Faircloth, James B., Louis M. Capella, & Bruce L. Alford. 2001. "The effect of brand attitude and brand image on brand equity." *Journal of Marketing Theory and Practice* 9(3): 61–75.

Family, Leila, Guili Zheng, Maritza Cabezas, Jennifer Cloud, Shelly Hsu, Elizabeth Rubin, Lisa V. Smith, & Tony Kuo. 2019. "Reasons why low-income people in urban areas do not drink tap water." *Journal of the American Dental Association* 150(6): 503–513.

Favero, Nathan, & Minjung Kim. 2020. "Everything is relative: How citizens form and use expectations in evaluating services." *Journal of Public Administration Research & Theory* 31(3): 561–577.

Feldkamp, Kaleigh. 2018. "Columbia voters approve bond issue by large margins." *Columbia Missourian*, January 20. www.columbiamissourian .com/news/elections/columbia-voters-approve-water-bond-issue-by-large-margin/article_63570d02-9a75-11e8-865f-8fa42629aa63.html.

Feldkamp, Kaleigh, and Matthew Hall. 2018. "Voters to decide $42.8 million water bond issue Tuesday." *Columbia Missourian*, January 20. www.columbiamissourian.com/news/elections/voters-to-decide-42-8-million-water-bond-issue-tuesday/article_d1145fc0-941c-11e8-8240-17bb81ddcb03.html.

Filer, John E., Lawrence W. Kenny, and Rebecca B. Morton. 1991. "Voting laws, educational policies, and minority turnout." *Journal of Law and Economics* 34(2): 371–393.

Fiorina, Morris P. 1978. "Economic retrospective voting in American national elections: A micro-analysis." *American Journal of Political Science* 22(2): 426–443.

Fonger, Ron. 2018. "EPA whistleblower says he warned Michigan DEQ it was wrong about Flint Water." Mlive.com, January 27. www.mlive .com/news/flint/2018/08/epa_whistleblower_testifies_de.html.

Fox, Susannah, & Oliver Lewis. 2001. *Fear of Online Crime: Americans Support FBI Interception of Criminal Suspects' Email and New Laws to Protect Online Privacy*. Washington, DC: Pew Internet & American Life Project.

Foxall, Gordon R., Jorge M. Oliveira-Castro, & Teresa C. Schrezenmaier. 2004. "The behavioral economics of consumer brand choice: Patterns of reinforcement and utility maximization." *Behavioural Processes* 66 (3): 235–260.

Foxall, Gordon R., & Teresa C. Schrezenmaier. 2003. "The behavioral economics of consumer brand choice: Establishing a methodology." *Journal of Economic Psychology* 24(5): 675–695.

Franzese, Robert J., & Jude C. Hays. 2008. "Empirical models of spatial interdependence." In Janet Box-Steffensmeier, Henry Brady, & David Collier (Eds.), *Oxford Handbook of Political Methodology*. Oxford: Oxford University Press.

Fukuyama, Francis. 1995. *Trust: The Social Virtues and the Creation of Prosperity*. New York: Free Press.

Garcia, Bianca, & Manuel Hernandez Jr. 2011. "Water Commodification in the Lower Rio Grande Valley, Texas." Undergraduate Research Scholars' thesis, Texas A&M University.

Garcia, John A. 1986. "The Voting Rights Act and Hispanic political representation in the Southwest." *Publius: The Journal of Federalism* 16(4): 49–66.

Garrett, Olivia. 2018. "$42.8 million water bond would pay for treatment plant expansion." *Columbia Missourian*, January 5. www.columbiamissourian.com/news/local/million-water-bond-would-pay-for-treatment-plant-expansion/article_7d189a8a-5065-11e8-9e2c-6fa10de60664.html.

Gelbach, Scott. 2006. "A formal model of exit and voice." *Rationality and Society* 18(4): 395–418.

Gironi, Fausto, & Vincenzo Piemonte. 2011. "Life cycle assessment of polylactic acid and polyethylene terephthalate bottles for drinking water." *Environmental Progress & Sustainable Energy* 30(3): 459–468.

Gitlitz, Jennifer, & Pat Franklin. 2007. "Water, water everywhere: The growth of noncarbonated beverages in the United States." Container Recycling Institute. https://www.container-recycling.org/assets/pdfs/reports/2007-waterwater.pdf.

Gleick, Peter H. 2010. *Bottled and Sold: The Story behind Our Obsession with Bottled Water*. Washington, DC: Island Press.

Gleick, Peter H., & Heather S. Cooley. 2009. "Energy implications of bottled water." *Environmental Research Letters* 4(1): 014009.

Goetz, Stephan J., & Sundar S. Shrestha. 2009. "Explaining self-employment success and failure: Wal-Mart versus Starbucks, or Schumpeter versus Putnam." *Social Science Quarterly* 90(1): 22–38.

Goldman Environmental Prize. 2018, April 22. "Leanne Walters, 2018 Goldman Environmental Prize, United States." [Video] YouTube. www.youtube.com/watch?v=hpFNG8DDTrs&feature=emb_title.

2018. "LeAnne Walters: 2018 Goldman Prize Recipient North America." www.goldmanprize.org/recipient/leeanne-walters/.

Gonzalez, Ana. 2021. "This Texas H-E-B allowed customers to pick out groceries for free during the winter freeze." Click2Houston.com, February 23. www.click2houston.com/news/texas/2021/02/23/this-texas-h-e-b-allowed-customers-to-pick-out-groceries-for-free-during-winter-freeze/.

Gormley, William T., & David L. Weimer. 1999. *Organizational Report Cards*. Cambridge, MA: Harvard University Press.

Graydon, Ryan Christopher, Paola Andrea Gonzalez, Abdiel Elias Laureano-Rosario, & Guillermo Reginald Pradieu. 2019. "Bottled water versus tap water." *International Journal of Sustainability in Higher Education* 20(4): 654–674.

Green, Bernard Lee, Richard Maislak, Min Qui Wang, Marcia F. Britt, & Nonie Ebeling. 1997. "Participation in health education, health promotion, and health research by African Americans: Effects of the Tuskegee syphilis experiment." *Journal of Health Education* 28(4): 196–201.

Grodzins, Morton. 1964. *The American System*. Chicago: Rand McNally.

Grofman, Bernard, and Lisa Handley. 1991. "The impact of the Voting Rights Act on black representation in southern state legislatures." *Legislative Studies Quarterly* 16(1): 111–128.

Hajnal, Zoltan, Nazita Lajevardi, and Lindsay Nielson. 2017. "Voter identification laws and the suppression of minority votes." *Journal of Politics* 79(2): 363–379.

Hajnal, Zoltan L., and Paul G. Lewis. 2003. "Municipal institutions and voter turnout in local elections." *Urban Affairs Review* 38 (5): 645–668.

Handley, Lisa, Bernard Grofman, & Wayne Arden. 1998. "Electing minority-preferred candidates to legislative office." In Bernard Grofman, ed., *Race and Redistricting in the 1990s*. New York: Algora, 13–38.

Hansen, Katy, Shadi Eskaf, & Megan Mullin. 2022. "Avoiding punishment? Electoral accountability for local fee increases." *Urban Affairs Review* 58(3): 888–906.

Heckman, James J. 1979. "Sample selection bias as a specification error." *Econometrica* 47(1): 153–161.

Hendry, David. F. 1995. *Dynamic Econometrics*. Oxford: Oxford University Press.

Hetherington, Marc J. 2005. *Why Trust Matters: Declining Political Trust and the Demise of American Liberalism*. Princeton, NJ: Princeton University Press.

Hillier, Amy E. 2003. "Redlining and the Home Owners' Loan Corporation." *Journal of Urban History* 29(4): 394–420.

Hine, Thomas. 1995. "Glacier's technology is a public water woe." *Albany Times Union*, September 25, C1.

Hird, John A., & Michael Reese. 1998. "The distribution of environmental quality: An empirical analysis." *Social Science Quarterly* 79(4): 693–716.

Hirschman, Albert O. 1970. *Exit, Voice, and Loyalty: Reponses to Decline in Firms, Organizations, and States.* Cambridge, MA: Harvard University Press.

Hirschman, Elizabeth, Stephen Brown, & Pauline Maclaran. 2007. *Two Continents, One Culture: The Scotch-Irish in Southern Appalachia.* Johnson City, TN: Overmountain Press.

Hobson, Wendy L., Miguel L. Knochel, Carrie L. Byington, Paul C. Young, Charles J. Hoff, & Karen F. Buchi. 2007. "Bottled, filtered, and tap water use in Latino and Non-Latino children." *Archives of Pediatrics & Adolescent Medicine* 161(5): 457–461.

Howell, Junia, & Elizabeth Korver-Glenn. 2020. "The Increasing Effect of Neighborhood Racial Composition on Housing Values, 1980–2015." *Social Problems* 68(4): 1051–1071.

Howell, Susan E. 2007. *Race, Performance, and Approval of Mayors.* New York: Palgrave MacMillan.

Hu, Zhihua, Lois Wright Morton, & Robert Mahler. 2011. "Bottled water: United States consumers and their perceptions of water quality." *International Journal of Environmental Research and Public Health* 8 (2): 565–578.

Huerta-Saenz, Lina, Matilde Irigoyen, Jorge Benavides, & Maria Mendoza. 2012. "Tap or bottled water: Drinking preferences among urban minority children and adolescents." *Journal of Community Health* 37(1): 54–58.

Hughes, Jeff, Richard Whisnant, Lynn Weller, Shadi Eskaf, Matthew Richardson, Scott Morrissey, & Ben Altz-Stamm. 2005. *Drinking Water and Wastewater Infrastructure in Appalachia.* Chapel Hill: UNC Environmental Finance Center.

Hughes, Sara. 2021. "Flint, Michigan, and the politics of safe drinking water in the United States." *Perspectives on Politics* 19(4): 1219–1232.

Hughes, Sara, Stephanie Pincetl, & Christopher Boone. 2013. "Triple exposure: Regulatory, climatic, and political drivers of water management changes in the city of Los Angeles." *Cities* 32: 51–59.

Ikem, Abua, Seyi Odueyungbo, Nosa O. Egiebor, & Kafui Nyavor. 2002. "Chemical quality of bottled waters from three cities in Eastern Alabama." *Science of the Total Environment* 285(1): 165–175.

Ireland, Patrick R. 2014. "Cracker craic: The politics and economics of Scots-Irish cultural promotion in the USA." *International Journal of Cultural Policy* 20(4): 399–421.

Javidi, Ariana, & Gregory Pierce. 2018. "U.S. households' perception of drinking water as unsafe and its consequences: Examining alternative choices to tap." *Water Resources Research* 54(9): 6100–6113.

Jefferson, Greg. 2021. "Opinion: Why H-E-B comes through in a crisis when Texas government doesn't." *San Antonio Express-News*, February 19. www.houstonchronicle.com/business/article/H-E-B-winter-storm-Abbott-Texas-power-grid-15964779.php.

Jensen, Vivian, Tarrah Henrie, Jeannie Darby, & Janet Clements. 2020. "An affordability assessment of consolidated management of nitrate treatment." *AWWA Water Science* 2(6): e1209.

Jepson, Wendy. 2012. "Claiming space, claiming water: Contested legal geographies of water in South Texas." *Annals of the Association of American Geographers* 102(3): 614–631.

Jepson, Wendy, & Heather Lee Brown. 2014. "'If no gasoline, no water': Privatizing drinking water quality in South Texas colonias." *Environment and Planning A* 46(5): 1032–1048.

Jepson, Wendy, & Emily Vandewalle. 2016. "Household water insecurity in the global north: A study of rural and periurban settlements on the Texas-Mexico border." *Professional Geographer* 68(1): 66–81.

Johnson, Branden B. 2000. "Utility customers' views of the Consumer Confidence Report of Drinking Water Quality." *RISK: Health, Safety & Environment* 11(4): 309–328.

Jungbluth, Niels. 2005. "Comparison of the environmental impact of tap water vs. bottled mineral water." Zürich: Swiss Gas and Water Association.

Kanouse, David E., & L. Reid Hanson Jr. 1972. "Negativity in evaluations." In Edward E. Jones, David E. Kanouse, Richard E. Nesbitt, Stuart Valins, and Bernard Weiner, eds., *Attribution: Perceiving the Causes of Behavior*. Morristown, NJ: General Learning, 47–62.

Kane, Joseph W. 2018. "Water affordability is not just a local challenge, but a federal one too." *The Avenue* (blog), Brookings Institution, January 25. https://www.brookings.edu/blog/the-avenue/2018/01/25/water-affordability-is-not-just-a-local-challenge-but-a-federal-one-too/.

Kang, Minjeong, & Young Eun Park. 2017. "Exploring trust and distrust as conceptually and empirically distinct constructs: Association with symmetrical communication and public engagement across four pairings of trust and distrust." *Journal of Public Relations Research* 29(2–3): 114–135.

Keller, Kevin Lane. 1993. "Conceptualizing, measuring, and managing customer-based brand equity." *Journal of Marketing* 57(1): 1–22.

Kettl, Donald F. 2017. *Can Governments Earn Our Trust?* Malden, MA: Polity Press.

2019. "From policy to practice: From ideas to results, from results to trust." *Public Administration Review* 79(5): 763–767.

Kettl, Donald F., & Anne Khademian. 2020. "Building trust in government one problem at a time: Public administration needs a new social contract." *Government Executive*, July 14. www.govexec.com/management/2020/07/building-trust-government-one-problem-time/166878/.

Konisky, David M. 2009. "Inequities in enforcement? Environmental justice and government performance." *Journal of Policy Analysis and Management* 28(1): 102–121.

Konisky, David M., & Christopher Reenock. 2013. "Compliance bias and environmental (in)justice." *Journal of Politics* 75 (2): 506–519.

Konisky, David M., & Tyler S. Schario. 2010. "Examining environmental justice in facility-level regulatory enforcement." *Social Science Quarterly* 91(3): 835–855.

Konisky, David M., & Manuel P. Teodoro. 2016. "When governments regulate governments." *American Journal of Political Science* 60(3): 559–574.

Koran, Mario. 2019. "Californians are turning to vending machines for safer water. Are they being swindled?" *The Guardian*, December 2. https://www.theguardian.com/us-news/2019/dec/02/california-water-vending-machines-quality.

Krause, George A., & James A. Douglas. 2005. "Institutional design versus reputational effects on bureaucratic performance: Evidence from US government macroeconomic and fiscal projections." *Journal of Public Administration Research and Theory* 15(2): 281–306.

Krishnamurthi, Lakshman, & Sudha P. Raj. 1991. "An empirical analysis of the relationship between brand loyalty and consumer price elasticity." *Marketing Science* 10(2): 172–183.

Krometis, Leigh-Anne, Hannah Patton, Austin Wozniak, and Emily Sarver. 2019. "Water scavenging from roadside springs in Appalachia." *Journal of Contemporary Water Research & Education* 166(1): 46–56.

Lakhani, Nina. 2020. "'It smells bad, it tastes bad': How Americans stopped trusting their water." *The Guardian*, September 22. www.theguardian.com/us-news/2020/sep/22/martin-county-kentucky-tap-water.

Lane, Vicki, & Robert Jacobson. 1995. "Stock market reactions to brand extension announcements: The effects of brand attitude and familiarity." *Journal of Marketing* 59(1): 63–77.

Lanz, Bruno, & Allan Provins. 2016. "The demands for tap water quality: Survey evidence on water hardness and aesthetic quality." *Water Resources and Economics* 16: 52–63.

Lassar, Walfried, Banwari Mittal, & Arun Sharma. 1995. "Measuring customer-based brand equity." *Journal of Consumer Marketing* 12(4): 11–19.

Lasswell, Harold D. 1936. *Politics: Who Gets What, When, How.* New York: Whittlesey House.

Lau, Richard R. 1985. "Two explanations for negativity effects in political behavior." *American Journal of Political Science* 29(1): 119–138.

Lee, Mordecai. 2011. *Congress vs. the Bureaucracy: Muzzling Agency Public Relations.* Norman: University of Oklahoma Press.

Lee, Shinwoo. 2018. "Employee turnover and organizational performance in US federal agencies." *American Review of Public Administration* 48(6): 522–534.

Lee, Soo-Young, & Andrew B. Whitford. 2013. "Assessing the effects of organizational resources on public agency performance: Evidence from the US federal government." *Journal of Public Administration Research & Theory* 23(3): 687–712.

Leighley, Jan E., & Arnold Vedlitz. 1999. "Race, ethnicity, and political participation: Competing models and contrasting explanations." *Journal of Politics* 61(4): 1092–1114.

Lerman, Amy E. 2019. *Good Enough for Government Work: The Public Reputation Crisis in America (and What We Can Do to Fix It).* Chicago: University of Chicago Press.

LeRoux, Kelly, & Sanjay K. Pandey. 2011. "City managers, career incentives, and municipal service decisions: The effects of managerial progressive ambition on interlocal service delivery." *Public Administration Review* 71(4): 627–636.

Levêque, Jonas G., & Robert C. Burns. 2017. "Predicting water filter and bottled water use in Appalachia: A community-scale case study." *Journal of Water & Health* 15(3): 451–461.

2018. "Drinking water in West Virginia (USA): Tap water or bottled water – what is the right choice for college students?" *Journal of Water & Health* 16(5): 827–838.

Levi, Margaret, & Laura Stoker. 2000. "Political trust and trustworthiness." *Annual Review of Political Science* 3(1): 475–507.

Levin, Ronnie B., Paul R. Epstein, Tim E. Ford, Winston Harrington, Erik Olson, & Eric G. Reichard. 2002. "US drinking water challenges in the twenty-first century." *Environmental Health Perspectives* 110 (Suppl 1): 43–52.

Lewin, Philip G. 2017. "'Coal is not just a job, it's a way of life': The cultural politics of coal production in central Appalachia." *Social Problems* 66 (1): 51–68.

Li, Yanmei, Mary V. Wenning, & Hazel A. Morrow-Jones. 2013. "Differences in neighborhood satisfaction between African American and white homeowners during the early 2000s." *Housing and Society* 40(2): 124–149.

Lilly, Jessica, Roxy Todd, & Eric Douglas. 2019. "Beneath the surface – drinking water inside Appalachia." *Inside Appalachia Podcast.* WV Public Broadcasting, May 3. www.wvpublic.org/podcast/inside-appala chia/2019-05-03/beneath-the-surface-drinking-water-inside-appalachia.

Locke, John. [1690] 1980. *Second Treatise of Civil Government.* Indianapolis: Hackett.

Logan, Michael F. 2006. *Desert Cities: The Environmental History of Phoenix and Tucson.* Pittsburgh, PA: University of Pittsburgh Press.

Lowi, Theodore J. 1972. "Four systems of policy, politics, and choice." *Public Administration Review* 32(4): 298–310.

Lurie, Julia. 2016. "Meet the mom who helped expose Flint's toxic water nightmare." *Mother Jones*, November 3. www.motherjones.com/polit ics/2016/01/mother-exposed-flint-lead-contamination-water-crisis/.

Lyons, William E., David Lowery, & Ruth Hoogland DeHoog. 1992. *The Politics of Dissatisfaction: Citizens, Services and Urban Institutions.* New York: Routledge.

MacDonald, Jason A., & William W. Franko Jr. 2007. "Bureaucratic capacity and bureaucratic discretion: Does Congress tie policy authority to performance?" *American Politics Research* 35(6): 790–807.

Madin, Elizabeth M. P., Joshua S. Madin, & David J. Booth. 2011. "Landscape of fear visible from space." *Scientific Reports* 1(1): 1–4.

Mahajan, Vijay, Vithala R. Rao, & Rajendra K. Srivastava. 1994. "An approach to assess the importance of brand equity in acquisition decisions." *Journal of Product Innovation Management* 11(3): 221–235.

Makropoulos, Christos K., & David Butler. 2010. "Distributed water infrastructure for sustainable communities." *Water Resources Management* 24(11): 2795–2816.

Marcillo, Cristina E., & Leigh-Anne H. Krometis. 2019. "Small town, big challenges: Does rurality influence Safe Drinking Water Act compliance?" *AWWA Water Science* 1(1): e1120.

Marschall, Melissa, & Parul R. Shah. 2007. "The attitudinal effects of minority incorporation: Examining the racial dimensions of trust in urban America." *Urban Affairs Review* 42(5): 629–658.

Marshall, Burke. 1961–1965. Personal Papers, Assistant Attorney General Files, 1958–1965. Writings, Speeches and Interviews, Speeches and interviews: Federal Protection of Negro Voting Rights. National Archives. www.jfklibrary.org/asset-viewer/archives/BMPP/013/BMPP-013-008.

Mason, Sherri A., Victoria G. Welch, & Joseph Neratko. 2018. "Synthetic polymer contamination in bottled water." *Frontiers in Chemistry* 6: 407.

Massey, Douglas, & Nancy A. Denton. 1993. *American apartheid: Segregation and the making of the underclass.* Cambridge, MA: Harvard University Press.

McCrary, Peyton. 2005. "How the Voting Rights Act works: Implementation of a civil rights policy, 1965–2005." *SCL Review* 57: 785–825.

McCubbins, Mathew D., & Thomas Schwartz. 1984. "Congressional oversight overlooked: Police patrols versus fire alarms." *American Journal of Political Science* 28(1): 165–179.

McGuire, Michael J. 2013. *The Chlorine Revolution: The History of Water Disinfection and the Fight to Save Lives.* Denver, CO: American Water Works Association.

McSpirit, Stephanie, & Caroline Reid. 2011. "Residents' perceptions of tap water and decisions to purchase bottled water: A survey analysis from the Appalachian, Big Sandy coal mining region of West Virginia." *Society and Natural Resources* 24(5): 511–520.

Meehan, Katie, Jason R. Jurjevich, Nicholas M. J. W. Chun, & Justin Sherrill. 2020. "Geographies of insecure water access and the housing–water nexus in US cities." *PNAS* 117(46): 28700–28707.

Meier, Kenneth J., Nathan Favero, & Mallory Compton. 2016. "Social context, management, and organizational performance: When human capital and social capital serve as substitutes." *Public Management Review* 18(2): 258–277.

Meier, Kenneth J., & Alisa Hicklin. 2008. "Employee turnover and organizational performance: Testing a hypothesis from classical public administration." *Journal of Public Administration Research & Theory* 18(4): 573–590.

Merriam-Webster Online Dictionary. 2021. "Hyperopia." www.merriam-webster.com/dictionary/hyperopia?utm_campaign=sd&utm_medium=serp&utm_source=jsonld.

Mettler, Suzanne. 2007. *Soldiers to Citizens: The G.I. Bill and the Making of the Greatest Generation.* New York: Oxford University Press.

   2011. *The Submerged State: How Invisible Government Policies Undermine American Democracy.* Chicago: University of Chicago Press.

Mill, John Stuart. 1861. *Considerations on Representative Government.* London: Parker, Son, and Bourn.

Minkoff, Scott L. 2016. "NYC 311: A tract-level analysis of citizen–government contacting in New York City." *Urban Affairs Review* 52 (2): 211–246.

Mitchell, Bruce, & Juan Franco. 2016. "HOLC 'redlining' maps: The persistent structure of segregation and economic inequality." National

Community Reinvestment Coalition. https://ncrc.org/wp-content/uploads/dlm_uploads/2018/02/NCRC-Research-HOLC-10.pdf.

Moffitt, Susan L. 2010. "Promoting agency reputation through public advice: Advisory committee use in the FDA." *Journal of Politics* 72(3): 880–893.

Montgomery, David, Rick Rojas, and Guilia McDonnell Nieto del Rio. 2021. "Texas needed food and comfort after a brutal storm. As usual, they found it at H-E-B." *New York Times*, February 22. www.nytimes.com/2021/02/22/us/texas-heb-winter-storm.html.

Myers, Adrian. 2010. "Camp Delta, Google Earth and the ethics of remote sensing in archaeology." *World Archaeology* 42(3): 455–467.

National Archives. n.d. An act to enforce the Fifteenth Amendment to the Constitution of the United States and for other purposes, August 6, 1965; Enrolled Acts and Resolutions of Congress, 1789–; General Records of the United States Government; Record Group 11. www.ourdocuments.gov/doc.php?flash=false&doc=100#.

National Research Council. 1997. *Safe Water from Every Tap*. Washington, DC: National Academies Press.

Nelson, Robert K., LaDale Winling, Richard Marciano, Nathan Connolly, et al. 2020. "Mapping inequality." In *American Panorama*, eds. Robert K. Nelson and Edward L. Ayers. October 20. https://dsl.richmond.edu/panorama/redlining.

Nickels, Ashley E. 2019. *Power, Participation, and Protest in Flint, Michigan*. Philadelphia: Temple University Press.

Nickels, Ashley E., Amanda D. Clark, & Zachary D. Wood. 2020. "How municipal takeovers reshape urban democracy: Comparing the experiences of Camden, New Jersey and Flint, Michigan." *Urban Affairs Review* 56 (3): 790–822.

Nuamah, Sally A. 2021. "The cost of participating while poor and black: Toward a theory of collective participatory debt." *Perspectives on Politics* 19(4): 1115–1130.

Obama, Barack. 2006. "An honest government – A hopeful future." Address at the University of Nairobi, August 28.

Olson, Mancur. 1965. *The Logic of Collective Action*. Cambridge, MA: Harvard University Press.

O'Toole, Laurence J., Jr., & Kenneth J. Meier. 2009. "The human side of public organizations: Contributions to organizational performance." *American Review of Public Administration* 39(5): 499–518.

Patel, Ami. 2019. "By the bottle: Who is drinking bottled water in Philly (and why does it matter)?" ImpactED blogpost, University of Pennsylvania. http://web.sas.upenn.edu/impact-ed/2019/07/09/by-the-bottle-who-is-drinking-bottled-water-in-philly-and-why-does-it-matter/.

Patton, Hannah, Leigh-Anne Krometis, & Emily Sarver. 2020. "Springing for safe water: Drinking water quality and source selection in central Appalachian communities." *Water* 12(3): 888.

Pauli, Benjamin J. 2019. *Flint Fights Back: Environmental Justice and Democracy in the Flint Water Crisis.* Cambridge, MA: MIT Press.

Peeters, Rik, Anat Gofen, & Oliver Meza. 2020. "Gaming the system: Responses to dissatisfaction with public services beyond exit and voice." *Public Administration* 98(4): 824–839.

Percy, Stephen L., Brett W. Hawkins, & Peter E. Maier. 1995. "Revisiting Tiebout: Moving rationales and interjurisdictional relocation." *Publius: The Journal of Federalism* 25(4): 1–17.

Pierce, Gregory, & Silvia Gonzalez. 2017. "Mistrust at the tap? Factors contributing to public drinking water (mis)perception across US households." *Water Policy* 19(1): 1–12.

Pierce, Gregory, Sylvia R. Gonzalez, Peter Roquemore, & Rebecca Ferdman. 2019. "Sources of and solutions to mistrust of tap water originating between treatment and the tap: Lessons from Los Angeles County." *Science of the Total Environment* 694: 133646.

Pip, Eva. 2000. "Survey of bottled drinking water available in Manitoba, Canada." *Environmental Health Perspectives* 108(9): 863–866.

Pohlar, Christopher. 2010. "The water tower: A new image in the urban landscape." Master's thesis, University of Cincinnati.

Porter, Ethan. 2020. *The Consumer Citizen.* New York: Oxford University Press.

Postel, Sandra. 1999. *Pillar of Sand: Can the Irrigation Miracle Last?* New York: Norton.

President's Appalachian Regional Commission. 1964. *Appalachia: A report by the President's Appalachian Regional Commission.* Washington, DC: US Department of Commerce.

Putnam, Robert D. 1993. *Making Democracy Work.* Princeton, NJ: Princeton University Press.

Putnam, Robert D., Robert Leonardi, & Raffaella Y. Nanetti. 1988. "Institutional performance and political culture: Some puzzles about the power of the past." *Governance* 1(3): 221–242.

Putnam, Robert D., Robert Leonardi, Raffaella Y. Nanetti, & Fanco Pavoncello. 1983. "Explaining institutional success: The case of Italian regional government." *American Political Science Review* 77(1): 55–74.

Redman, Russell. 2021. "H-E-B steps up with $1 million in aid for Texas after devastating winter storm." *Super Market News*, February 24. https://www.supermarketnews.com/issues-trends/h-e-b-steps-1-million-aid-texas-after-devastating-winter-storm.

Reinsch, Paul D. 2016. "The city of Saginaw: A historical water treatment facility and system perspective." *Journal AWWA* 108(12): 68–73.

Rice, Rip G., ed. 1985. *Safe Drinking Water: The Impact of Chemicals on a Limited Resource*. Boca Raton, FL: Lewis.

Ringquist, Evan J. 2005. "Assessing evidence of environmental inequities: A meta-analysis." *Journal of Policy Analysis and Management* 24(2): 223–247.

Risse, Mathias. 2014. "The human right to water and common ownership of the earth." *Journal of Political Philosophy* 22(2): 178–203.

Rivard, Ry. 2019. "Water vending businesses tap into customer fears over water quality." *Voice of San Diego*, September 30. https://voiceofsandiego.org/2019/09/30/water-vending-businesses-tap-into-customer-fears-over-water-quality/.

Rodwan, John G., Jr. 2020. "Bottled water 2019: Slower but notable growth." *Bottled Water Reporter* 60(4): 13–20.

Rosenthal, Aaron. 2021. "Submerged for some? Government visibility, race, and American political trust." *Perspectives on Politics* 19(4): 1098–1114 .

Rosinger, Asher Y., Kirsten A. Herrick, Amber Y. Wutich, & Jonathan S. Yoder. 2018. "Disparities in plain, tap and bottled water consumption among US adults: National Health and Nutrition Examination Survey (NHANES) 2007–2014." *Public Health Nutrition* 21(8): 1455–1464.

Rosinger, Asher Y., & Sera L. Young. 2020. "In-home tap water consumption trends changed among US children, but not adults, between 2007 and 2016." *Water Resources Research* 56(7): e2020WR027657.

Rossi, Peter Henry, Richard A. Berk, & Bettye K. Eidson. 1974. *Roots of Urban Discontent: Public Policy, Municipal Institutions, and the Ghetto*. New York: Wiley.

Rowat, Donald C. 1964. "Ombudsmen for North America." *Public Administration Review* 24(4): 230–233.

Roy, Siddhartha, Katherine Phetxumphou, Andrea M. Dietrich, Paul A. Estabrooks, Wen You, & Brenda M. Davy. 2015. "An evaluation of the readability of drinking water quality reports: A national assessment." *Journal of Water & Health* 13(3): 645–653.

Rundle, Andrew G., Michael D. M. Bader, Catherine A. Richards, Kathryn M. Neckerman, & Julien O. Teitler. 2011. "Using Google Street View to audit neighborhood environments." *American Journal of Preventive Medicine* 40(1): 94–100.

Rusbult, Caryl E., Isabella M. Zembrodt, & Lawanna K. Gunn. 1982. "Exit, voice, loyalty, and neglect: Responses to dissatisfaction in romantic involvements," *Journal of Personality and Social Psychology* 42(6): 1230–1242.

Sass, Tim R., and Stephen L. Mehay. 1995. "The Voting Rights Act, district elections, and the success of black candidates in municipal elections." *Journal of Law and Economics* 38(2): 367–392.

Saylor, Amber, Linda Stalker Prokopy, & Shannon Amberg. 2011. "What's wrong with the tap? Examining perceptions of tap water and bottled water at Purdue University." *Environmental Management* 48(3): 588–601.

Schaider, Laurel A., Lucien Swetschinski, Christopher Campbell, & Ruthann A. Rudel. 2019. "Environmental justice and drinking water quality: Are there socioeconomic disparities in nitrate levels in US drinking water?" *Environmental Health* 18(1): 3.

Scherzer, Teresa, Judith C. Barker, Howard Pollick, & Jane A. Weintraub. 2010. "Water consumption beliefs and practices in a rural Latino community: Implications for fluoridation." *Journal of Public Health Dentistry* 70(4): 337–343.

Schuit, Sophie, and Jon C. Rogowski. 2017. "Race, representation, and the Voting Rights Act." *American Journal of Political Science* 61(3): 513–526.

Schwartzstein, Peter. 2020. "Merchants of thirst." *New York Times*, January 12, B1.

Scott, Shaunna L., Stephanie McSpirit, Sharon Hardesty, & Robert Welch. 2005. "Post disaster interviews with Martin County citizens: "Gray clouds" of blame and distrust." *Journal of Appalachian Studies* 11 (1&2): 7–29.

Scott, Tyler A., Tima Moldogaziev, & Robert A. Greer. 2018. "Drink what you can pay for: Financing infrastructure in a fragmented water system." *Urban Studies* 55(13): 2821–2837.

Scutchfield, F. Douglas, Evelyn A. Knight, Ann V. Kelly, Michelyn W. Bhandari, & Ilie Puiu Vasilescu. 2004. "Local public health agency capacity and its relationship to public health system performance." *Journal of Public Health Management and Practice* 10(3): 204–215.

Sharp, Renee, & Bill Walker. 2002. "Is water from vending machines really 'chemical-free'?" Environmental Working Group. https://static.ewg.org/reports/2002/IsWaterFromVendingMachinesReallyChemicalFree.pdf?_ga=2.56827242.1713316250.1574645644-166706387.1573012901.

Shi, Irene M., Eric S. Weintraub, & Deborah A. Gust. 2006. "Parents concerned about vaccine safety: Differences in race/ethnicity and attitudes." *American Journal of Preventative Medicine* 31(3): 244–251.

Siegel, Seth M. 2019. *Troubled Water: What's Wrong with What We Drink*. New York: Thomas Dunne.

Simon, Herbert A. 1985. "Human nature in politics: The dialogue of psychology with political science." *American Political Science Review* 79(2): 293–304.

Simon, Carol J., & Mary W. Sullivan. 1993. "The measurement and determinants of brand equity: A financial approach." *Marketing Science* 12 (1): 28–52.

Solis, Miriam. 2020. "Conditions and consequences of ELULU improvement: Environmental justice lessons from San Francisco, CA." *Journal of Planning Education and Research.* https://doi.org/10.1177% 2F0739456X20929407.

Stigler, George J. 1971. "The theory of economic regulation." *Bell Journal of Economics & Management Science* 2(1): 3–21.

Stewart, Emily. 2018. "2018's record-setting voter turnout, in one chart." *Vox*, November 19. www.vox.com/policy-and-politics/2018/11/19/ 18103110/2018-midterm-elections-turnout.

Sugrue, Thomas J. 2005. *The Origins of the Urban Crisis.* Rev. ed. Princeton, NJ: Princeton University Press.

Switzer, David. 2019a. "Citizen partisanship, local government, and environmental policy implementation." *Urban Affairs Review* 55 (3): 675–702.

2019b. "Getting off the (water) bottle: Constraining or embracing individual liberty in pursuit of the public interest." *Ethics, Policy & Environment* (early view).

Switzer, David, & Manuel P. Teodoro. 2017. "The color of drinking water: Class, race, ethnicity, and Safe Drinking Water Act compliance." *Journal AWWA* 109(9): 40–45.

2018. "Class, race, ethnicity, and justice in Safe Drinking Water Act compliance." *Social Science Quarterly* 99(2): 524–535.

Switzer, David, Manuel P. Teodoro, & Stuart Karasik. 2016. "The human capital resource challenge: Recognizing and overcoming small utility workforce obstacles." *Journal AWWA* 108(8): e416–424.

Szasz, Andrew. 2007. *Shopping Our Way to Safety.* Minneapolis: University of Minnesota Press.

Taylor, Cedric, Daniel Bracken, Eric Limarenko, & Don Blubaugh (producers) & Cedric Taylor (director). 2018. *Nor Any Drop to Drink: Flint's Water Crisis* [video file]. Retrieved from www.noranydropfilm.com/.

Teaford, Jon C. 1984. *The Unheralded Triumph: City Government in America, 1870–1900.* Baltimore: Johns Hopkins University Press.

Timmins, Christopher. 2002. "Does the median voter consume too much water? Analyzing the redistributive role of residential water bills." *National Tax Journal* 55(4): 687–702.

Tobler, Waldo R. 1970. "A computer movie simulating urban growth in the Detroit region." *Economic Geography* 46(Suppl 1): 234–240.

Tocqueville, Alexis de. [1835]. *Democracy in America*. New York: Library of America.

Torney-Purta, Judith, Carolyn Henry Barber, & Wendy Klandl Richardson. 2004. "Trust in government-related institutions and political engagement among adolescents in six countries." *Acta Politica* 38(4): 380–406.

Tucker, Phillip T. 2015. *How the Irish Won the American Revolution: A New Look at the Forgotten Heroes of America's War of Independence*. New York: Simon & Schuster.

Turner, Patricia. 1993. *I Heard It through the Grapevine: Rumor in African-American Culture*. Berkeley: University of California Press.

Teodoro, Manuel P. 2011. *Bureaucratic Ambition: Careers, Motives, and the Innovative Administrator*. Baltimore: Johns Hopkins University Press.

2018. "Measuring household affordability for water and sewer utilities." *Journal AWWA* 110(1): 13–22.

2019. "Water and sewer affordability in the United States." *AWWA Water Science* 1(2): e1129.

Teodoro, Manuel P., & David Switzer. 2016. "Drinking from the talent pool: A resource endowment theory of human capital and agency performance." *Public Administration Review* 76(4): 564–575.

Teodoro, Manuel P., Mellie Haider, & David Switzer. 2018. "US environmental policy implementation on tribal lands: Trust, neglect, and justice." *Policy Studies Journal* 46(1): 37–59.

Teodoro, Manuel P., & Seung-Ho An. 2018. "Citizen-based brand equity: A model and experimental evaluation." *Journal of Public Administration Research and Theory* 28(3): 321–338.

Teodoro, Manuel P., & Robin Rose Saywitz. 2020. "Water and sewer affordability in the United States: A 2019 update." *AWWA Water Science* 2(2): e1176.

Teodoro, Manuel P., Youlang Zhang, & David Switzer. 2020. "Political decoupling: Private implementation of public policy." *Policy Studies Journal* 48(2): 401–424.

Turkowitz, Julie. 2016. "Denver tries to persuade Latino immigrants to trust tap." *New York Times*, April 1, A13.

Tyler, Tom R., & Yuen J. Huo. 2002. *Trust in the Law: Encouraging Public Cooperation with the Police and Courts*. New York: Russell Sage.

University of California. 2020. *Statewide Database* (2016 election data) [Data set]. https://statewidedatabase.org/.

Unrine, Jason M. 2020. "The Martin County Kentucky Community-Engaged Drinking Water Health Pilot Study." Preliminary Technical Report, University of Kentucky.

Valelly, Richard M. 2004. *The Two Reconstructions: The Struggle for black Enfranchisement*. Chicago: University of Chicago Press.

van den Bekerom, Joris van der Voet, & Johan Christensen. 2020. "Are citizens more negative about failing service delivery by public than private organizations? Evidence from a large-scale survey experiment." *Journal of Public Administration Research & Theory* 31(1): 128–149.

Van Roosbroek, Steven, & Steven Van de Walle. 2008. "The relationship between ombudsman, government, and citizens: A survey analysis." *Negotiation Journal* 24(3): 287–302.

Van Ryzin, Gregg G. 2004a. "Expectations, performance, and citizen satisfaction with urban services." *Journal of Policy Analysis and Management* 23(3): 433–448.

Van Ryzin, Gregg G. 2004b. "The measurement of overall citizen satisfaction." *Public Performance & Management Review* 27(3): 9–28.

2007. "Pieces of a puzzle: Linking government performance, citizen satisfaction, and trust." *Public Performance & Management Review* 30(4): 521–535.

2011. "Outcomes, process, and trust of civil servants." *Journal of Public Administration Research & Theory* 21(4): 745–760.

2015. "Service quality, administrative process, and citizens' evaluation of local government in the US." *Public Management Review* 17(3): 425–442.

Van Ryzin, Gregg G., Stephen Immerwahr, & Stan Altman. 2008. "Measuring street cleanliness: A comparison of New York City's scorecard and results from a citizen survey." *Public Administration Review* 68(2): 295–303.

Van Ryzin, Gregg G., Douglas Muzzio, & Stephen Immerwahr. 2004. "Explaining the race gap in satisfaction with urban services." *Urban Affairs Review* 39(5): 613–632.

Vega, Margaret Brown, Nathan Craig, & Gerbert Asencios Lindo. 2011. "Ground truthing of remotely identified fortifications on the Central Coast of Peru," *Journal of Archaeological Science* 38(7): 1680–1689.

Vega, Solmaria Halleck, & J. Paul Elhorst. 2015. "The SLX model." *Journal of Regional Science* 55(3): 339–363.

Velasco, Teresa. 2021. "'H-E-B for governor': Texans praise H-E-B for winter storm response." MySA.com, February 18. www.mysanantonio.com/galleries/article/H-E-B-for-governor-Texans-praise-H-E-B-for-15961527.php.

Verba, Sidney, Kay Lehman Schlozman, Henry Brady, & Norman H. Nie. 1993. "Race, ethnicity, and political resources." *British Journal of Political Science* 23(4): 453–497.

Virginia Tech University. 2020. "US water study." November 5. https://crowdfund.vt.edu/project/9102.

Viscusi, W. Kip, Joel Huber, & Jason Bell. 2015. "The private rationality of bottled water drinking." *Contemporary Economic Policy* 33(3): 450–467.

Wagner, Martin, & Jörg Oehlmann. 2009. "Endocrine disruptors in bottled mineral water: Total estrogenic burden and migration from plastic bottles." *Environmental Science and Pollution Research* 1(3): 278–286.

Ward, Michael. D., & Kristian S. Gleditsch. 2008. *Spatial Regression Models* (Vol. 155). New York: Sage.

Warner, Mildred E. 2009. *Local Government Infrastructure and the False Promise of Privatization.* New York: The Century Foundation.

Watermill Express. 2017. "Watermill Express soars to new heights on Entrepreneur Magazine's 38th Annual Franchise 500 List." Franchising. com, February 28. www.franchising.com/news/20170228_watermill_express_soars_to_new_heights_on_entrepre.html.

West, Darrel M. 2004. "E-government and the transformation of service delivery and citizen attitudes." *Public Administration Review* 64(1): 15–27.

Westerhoff, Paul, Panjai Prapaipong, Everett Shock, & Alice Hillaireau. 2008. "Antimony leaching from polyethylene terephthalate (PET) plastic used for bottled drinking water." *Water Research* 42(3): 551–556.

Whitten, Guy D., Laron K. Williams, & Cameron Wimpy. 2021. "Interpretation: The final *spatial* frontier." *Political Science Research and Methods* 9(1): 140–156.

Wies, Jennifer R., Alisha Mays, Shalean M. Collins, & Sera L. Young. 2020. "'As long as we have the mine, we'll have water': Exploring water insecurity in Appalachia." *Annals of Anthropological Practice* 44(1): 65–76.

Willcoxon, Nicole. 2017. "The Voting Rights Act in North Carolina: Turnout, registration, access, and enforcement." PhD dissertation, University of California, Berkeley.

Wilson, James Q. 1974. "The politics of regulation." In James W. McKie, ed., *Social Responsibility and the Business Predicament.* Washington, DC: Brookings Institution Press, 135–168.

Wimpy, Cameron, Laron K. Williams, & Guy D. Whitten. 2021. "X marks the spot: Unlocking the treasure of spatial-X models." *Journal of Politics* 83(2): 722–739.

Winter, Soren C., & Peter J. May. 2001. "Motivation for compliance with environmental regulations." *Journal of Policy Analysis and Management* 20(4): 675–698.

Wright, Will, Coyne, Caity & Molly Born. 2018. "Stirring the waters: Investigating why many in Appalachia lack reliable, clean water." *Lexington Herald Leader*, December 6. www.kentucky.com/news/local/watchdog/article222656895.html.

Yee, Alex Thiam Koon, Richard T. Corlett, Soo Chin Liew, & Hugh T. W. Tan. 2011. "The vegetation of Singapore: An updated map." *Gardens' Bulletin Singapore* 63(1&2): 205–212.

York, Abigail M., Allain Barnett, Amber Wutich, & Beatrice I. Crona. 2011. "Household bottled water consumption in Phoenix: A lifestyle choice." *Water International* 36(6): 708–718.

Young, Dennis R. 1972. "Exit and voice in organization of public services." *Information (International Social Science Council)*, 13(3): 49–65.

Zenou, Yves, & Nicolas Boccard. 2000. "Racial discrimination and redlining in cities." *Journal of Urban Economics* 48(2): 260–285.

Zwick, William R., & Wayne F. Velicer. 1982. "Factors influencing four rules for determining the number of components to retain." *Multivariate Behavioral Research* 17(2): 253–269.

# Index

Affordable Care Act (ACA), 50
American Community Survey (ACS), 141
American Consumer Satisfaction Index (ACSI), 47
American Society of Civil Engineers, 26
American Water Works Association, 225
Appalachian Regional Commission, 160, 163
Appalachian Regional Development Act (ARDA), 155, 160
Aqua America, 214
Aquafina, 8
architecture, 226, 228
Arrowhead, 8
assimilation, 153

basic services. *See also* utilities
    actual quality of, 3, 194, 199, 208, 214
    commercial production of, 37
    equity of, 199, 206–207, 210
    evaluation of, 202, 206, 208, 223, 225, 229
    and government legitimacy, 1–2, 28, 31, 33, 35, 69, 191, 193–194, 196, 210
    interruptions in, 86
    and local governments, 209
    patterns of failure, 197
    perceptions of, 52
    provision of, 36, 71, 174, 179, 199
    responsibility for, 36, 98, 125, 198
    spending on, 179, 181, 189, 210
    and state government, 210
Bell, Jason, 25
Bliss, Laura, 143–144
boil water advisories, 164
Boston, MA, 203

bottled water. *See also* commercial water
    availability of, 87
    correlation with voter turnout, 141, 143, 180
    costs of, 8–9
    demand for, 106, 108, 135, 158, 163, 174
    environmental impacts of, 8–9
    and income level, 16
    perceptions of, 13, 27
    and political participation, 139
    profitability of, 159
    proliferation of, 158, 166
    and race, 25
    reliance on, 164
    sources of, 27
    spending on, 4, 141, 143, 166
branding, 42, 62
Brentwood Associates, 145
Bridges, Amy, 167
Bureau of Labor Statistics, 140
Burns, Robert, 165

California Environmental Health Tracking Program, 187
Carpenter, Daniel, 50
chlorination, 6
cholera, 5
citizen-consumers. *See also* political engagement, democracy, government, exit, *and* voice
    advocacy for, 228
    alienation of, 147
    choices by, 35, 37, 55–56, 58, 86, 99, 126, 128
    identity of, 105–106, 108, 124
    and political engagement, 2, 5, 30, 38, 140, 145, 152, 176–177, 186
    power of, 177

For EU product safety concerns, contact us at Calle de José Abascal, 56–1°,
28003 Madrid, Spain or eugpsr@cambridge.org.

www.ingramcontent.com/pod-product-compliance
Ingram Content Group UK Ltd.
Pitfield, Milton Keynes, MK11 3LW, UK
UKHW020400140625
459647UK00020B/2563